BEYOND THE
BALANCE SHEET

BEYOND THE BALANCE SHEET

Geoffrey Holmes and Robin Dunham

WOODHEAD-FAULKNER

New York London Toronto Sydney Tokyo Singapore

First published 1994 by
Woodhead-Faulkner (Publishers) Limited
Campus 400, Maylands Avenue
Hemel Hempstead
Hertfordshire, HP2 7EZ
A division of
Simon & Schuster International Group

Printed and bound in Great Britain by
Redwood Books, Trowbridge, Wiltshire

British Library Cataloguing in Publication Data

A catalogue record for this book is available from
the British Library

ISBN 0-85941-752-2

1 2 3 4 5   98 97 96 95 94

CONTENTS

		Page
Preface		*ix*

1. Personal skills — 1

Develop a healthy scepticism. Reading between the lines of brokers' circulars. Things companies don't tell you. Use your eyes and ears. Take a walk down the High Street. It's not what you know but whom you know.

2. The quick look — 6

A two-stage approach. Getting a first impression. The same ... but different. Case study: Wilding Office Equipment. Commentary. With hindsight.

3. The longer look — 13

Where do you start? Forming the right habits. Why invest in equities at all? How to choose a sector. Assessing a company's prospects. Developing useful key ratios.

4. The company visit — 17

Seize any opportunity. Prepare thoroughly. Meet the management. Visit the factory. Try to attend annual general meetings. Insider dealing.

5. Presentation — 20

Methods of presentation. Accounts and tables. In the balance sheet. Standards of graphic presentation. Ways of conveying information. Information presented graphically. Demonstrating growth.

6. Preparing an in-depth report — 25

Essential reference material. Adopt a standard format. Why is so much information necessary?

7. Cash flow statements and the projection of future capital needs — 29

How to read a cash flow statement. Consider separately each standard heading. Consider the document as a whole. The Financial Review. Future capital requirements. Case study: Lucas.

8. Finding the money — 36

At the drop of a hat. Internal sources versus external. Relations with banks. Shares or loan capital: the choice. The effects of gearing. Cost of capital. Unusual capital instruments. Accounting for capital instruments. Yellow Book requirements. Off balance sheet finance. Factoring. Leases and hire purchase contracts. Case study: Asda.

9.   Impending disaster and how to spot it   46

Failure: size and age are a factor. Companies can grow *too* fast. Overambitious ill-timed acquisitions. Expanding too fast. Excessive and short-term borrowings. Dominant characters and a resigning board. Other warning signs. Learning from inspectors' reports. Scientific methods of predicting failure. What goes up ... Danger signals. Down but not out.

10.   Profit improvement   51

Some companies have it – others don't. Using consultants. Improving the existing business. Other ways of improving profitabilty. Ratios to watch. Case study: Abbey Crest. Reducing net interest payable. More questionable improvements. Cash flow effects of profit improvement.

11.   Reporting financial performance   57

FRS 3 summarised. Statement of total recognised gains and losses. Reconciliation of movements in shareholders' funds. Transitional problems. Earnings per share. Notional, or underlying, earnings.

12.   Acquisitions and mergers   63

Why companies make acquisitions. Visionary / opportunistic acquisitions. Keys to success. Post-acquisition audit. Deferred consideration. Fair value adjustments. Where to look for information on acquisitions and mergers. Case Study: Inchcape. FRED 6.

13.   Discontinued operations and disposals   71

Why groups dispose of subsidiaries. Why companies resort to closure. Changes in 'shape'. Reporting discontinued operations. Management buyouts. Demergers. Keeping track. Treatment of goodwill on disposal of a business.

14.   Group philosophy; methods of controlling a large group   76

Five key factors to consider. Independence. The role of the Finance Director. Non-executive directors. Transparency. Succession. Rationale. Controlling the larger group. What kind of group is it? Styles of strategic management. The analyst's concern with style.

15.   Foreign operations and currency risk   81

UK companies trading abroad. Why companies buy and sell overseas. Swaps, interest caps and the foreign exchange forward market. Playing the currency markets. The financial review and foreign exchange. Foreign registered subsidiaries. Why groups have foreign subsidiaries. Types of investment in foreign companies. Methods of organising foreign operations. Accounting treatment of overseas activities. In the accounts of the individual company. In the group accounts. High inflation and hyperinflation. The temporal method.

16.   Pensions and pension funds   91

The problem with pensions. Who calls the tune? Can one really rely on the trustees? Inflation is a key problem. Who owns a surplus (and who makes good any deficit)? Pressure to reduce surpluses. Things to look out for. Pension schemes and the acquirer. Self-investment. Sex equality and other recent developments. Pension costs and the concept of prudence. Pension law reform.

17.   Effects of inflation   98

Why the present position is unsatisfactory. Inflation is difficult to measure. Depreciation is insufficient. Is revaluation the solution? Rents in an inflationary period. Gains on borrowed money. Stock and stock profits. Effect of inflation on other components of working capital. Adjusting figures in historical summaries. Accounting for inflation.

18. **Interim reports**   104

Uses and shortcomings. A shame there is no balance sheet. Audit and the true and fair view. Do interim reports give warning of impending disaster? The seasonal business. Using the interim statement. The Cadbury report. Would Quarterly Statements be better?

19. **Sectors and segments**   109

Getting to grips with a sector. How sectors differ. Companies come in all shapes and sizes. Where to start. Segmental analysis. Using segmental information. The media. Case study: Courts.

20. **Building materials and merchants, building and construction**   115

General overview. Building materials and merchants: manufacture, extractive activities, merchants. Contracting and construction. What to look for in construction company accounts.

21. **Leisure and hotels**   122

Overview of the sector. Hotels and catering. Accounting features of hotels. Gaming. Package tours and holidays.

22. **Retailers, food and retailers, general**   126

Overview of the sectors. Grasping the essentials. Stores. Points to look for in the accounts of stores companies. Points to look for in the accounts of food retailers and supermarkets.

23. **Utilities**   130

General overview. Privatised utilities. Electricity. Water. Telecommunications.

24. **Pharmaceuticals and health care**   134

General overview. What to look for in the reports and accounts of pharmaceutical companies. What to look for in the reports and accounts of health care companies. Case study: Medeva.

25. **Oil, integrated, development and production, gas distribution**   140

General overview. Exploration and development expenditure. Successful efforts. Full cost accounting. Points to look for in the accounts. Impairment: ceiling tests. Abandonment and site restoration. Taxation of oil companies. Oil reserves. Financing arrangements. Capitalisation of interest. Integration. Effect of foreign exchange rates. Environmental costs. Effects of FRS 3.

26. **Banks and Merchant Banks**   145

General overview. Banks come in all sorts and sizes. Central banks and bank supervision. Banks face developing competition. Reports and accounts of banks. Points to look for.

27. **Insurance and life assurance**   152

General overview. How insurance and assurance work. Things to look for in the accounts of insurance companies. A ratio to watch. The accounts. Domestic breakdown insurance. Insurance brokers.

28. **Property**   159

General overview of the sector. What makes property an attractive investment? How property ownership is organised. Property valuation. What property companies do. What to search for in property company accounts. Net asset value. Useful ratios. Things to look out for.

Index   170

PREFACE

'So may the outward shows be least themselves:
The world is still deceived with ornament.' – *William Shakespeare*

Beyond the Balance Sheet provides a second stage introduction to the understanding and interpretation of published accounts. While written especially with the needs of investment analysts in mind, it should prove useful to fund managers, bankers and merchant bankers, accountants and private investors, directors and managers, indeed to anyone with a basic knowledge of how to prepare accounts, seeking a better understanding of what makes businesses tick. Knowing how to prepare accounts is not at all the same thing as getting to grips with (and behind) accounts produced by others. Indeed, history is littered with examples of people who, in the widest sense, invested in businesses which they thought they understood but which experience showed they didn't.

A second stage work, it assumes a basic understanding of the terminology of accounting and the business world equivalent to that gained from study of its companion volume *Interpreting Company Reports and Accounts* by Holmes and Sugden (Woodhead-Faulkner Ltd). Occasionally, where that is helpful, it contains cross references to that work.

When speaking of a distinguished accountant, or man of eminence in the business world, it is sometimes said that 'he can read a balance sheet like a book'. In the authors' opinion, that is without doubt an exaggeration; and if he himself believes this, it is a delusion.

'A balance sheet provides a sort of instant snapshot of a business', people sometimes suggest. Though there is certainly an element of truth in this – the information it provides, like a snapshot, relates to only a single point in time. And if it is a photograph, it is a relatively poor one. It is somewhat out of focus; and gives a partial view of a wide landscape much of the detail of which is impossible to make out. And we all know how, by the accidental, or even deliberate, choice of an odd viewpoint, or by the use of a lens of different focal length, a camera can be made to lie – and so provide a picture quite unlike that perceived with the human eye. Nevertheless, much can be gleaned from a study of reports and accounts, as many successful fund managers, businessmen and investors have proved.

Over the years accountants have argued amongst themselves as to whether the profit and loss account or the balance sheet is the more important; and opinion has swung from one to the other. Cash flow statements present another claim for supremacy.

In fact each has its place; as do the chairman's statement, the report of the directors, the auditors' report, and any 5–10 year summary.

To really understand a company or group, and assess its prospects, one needs to look far beyond the annual report. Factories and offices are not provided (as some business sites are) with convenient peepholes in the wall so that those interested can see how things are shaping up. But there is a mass of information available.

Beyond the Balance Sheet tells you how to observe, to question, to listen, to assess whether a company, and those who manage it, have what it takes, or are doomed to failure.

One needs all the help – and all the information – one can get. It is with this in mind that we ask readers to embark on the exciting journey to those interesting lands which lie *Beyond the Balance Sheet*.

The book reflects the law, accounting standards, market capitalisations of companies and sectors as they stood on 31 January 1994.

GEOFFREY HOLMES
ROBIN DUNHAM

Chapter 1

PERSONAL SKILLS

Develop a healthy scepticism

In researching a company perhaps the most important thing to have is a healthy streak of scepticism. Don't rely solely on what a company's board tells you in its report and accounts. Remember that it is an important part of the directors' duty to sustain public confidence in the company.

Most major companies, and many smaller ones, today employ public relations and design consultants who earn their living by creating the right impression for their client. Make allowance for that. Don't believe all the hype and press puffs about success.

Remember too, that it is the job of the company's broker to show the company in a good light and promote the market in its shares. Brokers in general, and a company's own broker in particular, are reluctant to criticise a company in writing. They avoid, if they can, putting out a straight SELL recommendation note, lest they offend the management and get cut off from future contact or, in the case of the company's broker, get sacked.

A classic case of a chairman's reaction to unwelcome criticism concerned the late Robert Maxwell. As a *Daily Telegraph* article on Maxwell, entitled 'Yes, he was a crook', explained:

MAXWELL *Extract from* Daily Telegraph *5 December 1991*

Any employee with the courage to question ... the great man's judgement risked dismissal. City analysts fared no better. Derek Terrington, a media analyst at stockbrokers UBS Phillips & Drew, wrote a circular on the flotation of Mirror Group Newspapers last May. The price, described by Maxwell as a bargain even a one-eyed Albanian could see, was 125p, but Terrington's circular was headed 'Can't Recommend A Purchase'. Terrington was right, and the price collapsed immediately, but

the acronym had incensed Maxwell, who forced UBS Phillips & Drew to withdraw the circular. Terrington has since left the firm.

Maxwell's technique for suppressing criticism was well described by David Hooper, a solicitor specialising in libel, in an article entitled 'How the libel laws helped Maxwell get away with it', published in the *Daily Telegraph* two days later:

MAXWELL *Extract from* Daily Telegraph *7 December 1991*

Maxwell ... fired off writs in staggering numbers. He knew that the recipient of the writ would have to spend substantial sums proving what was said was true or fair comment on a matter of public interest. He knew, too, that the person he sued would be reluctant to spend such sums and would be happy, if only for economic reasons, to pay a modest sum in damages and costs and make a public apology to get out of the libel action. He also knew that the defendant would soon discover, if he did not know it already, that witnesses would be reluctant to give evidence against a man of his power, particularly if they earned their livelihood in journalism or printing. The result was that editors tended to spike stories critical of Maxwell.

Reading between the lines of brokers' circulars

From time to time you do get warnings from brokers' notes. But research shows that BUY recommendations outnumber SELL recommendations in stockbrokers' notes by more than ten to one. It is usually necessary to do a certain amount of reading between the lines.

If you are a fund manager or major corporate or private investor, you may be in a position to talk directly to the analyst. By all means do so, if you can. On a one to one basis he may be prepared to speak out more directly. In any case, be on the look out for euphemisms for SELL, eg 'Long term buy', which means 'do not buy at the present price'. Other synonyms are 'Expensive' and 'Fully Valued'. 'Take Profits' is far less offensive than that dreaded four letter word since it implies that the company must have done well at some time for there to be any profits to take.

While there are plenty of companies where management is prepared to take fair comment, there are others, alas, who get quite unpleasant when criticised. For example:

POLLY PECK *Extract from 'Polly's dying threat'* Sunday Express *18 November 1990*

Last April [1990], Polly Peck told a stockbroking firm to sack an analyst who pointed out the company's weaknesses ...

The analyst for Societe General Strauss Turnbull made a private report to the firm's market-makers saying that Polly Peck's shares were overvalued, its debts might be higher than the City believed, and some Nadir [Polly Peck's chairman] acquisitions could be worth less than claimed.

A Polly Peck director told the analyst's boss the document was inaccurate and he must 'get rid of' the analyst. He threatened to remove Polly Peck's business from the firm's parent Societe General if the report was not withdrawn.

Mr Nadir was, admittedly, an extreme example, but it is just this sort of company – often one with a dominating chairman/chief executive – that you want to identify. Such a man will probably surround himself with 'yes-men', and in the long run is likely, like Asil Nadir, to come a cropper.

In October 1990, six months after the Strauss Turnbull incident, Polly Peck announced that it was halting payments to its bankers due to liquidity problems. Three weeks later it was in administration.

Things companies don't tell you

Chairmen are always happy to tell you about things that are going well, but often omit to mention things which aren't so good. Look out when a chairman's annual review tells you how well they are doing in activities A, B and D, but glosses over or even makes no mention of C.

Note carefully cases where what is said does not appear to stand up. For example, the Chairman of BURNETT & HALLAMSHIRE, a UK open-cast coal mining company, said in his 1984 statement that 'Your board has taken steps to ensure that financial exposure in California is reduced.' But in the same report the Review of Opertions said that 'Two prime office development sites were acquired dur-

ing the year ... in Los Angeles', which hardly tied up with reducing financial exposure in California. It subsequently transpired that the Group had borrowed heavily off-balance-sheet to put huge sums of money into a totally unrelated and geographically remote business that was soon to drag the company under.

So, if you find even the tiniest clue that the chairman/MD/FD is being economical with the truth, tread very warily indeed and assume his motives to be guilty ones unless and until they are proved innocent.

Leopards do not change their spots. Learn what you can of the history of those with whom you are dealing. Years ago, in the 1950s, when a City scandal broke centring on a wealthy, and up till then highly regarded, chairman, who had a nice town house in Chelsea and a large farm in Hampshire, a wise old broker told us 'We always knew he was bent, he got fined for watering the milk during the war.'

Beware too of the Chairman or Chief Executive who says that *his* company is going to buck the trend. For example, in 1988 MC CARTHY & STONE, the housebuilder which specialises in retirement homes, reported pre-tax profits up from £24.9m to £34.1m and the chairman's statement told us:

MC CARTHY & STONE *Extract from 1988 chairman's statement*

Outlook
The recent rise in interest rates seem to have marked the end of the sustained period of high demand and rapid price increases in the housing market. This is giving way to concern about the performance of the housebuilding industry in the immediate future. We do not share this concern.

In 1989 McCarthy & Stone's profits fell almost 80%, to £7.1m pre-tax, and the company plunged into a loss of £10.8m in 1990 (£16.9m in 1991 and £19.0m in 1992). Moral of the story: if a Chairman or Chief Executive says his company is going to buck the trend – don't necessarily believe him.

Some directors are born optimists, some are always cautious. Some will tell you bad news as well as good. Others are just available. It is important to decide quickly which is which.

Look out for press comments, especially those in the *FT*, including the Lex column, the *Investors' Chronicle* (which produces an invaluable quarterly index enabling you to read up their comments on a company over the past 2 or 3 years very easily) and the Questor column in the *Daily Telegraph*. The *Daily Mail* City pages, though smaller, are punchy and easy to read. But always remember, even an unfettered press may avoid offending the management of companies with large advertising budgets.

When directors resign, or are replaced, be on the look out for explanations, either on the part of the company or the director. While changes in a board of directors are normally announced in the financial press, explanation for them is, unfortunately but perhaps understandably, comparatively rare. The reader is left to put two and two together, in the hope of making five. But he should endeavour to do so, especially when it is: (i) the chief executive or (ii) the finance director or (iii) a non-executive director with a reputation for independence, who departs.

HI-TEC SPORTS *Extract from* Financial Times *18 March 1993*

Shares in Hi-Tec Sports, the sports and leisure wear company, yesterday headed back towards their all time low – touched in January – as the market reflects on Tuesday's resignation of the company's newly appointed non-executive directors.

'Sir Michael Edwardes, former chairman of British Leyland, and Mr Richard Fenhalls, chief executive of Henry Ansbacher, joined the Hi-Tec board in January and their sudden departure was largely overlooked by the stock market which was concentrating on the Budget ...

'When non-executives of this calibre resign simultaneously, one obviously draws a negative conclusion", one analyst said. Hi-Tec's position was not helped by the refusal of both sides to comment on the resignations.

'Sir Michael and Mr Fenhalls were appointed by Hi-Tec chairman and 54 per cent shareholder Mr Franz van Wezel ...

'But his choice of such high profile non-executives looks strange, as does their agreement to work under a man with a reputation for getting his own way.'

Watch out also for changes in directors' shareholdings, as reported to the Stock Exchange, and in disclosed stakes of 3% and over.

Use your eyes and ears

Common sense and using one's eyes and ears are vital. For example, if a motor manufacturer produces a crummy new model (as FORD did in the US with the Edsel years ago and BLMC did more recently with the Marina), it may be a good time to sell.

If, as more recently, you can get a 15% discount or a generous guaranteed minimum part exchange allowance on a new car, it must be bad news for motor distributors – but it may already be too late to sell, the market is likely to have absorbed the information.

But, if you notice a sudden drop off in custom at a particular retailer, or type of store, or an unexpected upsurge, you may just spot a trend before other people.

Study business fashion. When everyone is rushing into the latest 'growth' area (including banks eager to lend money), it is probably late in the day: supply is about to exceed demand, and that particular sector is about to fall out of bed.

Remember the way the banks paid over the odds to get into stockbroking, precisely at the time the stockbrokers' lucrative monopoly (the closed shop commission scale cartel) was being removed by 'Big Bang'; the way insurance companies vied with one another to take over estate agents as the housing market topped out; the way banks and building societies lent up to the hilt (even 100% +) on house mortgages just at the top of the 1988/89 property boom and the way video shops mushroomed just as every petrol station and CTN (confectionery, tobacco and newspaper) outlet was trying to find a few square feet of space to compete – just as two rival types of satellite TV were trying to cut each other's throat and to undercut the video market.

Some trends, once begun, go on for several years (even many) eg the growth of major food retailers, initially into High Street supermarkets, then into larger High Street outlets, and more recently into ever larger out of town superstores. Others, like the popularity of oil and gas exploration stocks in the 1970s and early 1980s (as oil prices soared), are much less lasting.

Take a walk down the High Street

Every visit to the High Street or the local trading estate is, to the analyst, a voyage of discovery – an opportunity:

1. To study companies in action;
2. To see how peoples' tastes and buying patterns are changing.

Every week make a practice of asking yourself:

1. Which shops look busy, and which do not?
2. Where is the quality of goods improving? or falling?
3. What is the level of stocks? Low stocks may be a sign of efficiency – but stocks so low that you cannot buy what you want may reflect pressure on working capital – and will certainly lose customers.
4. Are they attracting, or trying to attract, a new type of customer eg teenagers?
5. Are staff well-trained, polite, helpful, efficient, or indifferent to customer needs, chatting to themselves in a corner? What does that tell you about management?
6. Watch how staff handle complaints? Do they care whether customers are satisfied?

7. How much business are they doing? Less than last week or last year? Or more? Look at customers – who is buying what, where?

8. Who is building what, where? Is work going ahead or has construction stopped?

9. Where were the goods on display made: Taiwan, Malaysia, Japan, Germany, Spain? What does that imply about British manufacturers of the same type of goods? Which products are people buying – do they 'Buy British'? If not, why not?

10. Compare Sainsbury, Asda, Safeway and Tesco; which has the edge, for what, and why?

11. Which has the longer check-out queues? Which is the slowest to serve? And why: slowness of staff? slowness of the computer system? lack of a price on the goods?

12. Compare W.H. Smith, Woolworth and Toys-R-Us on price, choice and custom.

13. What has succeeded Cabbage Patch dolls, Ninja Turtles and Thunderbirds as toy of the year? And what will follow Trivial Pursuit and Nintendo?

14. Is trade in local pubs increasing, or falling? What proportion of turnover represents meals/snacks? And how do prices measure up against inflation?

15. Who is advertising what, how, where? And why? Is it an attempt to defend market share, if so against whom? Or are they trying to grab a *bigger* share – if so, at whose expense? Do you think they will succeed?

16. Look around for new cars: what do the registrations you see tell you about (i) the affluence of local people; (ii) recent car sales? Are people buying smaller cars because of increased tax on fuel; are companies buying less expensive cars because of changes in car benefits charges?

17. How many 'Closing down', 'In receivership', 'For sale' and 'To let' signs are there? What does that tell you about (i) trade; (ii) market rents; (iii) property values?

18. Is there a pattern to the closures – for example, have several local butchers been put out of business because people find it cheaper or more convenient to buy their meat at Sainsbury or Tesco?

19. How many 'Acquired for clients of XYZ' signs are there? Is business looking up?

20. When you pass the local travel agents: do they look busy? Are customers flocking to book holidays? Or are there significant price reductions to attract custom? How are bookings for conferences and functions at local hotels? When you travel, is your plane deserted?

Please do not regard this as a check list. It is not. To tell you to keep you eyes open would be unhelpful. We are simply outlining some of the things which we are looking for currently. Tomorrow the list will be different. What you have to do is to develop your own way of seeing the world – your own list of questions.

It's not what you know but whom you know

We would not go quite as far as that; for the more you know about a company, its products, methods, policies and plans, and the people who run it, the greater the edge you will have over the investor or analyst who has not done his homework.

But having the right network of contacts is very important. Don't be deceived, whom you know is not just a matter of where you went to school. It is a skill that has to be learned.

A key tool of the analyst (or the researcher or professional journalist) is his address book. Into it go the names and addresses and phone numbers (and in these days fax numbers) of those he meets. Cynically one might add, 'and who might be useful to him one day'.

More than that, he includes potential contacts – the name of the FD he didn't meet but whose name came up in conversation with the chairman. In this way you can say, quite truthfully, 'I was talking to your chairman (or perhaps even 'to Peter X') a few days ago, and he mentioned your name ... I wonder whether you are able help me.'

Some analysts make a point of finding out the name of a contact's secretary – and perhaps finding some minor reason to talk to her, to 'make his number', so building another useful bridge.

Try to make a habit of talking to people about competitors in the same trade. You can learn a lot.

We risk your thinking that we are stating the obvious – that in some way we are being patronising.

We are far from alone in adopting these techniques. To cite just one supporter: Peter Lynch retired in 1990 as manager of the (US) Fidelity Magellan Fund, which for years was America's top-ranked general equity mutual fund – a fund an investment of $1,000 in which in 1977 was worth $28,000 in 1990. Writing of three companies which made him a great deal of money, he says (page 118 of *Beating the Street*, published by Simon and Schuster, and well-worth reading in its entirety):
'Employees and shoppers in these stores could have seen the evidence with their own eyes, and learned the same details that Danoff [a retail analyst] and I did. The alert shopper has a chance to get the message about retailers earlier than Wall

Street does, and to make back all the money he or she ever spends on merchandise – by buying undervalued stocks.'

Another advocate of the principle, nearer home: 'After my initial due diligence, I always try to keep a watching brief over the few stocks that constitute my portfolio. Needless to say, I read about all major developments and keep an eye on Directors' share dealings. I also keep an eye on retail sales. Let me give you a recent example – after Psion introduced their new palm-top computers, they had some teething troubles, and a batch had to be withdrawn. While I was interested in the shares, whenever out shopping, I took the oportunity of dropping into a Dixons store and, under the guise of being a prospective customer, asked an assistant how Psion sales were progressing, if they were recommending anything better and whether or not they had any trouble with the product.' (Jim Slater, *The Zulu Principle*, published by Orion).

Practice

In the High Street, and on your local trading estate, indeed wherever you find yourself: observe carefully, listen attentively and note down any significant development that might impact on the sales, profitability and future of businesses around you.

If you have the chance, talk to assistants about the effects of their company having been recently taken over. Have things changed for the better – or for the worse? Has it really made any difference?

When you get home, take half an hour to jot down your conclusions.

Chapter 2

THE QUICK LOOK

A two-stage approach

We recommend a two-stage approach to the study of a report and accounts:

1. A quick look; then, if what you see is still of interest
2. A longer look; considered in Chapter 3.

In this way any company with which you are not happy can be discarded without undue waste of time. This is important. It is efficient. Getting to grips with a company – making an in-depth study of its report and accounts – is time-consuming, not something which can be done in a few moments. So the sooner that any duds are discarded, the better.

Getting a first impression

At first, you are likely to need at least 15 to 20 minutes to get any sort of feel for a company. With experience, just five minutes study in the case of a small company, and generally less than 10, may be all that is needed to reject a business or decide it is worth further study. It is all a matter of practice.

Before you even open the report, ask yourself how *you* feel about the sector. Is it cyclical? Is it currently unpopular – or is going through the roof? That alone certainly is not enough but it should, colour your views.

See what the market thinks of the company: consider the share price (both in absolute terms and as an index relatative) and the company's high/low, dividend yield and price earnings ratio.

On opening the report, obtain a general feel for the way in which the company has progressed (or otherwise) over the last few years by glancing at any table of 'Financial Highlights'. After that, this is the sequence we suggest:

DIRECTORS' REPORT:

1. Study the statement of the 'Principal activities of the company'. This often forms the first paragraph of the Directors' Report. It is usually somewhat generalised, but it does provide something to build upon. Unless you have a sound idea of what a company (group) does, you will find it difficult to come to meaningful conclusions.
2. Glance at the directors' shareholdings and stakes over 3%. Do they tell you anything?

PROFIT & LOSS ACCOUNT:

3. Has there been a sharp change in turnover? If so, check the Directors' Report for details of acquisitions and disposals.
4. Is the company making losses – or did the latest year show sharply lower profits? If so, why? What has gone wrong?
5. Is interest cover less than 5 – and falling? If so, that is a disturbing sign.
6. Are earnings per share rising or falling? If they are falling, has the company issued a large number of new shares during the year?

BALANCE SHEET:

7. Have equity shareholders' funds fallen? Study with care: (i) the statement of total recognised gains and losses; and (ii) the reconciliation of movements in shareholders' funds – required by FRS 3. Possible reasons for a fall are: an after tax loss; an uncovered dividend; write downs of property values against revaluation reserve; extraordinary items or prior year adjustments; adverse foreign currency translation differences; acquisitions (the writing off of goodwill) or

earn outs (additional performance related payments to vendors, which, since they bring no new tangible assets, represent additional goodwill).

8. Have borrowings – especially floating rate borrowings – increased sharply?

9. Are large amounts of borrowings soon due for repayment (or renegotiation)? If so, two possible difficulties may arise: (1) lenders may be unwilling to continue the facilities at all (eg bankers may already be struggling to recover lending to other companies in the same industry); or (2) it may be necessary to replace existing borrowings made at a modest fixed rate (eg a debenture or loan stock) with variable rate borrowings, possibly at a much higher rate

10. Contingent liabilities: Are payments likely to arise in the near future for earn-outs? Are there any guarantees, other than for borrowings of subsidiaries?

11. Post balance sheet events (eg rights issues, acquisitions or disposals).

CASH FLOW STATEMENT:

12. Was cash generated by operations? Negative cash generation by operations is a sure sign of strain.

13. When times are hard, cash is king. It is lack of available cash which is the killer (rather than inadequate profitability or even loss-making). How, therefore, have liquid resources changed? Study the notes. Is there any suggestion that the liquidity is under pressure? If so, check the chairman's statement for any comment about relationships with the company's bankers.

13. Has there been any significant expenditure on Goodwill. If so, check the Directors' Report for acquisition details.

HISTORICAL SUMMARY:

14. Are profits growing? Or are they static, or falling like a lead balloon?

AUDITORS' REPORT:

15. Take a quick glance to see if there anything significant eg a going-concern qualification? But don't expect the auditors to rock the boat. If they highlight a company's difficulties they will almost ensure its speedy demise. As a result: auditors' warnings often come too late.

In making a quick look, we follow up items into the notes to the accounts where it seems likely that they will shed valuable further light, *but only then*.

On the other hand, we do not regard our list as exhaustive: if other things stand out, we note them.

Summing up

Whether or not you decide the company is worth investigating further, spend a few moments to develop your conclusions.

Try, in a just a sentence or two to put the company into perspective:

(i) What sector is it in?
(ii) How does it rank in terms of size?
(iii) Why it is worth exploring further?
(iv) What loose ends did you find which would need further research?
(v) If you feel it is a company which should be left alone: why did you come to that conclusion?

A typical thumb-nail sketch might be: 'Grubby is a small West Midlands-based, effectively family-controlled contractor. It is suffering from the recent recession, has severe liquidity problems, and may not survive long enough to see a return to better times. Cheap, but not worth considering even as a recovery stock.'

The same ... but different

Investment analysis is indeed an art; and like any artist the analyst needs to develop a sense of perspective, and in particular to be able to relate one company to another, rather than consider it in isolation.

Just as a judge 'distinguishes' the facts in the case he has just heard from those in earlier cases, which he would otherwise be obliged to follow, so the analyst needs to look for differences between one company and another which is superficially similar.

Make a practice, therefore, even in taking a quick look, of considering competitors. By assessing their strengths, you will more easily spot the weaknesses of the company you are studying.

Case study: Wilding Office Equipment

Now give the following company a 'Quick Look', jot down the main points you notice, and then compare your commentary with that at the end of the chapter.

The extracts are given in the sequence in which they appear in the accounts, *not* in the sequence we have suggested for checking them.

WILDING OFFICE EQUIPMENT
When Wilding's 1990 accounts were published in March 1991, the *Financial Times* showed the 10p ordinary shares standing at 31p, giving a market capitalisation of about £5m, with a 1990–91 high / low of 112p / 20p.

Extracts from the report and accounts are to be found on pages 8 – 10.

Beyond the Balance Sheet

CHAIRMAN'S STATEMENT

Following the issue of shares referred to below, the gearing of the Group on a proforma basis as at 30 September 1990 was 86%, and the Group continues to receive positive support from its bankers [A].

DIRECTORS' REPORT

Principal activities and review of business developments
The principal activity of the Group is the sale and servicing of office equipment [B].

Fixed assets

The directors consider that the market value of the freehold and leasehold properties is in excess of book value but do not believe that the expense of a formal valuation is justified at this time [V].

Acquisitions

Open-Plan, which was acquired on 9 November 1988 achieved its target profit in the year under review and therefore a final consideration of £875,000 is payable to the vendors. This was satisfied by the issue and allotment of 2,573,529 Ordinary shares to the vendors on 25 January 1991.

Tyne & Wear Office Supplies Limited, which was acquired on 7 July 1988 has achieved its target profit and therefore a final consideration of £40,000 was paid to the vendors on 19 December 1990.

CONSOLIDATED PROFIT AND LOSS ACCOUNT
FOR THE YEAR ENDED 30 SEPTEMBER 1990

	Note	1990 £	1989 £
TURNOVER	[C]	54,064,943	50,554,836
Operating costs	[D]	54,018,541	49,752,360
TRADING PROFIT	[E]	46,402	802,476
Other income		6,345	51,682
Interest payable and similar charges	[F] 2cr	(637,821)	(344,854)
(LOSS) / PROFIT ON ORDINARY ACTIVITIES BEFORE TAXATION		(585,074)	509,304
Taxation		(192,928)	149,008
(LOSS) / PROFIT ON ORDINARY ACTIVITIES AFTER TAXATION		(392,146)	360,296
Retained profits at 30 September 1990		3,088,016	3,400,052
Dividend		(288,125)	(672,332)
RETAINED PROFIT AT 30 SEPTEMBER 1990		2,407,745	3,088,016
(LOSS) / EARNINGS PER SHARE	[G]	(2.4p)	2.3p

BALANCE SHEET AS AT 30 SEPTEMBER 1990 (GROUP)

		1990 £	1989 £
FIXED ASSETS			
Tangible assets	13	5,644,994	4,714,839
Intangible assets	[H] 15	378,990	473,000
		6,023,984	5,187,839
CURRENT ASSETS			
Stock		9,162,153	9,802,032
Debtors	17	8,464,795	9,447,246
Cash at bank and in hand		36,087	265,610
		17,663,035	19,514,888
CREDITORS – amounts falling due within one year [I]:			
Bank loans and overdrafts	18	3,419,876	3,090,939
Trade and other creditors	19	13,403,683	12,782,326
		16,823,559	15,873,265
NET CURRENT ASSETS		839,476	3,641,623
TOTAL ASSETS LESS CURRENT LIABILITIES		6,863,460	8,829,462
creditors – amounts falling due after more than one year:			
Hire purchase	20	332,137	498,773
Loan notes to be issued		–	875,000
PROVISIONS FOR LIABILITIES AND CHARGES	21	108,355	258,387
		6,422,968	7,197,302
CAPITAL AND RESERVES			
Called up share capital		1,600,864	1,600,864
Shares to be issued	23	875,000	–
Share premium account		1,133,466	1,133,466
Other reserves	25	405,893	1,374,956
Profit and loss a/c	11	2,407,745	3,088,016
	[J]	6,422,968	7,197,302

NOTES
7. INTEREST PAYABLE AND SIMILAR CHARGES

	1990 £	1989 £
Bank loans & overdrafts, net	379,100	209,510
Hire purchase and finance charges	155,293	135,344
Other interest payable	103,428	–
	637,821	344,854

8

CONSOLIDATED STATEMENT OF SOURCE AND APPLICATION OF FUNDS FOR THE YEAR ENDED 30 SEPTEMBER 1990

SOURCES OF FUNDS		1990 £	1989 £
FROM OPERATIONS			
(Loss) / Profit on ordinary activities before tax		(585,074)	509,304
Items not involving the movement of funds:			
Depreciation of tangible fixed assets		1,211,207	933,142
Profit on sale of tangible fixed assets		(67,568)	(73,824)
Amortisation of intangible assets		167,333	29,000
	[K]	725,898	1,397,622
OTHER SOURCES			
Issue of shares on acquisition of subsidiary		875,000	10,270,396
Proceeds of sale of fixed assets		173,288	101,954
Issue of loan notes		–	875,000
Tax refunded		–	389,443
Total sources of funds		1,774,186	13,034,415
FUNDS APPLIED			
Purchase of goodwill [L]		(969,063)	(8,425,768)
Purchase of tangible fixed assets	[N]	(2,247,082)	(3,734,288)
Payment of dividend		(672,332)	(559,611)
Payment of tax		(1,143,955)	(1,499,700)
Purchase of intangible fixed assets		(73,323)	(502,000)
Decrease in working capital		(3,331,569)	(1,686,952)
Arising from movements in:			
Stock	[M]	(639,879)	(43,520)
Debtors	[M]	(1,354,197)	1,538,299
Creditors		(779,033)	(660,235)
		(2,773,109)	834,544
Net liquid funds			
– bank overdraft		(328,937)	(2,731,329)
– bank and cash balance		(229,523)	209,833
		(558,460)	(2,521,496)
		(3,331,569)	(1,686,952)

14. INVESTMENT IN SUBSIDIARIES

	1990 £	1989 £
At 30 September 1989	11,690,864	381,766
Cost of shares acquired during the year	921,000	9,309,098
Provision made at 30 September 1990	(345,278)	–
Long term loan	(2,000,000)	2,000,000
At 30 September 1990	10,266,586	11,690,864

15. INTANGIBLE ASSETS

Deferred development costs of new furniture ranges [O]

At 1 October 1989	£473,000
Incurred in year	73,323
Amortised in year	(167,333)
At 30 September 1990	£378,990

19. TRADE AND OTHER CREDITORS - AMOUNTS FALLING DUE WITHIN ONE YEAR

		Group 1990 £	1989 £
...			
Deferred maintenance contract income		2,224,952	1,735,626
Loan notes	[P]	875,000	–
Taxation		–	815,104
Other creditors		210,754	531,696
...			

The loan notes are unsecured. £122,467 was repaid on 3 December 1990 and the balance of £752,533 is repayable in three equal instalments on 7 April, 1 June and 1 August 1991. They carry an interest rate of 1.5% pa below LIBOR to 30 November 1990, and thereafter 1.5% above National Westminster Bank base lending rate [Q].

23. SHARES TO BE ISSUED

Since the year end and pursuant to the agreement for the acquisition of Open-Plan Limited the final instalment to the vendors has been agreed at £875,000. As provided by the agreement this has been satisfied by the issue to the vendors of 2,573,529 new Ordinary shares of 10p each [R].

13. TANGIBLE FIXED ASSETS

	Freehold property	Short leasehold premises	Plant and equipment	Motor vehicles	Total
	£	£	£	£	£
Cost					
At 1 October 1989	1,322,034	2,078,863	1,544,244	2,774,166	7,719,307
Additions	-	935,206	466,024	845,852	2,247,082
Disposals	-	-	(65,756)	(486,676)	(552,432)
At 30 September 1990	1,322,034	3,014,069	1,944,512	3,133,342	9,413,957
Depreciation					
At 1 October 1989	9,517	716,277	875,047	1,403,627	3,004,468
Charge for year	32,686	237,291	260,755	680,475	1,211,207
Disposals	-	-	(43,793)	(402,919)	(446,712)
At 30 September 1990	42,203	953,568	1,092,009	1,681,183	3,768,963
Net book amounts					
At 30 September 1990	1,279,831	2,060,501	852,503	1,452,159	5,644,994
At 30 September 1989	1,312,517	1,362,586	669,197	1,370,539	4,714,839

25. OTHER RESERVES

	GROUP	
	1990	1989
	£	£
At 1 October 1989	1,374,956	–
Arising on issue of shares for acquisition of subsidiary company	–	9,800,724
Less: Goodwill written off [S]	(969,063)	(8,425,768)
At 30 September 1990	405,893	1,374,956

27. **PENSION COSTS**

The group operates a number of defined contribution schemes. The assets are held separately from those of the group. ... Pensions charge includes contributions paid by the Group ... £143,641 (1989 – £60,458) [X].

28. **PARTICULARS OF TRANSACTIONS INVOLVING DIRECTORS**

The Company rents two of its shops from the personal pension scheme of Mr T E Wilding. The rent is on normal commercial terms and amounted to £18,360 (1989 – £18,360).

Open-Plan Ltd rents one of its premises from a partnership in which Mr J F Nott is a partner. The rent is on normal commercial terms and amounted to £32,000 (1989 – £24,000).

Open-Plan Ltd trades with a company in which Mr J F Nott was a shareholder. The company produces artificial flower displays. During the year £27,228 (1989 – £15,182) has been invoiced to and £190,067 (1989 – £206,170) invoiced by this company on normal commercial terms. Mr J F Nott disposed of his shareholding in this company on December 18 1990; as a result he will receive over a period of between three and five years deferred consideration based in part upon the volume of purchases by Open-Plan Ltd from this company during that time [W].

REPORT OF THE AUDITORS

We have audited the accounts on pages 8 to 19 in accordance with Auditing Standards.

In our opinion the accounts give a true and fair view of the state of affairs of the Company and of the Group at September 30 1990 and of the loss and source and application of funds of the Group for the year then ended and have been properly prepared in accordance with the Companies Act 1985 [U].

FIVE YEAR RECORD FOR THE YEAR ENDED 30 SEPTEMBER 1990

	1990 £000	1989 £000	1988 £000	1987 £000	1986 £000
			[T]		
Turnover	54,065	50,555	41,423	30,849	22,207
(Loss) / Profit before tax	(585)	509	2,677	2,021	1,264
Taxation credit / (charge)	193	(149)	(995)	(741)	(498)
(Loss) / Profit after tax	(392)	360	1,682	1,280	766
(Loss) / Earnings per share (p)	(2.4)	2.3	15.0	11.7	7.9

Commentary

CHAIRMAN'S STATEMENT:

1. The Group continues to receive positive support from its bankers [A] – it certainly needs it.

DIRECTORS' REPORT:

2. Company sells and services office equipment [B].

PROFIT & LOSS ACCOUNT:

3. Turnover: growing, but not as fast as inflation [C].
4. Trading profit: almost wiped out [E].
5. Operating costs: out of control? or were they taken by surprise by recession? Were there any stock write-offs? [D].
6. Interest cover: 2.33 in 1989; uncovered in 1990 [F].
7. Earnings per share: Loss per share 2.4p (1989 eps 2.3p) [G].

BALANCE SHEET:

8. Equity shareholders' funds: fell [J]. Reasons: After tax loss; uncovered dividend; goodwill written off [S].
9. Borrowings increased sharply [I & P].
10. Loan Notes of £0.875m repayable in current year [P & Q].
11. There was no note on Contingent Liabilities.

FUNDS FLOW STATEMENT:

12. Funds generated by operations remain positive [K]. Reassuring sign. But doesn't a rising overdraft and falling cash suggest need for permanent capital?
13. Expenditure on Goodwill. Hefty acquisition in 1989 [L].

HISTORICAL SUMMARY:

14. Turnover continues to grow, but profits and eps peaked in 1988 [T]. In decline since despite acquisition and expansion. Why?

AUDITORS' REPORT:

15. Clean [U].

WE ALSO NOTICED:

16. Capitalisation of development costs of new products [H & O]. This is not prudent accounting.
17. Less money tied up in stock and debtors [M]: a good sign, unless forced upon the company by the bank.
18. Hefty outlay on additions to fixed assets. Looks as though they planned expansion but got their timing wrong [N].
19. Statement that freehold and leasehold land and buildings worth in excess of book value, but not worth the expense of revaluation (not uncommon) [V].
19. Transactions involving directors [W]. Always worth watching. These do not appear either unfair or threatening.
20. Sharp increase in pension contributions. On a company visit or other contact with the company it could be worth asking why [X].
21. Earn-out in 1990 [R].
22. The significant high / low range.

THUMB-NAIL SKETCH:

A smallish listed office equipment marketing and maintenance company which grew impressively from 1986 through to 1988. Expansion in 1989/90 came just at the wrong time and it now seems that Wilding probably paid too much for the subsidiaries acquired in 1989 (goodwill written off against reserves represented £8,425,768 of total cost of £10,270,396 (i.e. 82%).

With hindsight

Most people have 20:20 vision in hindsight, but it is, nevertheless, instructive to make a practice of following up one's analyses.

Let us see what happened to Wilding:

WILDING OFFICE EQUIPMENT *Extract from* Evening Standard *6 December 1991*

Pentos chairman Terry Maher has snapped up the struggling Wilding Office Equipment to add to his Rymans stationery and office furniture chain ...

At the same time as accepting the Pentos offer, Wilding announced a £2.9m loss for the year to 30 September against a £500,000 loss last time ...

Pentos is offering Wilding shareholders a mixture of shares and new Pentos warrants worth 20p a share against a closing price last night of 27p ...

The bid was 'successful', but that was not the end of the story.

PENTOS *Extract from the* Financial Times *5 March 1993*

Pentos, owners of specialist retailers Dillons, Ryman and Athena, has put its office furniture group up for sale as it reported a collapse in 1992 pre-tax profits from £15.2m to £4m.

The group also revealed that the £3.7m purchase of Wilding Office Equipment in December 1991, now merged with the Rymans chain, had resulted in a fair value provision of £12m.

Fair value provisions are necessary where the accounting principles of acquirer and acquired differ. Where valuations (eg of freeholds) are involved, an element of subjectivity enters into things. Hefty fair value provisions may be seen as a sign that management failed to do its homework properly, deceived itself, or was deceived. Often they are simply a convenient way of sweeping problems under the carpet.

Practice

Ability to get to grips with a company quickly and confidently comes only with practice.

Select a any company which interests you but:

1. Don't try to run before you can walk. Avoid choosing companies which are too big or whose group structure is too complex.
2. Don't expect all the companies you look at to be as interesting as Wilding. Like people, some companies are unambitious and just drift.
3. While the authors took less than 10 minutes to assess Wilding – though it took much longer to explain what they saw – don't expect to be able to work that fast straight away.

We cannot over-emphasise the importance of practice – of requesting accounts, talking to companies, atttending annual meetings, chatting to the directors, acquiring an instinct, knowing when to believe and when to be suspicious.

Without practice you will progress very slowly, if at all. But do remember, that it is only a quick look you are taking at this stage. You are not asked for a full analysis.

Start now: grab half a dozen annual reports and accounts and try out the quick look for yourself.

A company you might like to look at is Nobo Group – an office equipment company directly comparable with Wilding.

Chapter 3

THE LONGER LOOK

Where do you start?

Analysts differ in the way they approach an in depth study of a report and accounts. No one approach suits everyone.

Many start with the profit and loss account, homing in on turnover and profit from ordinary activities. Others look first at the earnings per share on the basis that they represent the best indicator of: (1) effective growth; (2) potential for both internally generated growth and dividend growth.

Those with a banking background tend to look first at the balance sheet. Or, taking the view that cash is king, the cash flow statement.

Yet others begin at the beginning and read the document from cover to cover.

Forming the right habits

It is important in making an in-depth study of a report and accounts:

1. *To use a consistent approach*, ie to get into the habit of reading through in a particular order which suits you and your purposes.
2. *To read everything*. Remember that it is the accounts *as a whole* which are required to give a true and fair view; and that information buried deep in a somewhat impenetrable note still forms part of that view. Recognise, too, that annual accounts have many limitations, some though not all of which can be overcome by directors who seek to be forthcoming in their review of activities, chairman's statement, financial review or directors' report.
3. *To read critically*, to listen for nuances, to notice when something expected is omitted (eg when there is no mention of a significant area of operations). Try to develop the ability

to detect inconsistencies or the need for further information, and to store these in your memory for future consideration – other sections of the report may shed further light, or they may simply add to your doubts.

People study reports and accounts for a variety of reasons. A few, very few, do so purely for pleasure. The vast majority have what may be termed a commercial reason, as investors or potential investors, analysts, fund managers, existing and potential lenders, suppliers, customers or employees. In broad terms what interests each of these groups is *risk*: absolute risk and risk relative to the market as a whole, to other sectors, to other companies and to other forms of investment; and *reward*.

In this Chapter we take the viewpoint of an analyst or substantial private or institutional investor prepared to devote time to the study of a particular business as an equity investor.

Before making or recommending any substantial investment in equities, he needs to ask himself:

1. Why should I (my client or company) invest in equities (rather than in, say, fixed interest securities, land or works of art)?
2. Why should I invest in *this* sector?
3. Why should I invest in *this* company rather than in one of its competitors?

Why invest in equities at all?

Investors generally seek:

1. Security of capital;
2. Security of income;
3. Reward.

But they may have other reasons; and the stress which they place on security and capital growth as against current income differs widely.

In times of inflation, the value of the annual income from a fixed interest security (be it a government stock, debenture, loan stock or preference share) falls in real terms year by year. Not only that, but if and when the stock is redeemed, the amount returned will, because of inflation, buy much less than it would have done when the investment was originally made.

Equities, on the other hand, represent investment in businesses and business assets, such as property, plant and machinery. Because of inflation the turnover and profits of such organisations, and the dividends they pay, tend to grow rather than remain fixed. 'Equities', it is suggested, 'provide a hedge against inflation'. This has given rise over the past 30–40 years to what is termed 'the cult of the equity' and the 'reverse yield gap'.

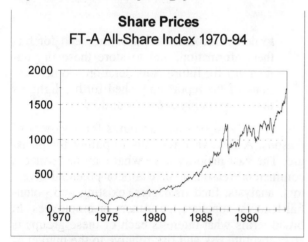

Share Prices
FT-A All-Share Index 1970-94

Example 3.1 FT–A All-Share Index 1970–94

Traditionally (ie until the 1950s) the dividend yield on equities was substantially *greater* than the yield on government stocks and other fixed interest securities, the difference representing the perceived additional risk attaching to equity investment. That position has reversed giving rise to what is termed the reverse yield gap. Forty or so years of inflation have ensured that few investors remember a situation when equities did not yield markedly less than fixed interest securities.

Equity investors today look not simply at dividend yield but at the total return:

Total return = Income + Capital Appreciation

They are prepared to pay heavily for growth of:

1. Capital value; and / or
2. Income.

For example, on 30 November 1992, the yield on irredeemable British Government Stocks was 8.9 per cent. The same day, GLAXO ordinary yielded 2.8 per cent. That is to say, GLAXO investors were not only prepared to take the additional risk of investing in equities rather than gilts but to suffer a 6.1 per cent reduction in yield - in the ex-

pectation that Glaxo would over the lifetime of their investment show growth in capital value (share price) and/or income sufficient to make this worth while.

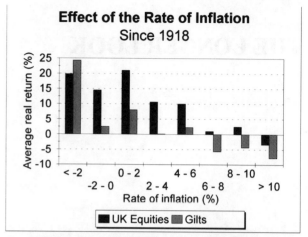

Effect of the Rate of Inflation
Since 1918

Example 3.2 Inflation is bad news whether you invest in Equities or Gilts (data: Barclays de Zoete Wedd Research Ltd based on experience since 1918)

Equity share values thus depend heavily upon the market's perception of: (1) inflation prospects and (2) growth prospects: (a) generally; and (b) of a particular share or sector. If inflation looks likely to be conquered or future growth begins to look less certain, share values fall, surprisingly rapidly.

Bearing this in mind, it is perhaps useful to express total return in more detail:

$$\text{Total return} = \text{Income} + \text{Sale proceeds} - \text{Cost of investment}$$

One can *measure* this only over the lifetime of the investment. Everything depends upon exit values. Until an investment is sold, and the net sale proceeds after selling costs and tax received, one can only estimate total return. Exit value risk is just one element of overall risk.

The in-depth study of either (1) a sector or (2) an individual company is, as we shall see, all about the assessment of risk.

How to choose a sector

Logically, people invest in a particular sector at a particular time in order:

1. To achieve a greater total return (to a particular time horizon, eg in the short term, or as a long-term investment) than would be provided by other sectors.

2. To obtain or maintain a portfolio with a particular balance.

Specialist funds exist which focus on one or more individual sectors, but it is generally unwise for private investors or pension funds to 'put all their eggs in one basket' in one company, or even to concentrate unduly on one sector, because of the risk. This explains the growing popularity of index funds aiming to replicate performance of the FTSE 100, that of smaller companies or of a particular country's stock market.

So, in considering a company we first consider *prospects for the sector*:

1. *Demand*: Is the company operating in a growth area – eg Pharmaceuticals (until recently)? – or an ex-growth area like Retailers? – or in a declining area like making machinery for the UK coal-mining industry?
2. *Cyclicity*: Is it a steady business in hard times as well as good, eg Food Manufacturers and Retailers, Electricity and Water? – or is demand likely to be curtailed in hard times eg Capital Goods? In an up-turn, will it precede or follow the general trend?
3. *Overcrowding*: Is there excess capacity in the UK eg Financial Services?
4. *Overseas competition*: This can vary from intense eg Motor Manufacturing and Textiles, to nil eg Ready-mixed concrete.

Only then do we focus on prospects for the individual company.

Assessing a company's prospects

In order to assess prospects for a particular company or group one needs to look at:

1. *Track record*: Has the company grown reasonably steadily of the last five years or is turnover in real terms static or even declining? If it has grown meteorically (see Chapter 9) is the growth balanced ie has the balance sheet kept pace with turnover growth or does the balance sheet look out of step? If the company has faced problems, has it tackled them successfully? Experience is a great teacher – if one is prepared to learn (and is given the chance).
2. *Products*: Has the company product strength or is it dependent on just one product or brand name? Are there barriers to entry (legal or the high capital investment involved) or has it technical advantages? Does it place a lot of emphasis on developing and launching new products, and has it a successful record in doing so?
3. *Assets*: Are there substantial tangible fixed assets eg does it own its own freeholds – and are they free to support borrowings or are they already encumbered? As one fund manager put it: 'I don't like companies where the assets go down in the lift and home at night'. He was talking about advertising agencies, but the same applies to all 'people' businesses.

4. *Operational risk*: Has the company high fixed costs, making it vulnerable to a fall in demand eg large manufacturing plants? Is its plant special purpose, making it dependent upon a particular product or is it general purpose, allowing it to adapt swiftly to a change in markets?
5. *Financial risk*: Do its operations generate cash, or absorb it? Is it heavily borrowed – particularly short term or at variable rate? Does it operate in an industry (eg property in the early 1990s) many companies in which have caused problems for the banks? However undeservedly, mud tends to rub off.
6. *Commercial risk*: Is the company heavily dependent on one customer or one type of customer? Does it undertake large, high risk, contracts? eg CONDER got into awful trouble in the early 1980s over a major contract with Iraq. More recently, it hit problems with wall cladding.
7. *Political risk*: Does it operate in politically risky or sensitive countries, and is any one of the countries very important to it? eg YUGOTOURS (Yugoslavia); POLLY PECK (Turkey and Turkish Zone of Cyprus); LONRHO (central and Southern Africa).
8. *Currency risk*: Where precisely are the assets and just where are the profits earned (and the cash generated)? Are there unmatched and unhedged borrowings (ie borrowins not covered by swaps or similar arrangements?
9. *Changes in shape (and / or strategy)*: This is a vital area which deserves consideration of a number of separate features:

   (i) Has the company made any acquisitions or disposals recently?
   (ii) Did those acquisitions represent a logical expansion of their existing area of expertise or an adventure into the unknown?
   (iii) How successful have past acquisitions been?
   (iv) Has it started up in new business areas or new geographical areas? Is it about to embark on a 'great leap forward'?
   (v) Does it pre-finance expansion (by rights issues, acquisitions for paper) or does it (like SOCK SHOP) do it all on overdraft?
   (vi) Are earn-outs pre-financed? Compare GOLD, GREENLEES TROTT and FKB and YELLOWHAMMER (see Chapter 9).
   (vii) When it introduces new capacity, does it reduce the risk by selling part of the capacity forward on long term contracts in order to cover fixed costs (as BOC)?

(viii) If there have been disposals, why? Was it a case of sifting through an acquisition and getting rid of the dross rather than trying to turn it round (quite reasonable)? Were companies acquired with a view to their being sold on (at a profit)? Or were the disposals simply past acquisitions which had failed? Has their been a strategic change – a decision to focus on a particular area with which the activities disposed of did not fit? Was it simply the sale of businesses which while profitble generated cash which could be employed more profitably elsewhere? Or was the need for cash desperate?

10. *Controlling shareholding*: If any one person or connected group of people have more than 50 per cent of the voting rights, you are entirely at their mercy. But control can also be exercised *de facto* by a family group with less than 50 per cent of the votes. If control is exercised through foreign trusts or a privately owned foreign company, or worse still by a group of interlocking foreign companies and trusts incorporated in tax havens with a low level of disclosure (the case with POLLY PECK), other shareholders are very vulnerable.

11. *Management*: Perhaps most important of all:

    (i) Have you any reason for not trusting the management?

    (ii) Have there been recent changes at the top eg STAKIS, GUINESS, BRITISH & COMMONWEALTH? If so why? Do they suggest changes in strategy may be imminent?

    (iii) Is it a 'one man band', or is there a good mix of age and experience on the Board? What is the second tier management like?

    (iv) Is the Board packed with superannuated politicians or other chums of the Chairman (consider MAXWELL)?

    (v) Nepotism. Is the son as good as the father? Has he the strength of personality, when necessary, to be independent?

12. *Directors' share purchases and sales*: Purchases (unless they represent the exercise of options at a price well below current market price) are an expression of confidence (though it could be misplaced) by insiders supposedly in the know. Equally, sales *may* represent an attempt to get out before it is too late. But they can simply be a restructuring of a director's investment portfolio: it is no

more reasonable for a director to tie up all his money in a single company than for anyone else. Equally, they may represent a change in domestic circumstances eg the purchase of country house prior to retirement.

13. *Share Price*: Consider recent price performance: Does the share look good value for the sector? Consider the share price chart: does it look 'toppy'? Take the case of FIRST TECHNOLOGY, a company highly dependent on the motor industry, and in particular VOLVO, which suffered with that industry in the 1988–92 recession.

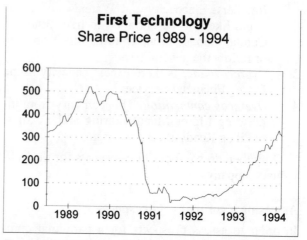

Example 3.3 Toppy in 1990? Then down, not out

Readers may find it useful to set out these points in the form of a checklist, and to apply it whenever they make a detailed study of a company.

Developing useful key ratios

Analysts have developed a host of ratios – operating and investment ratios – which are discussed in Chapter 24 of *Interpreting Company Reports and Accounts*. But ratios are not an end in themselves.

It is helpful to develop a standard series of ratios, ratios which you personally find useful and which can be used in discussing companies with colleagues. A few key ratios, like gross profit ratio, interest cover and earnings per share, apart, it is probably better to study the accounts in detail first, discover a feature of interest (or a problem) and only then quantify things with an appropriate ratio. If one begins by calculating a host of ratios, one is in danger of not seeing the wood for the trees.

Practice

Select any company, and work carefully through the checklist. Choose a company which particularly interests you. Failing that, obtain the report and accounts of PARK FOOD GROUP, a company widely tipped in 1991–93, despite the recession, who, amongst other things, produce and sell hampers.

Chapter 4

THE COMPANY VISIT

Seize any opportunity

Analysts often have the chance to visit a company and meet its senior management. So occasionally do substantial investors, and fund managers.

Major customers and potential customers too sometimes receive an invitation to look over the plant in an attempt to convince them of a supplier's efficiency. Suppliers may be offered such an opportunity.

Bankers and major lenders/venture capitalists such as *3i* who recognise that it is not a balance sheet but a company, its management, products and productive capacity that they are backing, often have, or make, the chance to see for themselves.

Such an opportunity should not be turned down lightly. To do so may well leave the advantage with the competition.

Nor should the company visit be regarded as a perk, as a day out, an escape from the office. Properly conducted, a company visit is hard work.

Prepare thoroughly

To take full advantage of a company visit it is necessary to prepare thoroughly. Before he sets out, the well-informed analyst (for simplicity we will refer to him as an analyst, though he could well be a banker or businessman) has studied the group or company history; knows something about the management team, their origins and background; has a file of recent press clippings (covering the past year) and has studied the group's published plans, its strengths and weaknesses.

More than this:

1. He knows where the competition lies, and
2. He has studied their published plans, and strengths, too.

Before visiting a company the analyst should:

1. Take a brief look at the company along the lines suggested in Chapter 2.
2. Work through the detailed checklist proposed in Chapter 3.

Inevitably, this process will raise an number of pertinent questions to which he would like the answer. If he is member of a group of visiting analysts from rival firms, he may decide it is best not to raise the question publicly, contenting himself instead with 'making his number' with management so that he is in a position to ask later, either by telephone or at the meeting if a moment presents itself. The important thing is not to impress your peers but to obtain information which they have not got.

Meet the management

The art in meeting management is to listen, rather than to talk; and to keep the flow going, rather than bring it to a premature halt. In an interview or as part of a small group, it pays to grunt, or say 'yes', or to raise one's eyebrows in mild disbelief, rather than interrupt the speaker. Few people, being interviewed, can resist a questioning look, or an unfilled silence, they tend to go on, to explain, to amplify, to defend themselves or their company.

Listen for nuances. But rather than pouncing immediately, store them up for possible use later.

Be careful not to allow a speaker who says: 'there are three reasons why we did so and so' to be interrupted and give only two. The third reason might just be the most revealing.

We frequently interview as a team; each armed with our own questions and maintaining our own tape record – for tape recorders do occasionally malfunction.

We also make a practice of renewing batteries before every interview. The cost in terms of time and embarrassment of the loss of a taped record far outweighs that of new batteries.

Before the interview, we undertake to send a draft of anything we write to be cleared by the interviewee before publication, on the strict understanding that the interviewee has the right to veto (or fine tune) any quotation – though not to interfere with our opinions.

So, if you are getting an 'exclusive' interview with the Chairman, Chief Executive or FD, sound him out ahead of the visit about taping the interview. Even the most skilled analyst, or professional journalist, finds it difficult, if not impossible, to write down accurately everything that is said, and at the same time to think up and be ready with a follow-up question. Use of a tape recorder removes part of the burden.

It also pays, even when one has tape backup, to make brief handwritten notes: (1) as a double safeguard and (2) as an index to the tape record.

Visit the factory

Rather than confining yourself to the office of the person you are seeing, take advantage of any offer of an opportunity to view the factory and offices, indeed actively seek such an opportunity. This again is not simply an interesting trip, a diversion, it is an opportunity to:

1. *Use your eyes:*

    (i) How old is the plant and machinery? Is it general purpose or special purpose machinery – is the company committed to one product or is there flexibility? Is it well maintained? Will it produce to high accuracy?

    (ii) How fully is the plant loaded? One joint author visited a printing company. After his visit, he remarked to the chairman: 'My eyes tell me that you are only 15% loaded. What are you doing to improve things?' An impertinent, subjective assessment, which drew the response: 'You are right, though we reckon it is nearer 25%, but we have certainly got to sell more. I, personally, am going out on the road on Monday.'

      Unfortunately, he had left it too late. Within three months the company was in liquidation.

    (iii) Does the plant look efficient? Or is there evidence, or even a suggestion, of waste or inefficiency?

2. *Use your ears.*
   Telephones that ring and are not answered tell one something of the organisation one is visiting – that customers, and potential customers do not matter; that top management does not control this aspect of customer relations, perhaps because it does not see the importance of efficient, considerate, customer relations, or does not care, or has more important matters to worry about – in one case we met, this was labour relations (we found that just as we met in another room half the workforce was being made redundant as part of a modernisation programme), but it could equally well have been staving off financial disaster.

   Staff are not always discreet. They tell you what they honestly think! Either explicitly or by their behaviour. If they are sulky – no response to your cheerful 'Good morning' – then industrial relations may not be too good.

   Should you follow up indiscretions by direct questions? Not if there is any chance of being given the information only on an 'off the record' basis. And certainly not when part of a large group, simply to show how clever you are. Instead, take the opportunity, after the visit, to write a thank you note to your host; and ask your question in that, so, hopefully, obtaining a personal reply, and at the same time building a contact.

3. *Watch the 'body language'.*
   How do managers behave: (1) to one another and (2) in one another's presence? Does their behaviour suggest, at one extreme, an autocratic chairman or chief executive who will brook no dissent, or at the other, a middle management which has the confidence of the board, and feels (1) free to speak up and (2) where necessary to act on its own initiative?

   On the factory floor, does the chief executive do all the talking, with the foreman and machine minders standing dutifully to attention? Or are you allowed to talk directly to the machine minder?

4. *Ask about the competition.*
   It's always worth asking about the competition for two reasons:

    (i) To get an idea of how management view their position in the market place, their strengths and weaknesses, and what they are doing to gain or reinforce competitive edge.

    (ii) Companies often know when a competitor is in serious trouble before it has become general knowledge. This may be useful background: next week you may be asked about that company. But it also provides information about the industry, its stresses and possible development.

It is sometimes said of an accountant that he has 'auditors' eyes'; that he is able to spot inconsistencies, and that somehow he knows where to look. This is not something one can acquire from a text book. Nor is it simply born of experience. It is a combination of inquisitiveness, dissatisfaction, suspicion, restlessness and of many skills, not least an ability continually to put two and two together in the knowledge, and expectation, that very occasionally they will make five. Analysts too need to develop 'analysts' eyes'; and there is no better way of doing this than visiting a company.

It is a useful discipline to make notes at the time and immediately on return to write them up and place them on file. If several individuals from the same firm or company go on the same visit, it is an interesting and instructive exercise for each independently to write up the visit, and then to exchange their file notes.

Firms which hold a morning meeting often expect reports of visits to be put before the next day's meeting. This has the threefold advantage of:

(i) Ensuring that visits are written up promptly;
(ii) Because such notes are on public record, improving their quality;
(iii) Building good internal communication of valuable information.

Try to attend annual general meetings

Annual meeting are time consuming; but they can provide an insight into management behaviour which the printed page does not. And they provide opportunities, though somewhat limited opportunities, to meet management personally.

Companies which hold their AGMs on site, rather than at an hotel or at an office in the City, will often invite those attending to go on a tour of their operations, and you can then get a real flavour of what the company is like. For example, BODY SHOP used to hold their AGM in their huge warehouse, on a Friday afternoon, with tea afterwards. The informal way in which Anita Roddick handed round cakes and chatted to everybody demonstrated how good she is with people.

If you had compared this with the last meeting of MAXWELL COMMUNICATION CORPORATION, where the dictatorial attitude of the Chairman came across all too loud and clear, you wouldn't have found it very difficult to decide which company not to put your money into.

If you attend an AGM (and if you are a serious investor, this is something you should make a habit of doing) and you find the management boot-faced and uncommunicative, be very cautious. At the other end of the scale, if the management seem just too optimistic (eg saying that they can 'buck the trend', when everybody knows the economy is turning down), be equally cautious. This applies particularly to companies run by a single dominant character (see Chapter 9).

Remember the story of the little old man in a shabby mackintosh who no sooner than the chairman got up at an AGM and said 'Things could not be better', shuffled out. When asked where he was going, the little man replied 'To sell my shares' – 'Why?' – 'Well if things could not be better, they can only get worse.'

Insider dealing

Until the share dealing scandals involving Boesky, Collier and Guinness (1986), insider dealing legislation tended to be seen by those who wanted to as largely irrelevant. Anyone visiting a company today would be well advised to study the provisions of Part V of the Criminal Justice Act 1993. The Stock Exchange has recently made it clear that visits and presentations to selected brokers/analysts /investors are beyond the pale unless information is released both publicly, and simultaneously.

Practice

Select at random a company which falls in terms of market capitalisation at the lower end of the FT-SE Actuaries Non-Financials index, preferably one that you have heard is rather good, and would like to know more about.

1. Find the name of the chairman. Write to him personally. Express interest in the company. Ask him for a copy of his company's latest accounts and interim statement, and for any other information which the shareholder relations department produces on its activities and products. Assess his response.

2. Work though the checklist in Chapter 3.

3. Imagine that you are invited to meet the chairman and tour the (a key) factory. Frame two series of questions:

   (i) questions of a general nature (which demonstrate your interest in the company and a broad knowledge of its products, activities, competition and problems);

   (ii) questions of a more challenging nature.

   The aim of the first series should be to encourage the chairman to talk, freely and without taking offence. The aim of the second is demonstrate, to yourself, your ability to get behind the published information – to probe omissions, inconsistencies and exaggerations.

Chapter 5

PRESENTATION

Methods of presentation

Presentation, more especially graphic presentation, is important to the analyst for four reasons:

1. People differ greatly in the ease with which they acquire information presented in different ways. Some find it easiest to understand and recall straight text; others – including most accountants – find that figures, and more especially tables of figure, are easy to understand and place in perspective. Yet others find that, to them, graphical methods create the most vivid and memorable impression. This is something we look at in more detail later in this chapter.
2. Standards exist for good presentation, both of numeric data and graphs. Fall below them and your presentation is likely not only to be unclear and/or unfair but to be mistrusted or even disregarded by readers.
3. Directors, and perhaps more especially their public relations advisers, are sometimes tempted distort their presentation in a deliberate attempt to hide unpleasant facts or simply to gild the lily. It is important to spot this since that will not only prevent the acceptance of inaccurate impressions but pin-point directors whose words, and actions, may be similarly bent.
4. Because layouts differ, it is easy to be misled, or to mislead oneself.

Accounts and tables

At one time it was quite common in accounts to find the *comparative figures* to the left of the narrative; and even when they were placed to the right they occasionally preceded those for the current year. The influence of the EC Fourth Directive, and the Companies Act 1985 formats to which it gave rise, ensure that the current year figures *virtually* always appear to the right of the narrative, followed by the corresponding figures. This makes it doubly important to watch out for exceptions. Such exceptions are perhaps most commonly found in takeover or merger documentation, where one needs to be especially on one's guard.

Brackets often trap the unwary since they are used in reports and accounts for several distinct purposes, and it is not always clear on first inspection in a particular case in which way they are being used.

They may indicate:

1. An item which is, by its nature, negative or adverse (ie which is deducted):

	£m
Ordinary Dividends	(72.7)
or	
Taxation	(54.8)

A sample of the 1991–1992 accounts of 50 listed companies taken at random showed 35 treating dividends in this way, 2 paying no dividend in either the current or the preceding year, and 13, including BRITISH LAND, BRITISH TELECOM, ROYAL BANK OF SCOTLAND, TESCO and GREAT UNIVERSAL STORES which do not bracket dividends, apparently assuming that the reader knows that dividends reduce the retained profits.

38 of the 50 companies bracketed a tax charge, 1 had no tax charge, and 11 did not.

In general companies were consistent, if they bracketed their tax charge, they also bracketed dividends paid or proposed. Which makes it all the more important to look out for exceptions like DAEJAN HOLDINGS.

DAEJAN HOLDINGS *Extract from profit and loss account to 31 March 1992*

	1992 £000	1991 £000
Profit on ordinary activities before taxation	16,218	16,356
Taxation on profit on ordinary activities	(5,753)	(6,199)
Profit on ordinary activities after taxation	10,465	10,157
Minority interests	(12)	(35)
Profit for the year	10,453	10,122
...		
Dividends: Interim 1,955		
Proposed final 2,118		

---

though it is doubtful whether this would confuse anyone.

2. An item for which the sign is reversed (often used if the corresponding figure is in one direction and the current year's in the other).

BLUE CIRCLE INDUSTRIES *Extract from the profit and loss account for 1990*

	1990 £m	1989 £m
Extraordinary items	(17.4)	23.3

Does this represent favourable or unfavourable extraordinary items in 1990? From this information alone we cannot tell.

Does it help to say that Blue Circle does not bracket items normally deducted (like tax or dividends)? No, companies are far from consistent. One needs either to read the supporting note, or do a quick calculation.

BLUE CIRCLE INDUSTRIES *Extract from the profit and loss account for 1990*

	1990 £m	1989 £m
Group share of profit after tax	141.6	163.0
Extraordinary items	(17.4)	23.3
Profit for the financial year	124.2	186.3

---

which makes it clear that in this case brackets represent 'adverse'. In our sample of 50, 25 companies used this convention, 21 had no extraordinary items, and 4 adopted the opposite convention (showing a loss unbracketed).

3. In text, either an aside or as a way of showing the corresponding figure for the previous period:

CLYDE PETROLEUM *Extract from Review of Operations for 1992*

In the Balmoral Field (Clyde 15%), gross production fell to 3,481 bopd from 10,588 bopd in 1991....

– which represents an aside. Compare with:

DUNTON GROUP *Extract from Note 21 of the 1992 accounts:*

The pension cost charge represents contributions payable by the company to the fund amounting to £13,662 (1991 £68,436).

– where the £68,436 is a positive figure for contributions but relates to the previous year.

In the balance sheet

Similar difficulties are found with 'signs' in the balance sheet. The specimen layouts provided in the Companies Acts show capital and reserves (when in credit) unbracketed and many companies (28 in our sample) did not bracket liabilities deducted from the 'assets side' (eg liabilities due within one year and deducted from current assets). But 22 did bracket such liabilities.

There is no uniformity either in the treatment of minority interests, though most companies bracket them in the profit and loss account (4 out of 30 with minority interests did not) and in the balance sheet most treat them as an addition to capital and reserves, and do not bracket them. But some companies (like PRUDENTIAL and FLEXTECH) deduct them in computing the net assets (Flextech brackets them, Prudential does not). So, brackets need to be treated with care. They do not always mean what they appear to at first glance.

Companies with subsidiaries are required to present both a company balance sheet and a consolidated balance sheet. Our sample suggests that just over half (28 out of 50) provide their company balance sheet and consolidated balance sheet on separate pages, invariably with the group balance sheet first. Indeed two of the sample presented their company balance sheet well away from the rest of their accounts ie after the notes on the group accounts.

Seventeen companies presented their group and company balance sheets side by side, 14 with the group accounts to the left, three (including BRITISH LAND and FORTE) with them to the right – a trap for the unwary, and one (PILKINGTON) with current year group, and current year holding company, on the left, with corresponding figures for both to the right.

Standards of graphic presentation

Generally accepted basic standards of graphic presentation are:

1. Axes and / or symbols used should be clearly defined either on the face of the chart or (very much second best) in the text. Be unambiguous, for example, do not say 'Turnover' but 'Turnover including VAT', if that is the case.
2. Scales should be chosen in such a way that they are both fair and appropriate.
3. The proportions (shape) of any chart should be both fair and appropriate eg not chosen in such a way as to magnify any improvement or reduce the effect of any adverse change.
4. A monetary, or quantity, axis (usually the *y*-axis) should where possible run continuously from a zero at the point at which it meets the time axis (usually the *x*-axis). Where this is not possible, the break in the axis should be clearly marked.
5. Three-dimensional representations, and shapes (such as barrels or corn cobs) which change size to represent changes in value, look nice but are best avoided, since it is difficult to tell whether changes in value are being represented by changes in height, in area or in volume.
6. Where growth over a period is being represented, the dates for the beginning and end of the period should be chosen fairly. For ex-

ample, spectacular growth would be exhibited by most unit trusts which took as their start the bottom of the 1973 bear market and compared it with the most recent market peak. That might be a *true* representation if the trust was actually set up in 1973, but it would still not provide a *fair* indication of average growth prospects.

7. While all points do not need to be plotted (eg every day's index), any smoothing should be fair, and not introduced in a deliberate attempt to hide volatility.
8. Data should be compiled on a consistent basis throughout. If not, any significant change should be noted.

Ways of conveying information

As we noted earlier, people differ in the ease with which they acquire information presented in different ways. Some find it easiest to understand and recall straight text. Most accountants find that figures, and more especially tables of figures, are easy to understand and place in perspective; many laymen do not. Others find that, to them, graphical methods create the most vivid and memorable impression.

It is important to know not only your own preferences in this regard but those of colleagues and others you wish to influence.

Consider carefully Example 5.1 which represents an extract from the 5 year summary of a mythical company, WunderMac plc.

Example 5.1 Extract from the Five Year Summary

WunderMac plc	1990	1991	1992	1993	1994
Turnover (£) excluding VAT	1191000	1244595	1314292	1942524	2031880
Profit from operations (£)	92898	108279	111714	134034	168646

If you try to form a detailed impression of how things have gone, you will probably find it quite difficult. The amounts are quite large. There is no punctuation in the figures, making them hard to construe. Look how much better the table looks with commas every three digits (see Example 5.2).

Example 5.2 Extract from an improved Five Year Summary

WunderMac plc	1990	1991	1992	1993	1994
Turnover (£) excluding VAT	1,191,000	1,244,595	1,314,292	1,942,524	2,031,880
Profit from operations (£)	92,898	108,279	111,714	134,034	168,646

which is much better, but still difficult. Only a bookkeeper needs figures to this level of accuracy.

Example 5.3 Extract from the Five Year Summary

WunderMac plc	1990	1991	1992	1993	1994
Turnover (£000) excluding VAT	1,191	1,245	1,314	1,943	2,032
Profit from operations (£000)	93	108	112	134	169

It is now easy to see that there has been steady growth in turnover, apart from 1993, when there was a sudden surge. Profits too improved markedly in 1993 and again in 1994. But that is still not a very sophisticated analysis. Let us present the same information in ratio terms (Example 5.4).

Example 5.4 Accounting ratios

WunderMac plc	1991	1992	1993	1994
Turnover growth Year on Year (%)	4.50	5.60	47.80	4.60
Profit growth Year on Year (%)	16.56	3.17	19.98	25.82

We are now in a position to put figures to our assessment. 'Turnover growth was around 5% throughout the period 1991–94, apart from 1993 which showed a spectacular 47.8%.' But we cannot leave it there. Turnover does not improve by that sort of percentage without a very good reason. Let us imagine that we find that increase was due to the acquisition of Wilson plc.

Profit growth was more erratic (1991 16.56%, 1992 only 3.17%). Since turnover was up 5.6%, margins must have been eroded. The turnover surge in 1993 of 47.8% did not work its way through to profits immediately – apparently Wilson took time to assimilate.

This immediately points the way to an analysis of margins.

Example 5.5 Analysis of margins

WunderMac plc	1990	1991	1992	1993	1994
Profit/turnover (%)	7.80	8.70	8.50	6.90	8.30

It seems that margins average about 8.3%, fell in 1993 but returned to that level in 1994 following the assimilation of Wilson – so there is scope for profit improvement.

Information presented graphically

Example 5.6 is a line graph which depicts WunderMac's turnover for the years 1990–94. While it makes the surge in 1993 very obvious it is not fair, since the y-axis does not go down to zero and there is no break symbol to warn one.

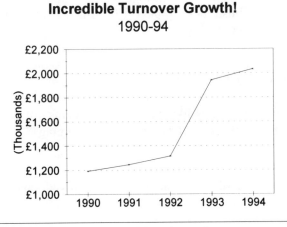

Example 5.6 What is incredible about it?

Example 5.7 depicts the same information in the form of a bar chart. At a glance, it is obvious that turnover is growing, steadily in 1991, 1992 and 1994, but there was a £700,000 surge in 1993.

Example 5.8, a line graph of the profit from operations, is striking, but it again represents unfair presentation since the y-axis does not start at zero.

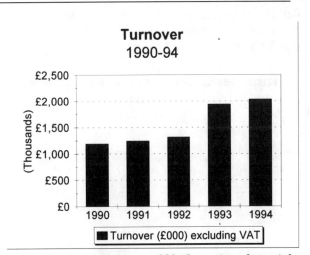

Example 5.7 No longer incredible, but quite substantial

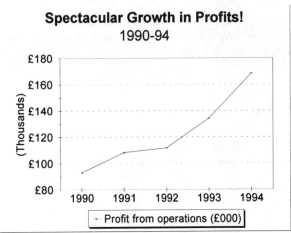

Example 5.8 Profit growth looks spectacular, but is it?

So any increase is magnified. Example 5.9 depicts the same information in the form of a bar chart.

The bar chart in Example 5.9, on the other hand, gives a clear picture of sales and profit growth and does not suffer from distorting effects – simply because a bar chart, by its nature, starts from zero.

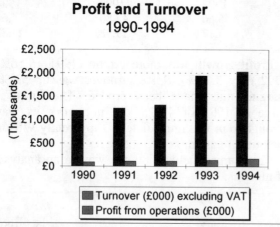

Profit and Turnover
1990-1994

Example 5.9 Profit growth, set against turnover as a bar chart, looks much less spectacular

Perhaps the clearest picture of trends is given by the three ratio charts. Study Examples 5.10, 5.11 and 5.12, with care, and see what they highlight.

Turnover Growth on Preceding Year
1991-94

Example 5.10 1993, it is clear, produced an abnormal, discrete, step in sales. One immediately asks: Why?

Sales Margin
1990-94

Example 5.11 But it also marked a low point in profit margins. One again asks oneself: Why?

Profit Growth on Preceding Year
1991-94

Example 5.12 Profit growth provides another perspective. Now, 1992, it seems, was the poor year!

Demonstrating growth

Many people use charts to demonstrate or depict growth; and this brings problems. Take the RPI. If inflation is said to be falling, the *pace* at which retail prices are increasing has reduced, but prices are still *growing*. Many people seem to be confused over this. We return to inflation in Chapter 17.

In a line graph, an upward straight line depicting, say, turnover represents turnover which is growing by the same *monetary amount* each period. One which depicts a uniform *rate* of growth (say 5% per annum) curves upwards.

If it is the *rate* of increase which is important, rather than its *absolute amount*, statisticians and analysts often use semi-logarithmic graph paper – see the illustration on page 139. But laymen often find this confusing.

This of course raises a question to which we shall return time and again: what do we mean by growth? What is it that we want to see grow?

Turnover growth which does not result in increased profits is like chasing moonbeams – it gets us nowhere. Is it net assets? Profits? Earnings?

Practice

Standards of presentation have improved greatly over the last few years. Nevertheless, unfair presentation still exists.

As an exercise, look critically at every graph or chart you see in a daily paper, magazine, report and accounts, or on television, and ask yourself:

1. Does the graph or chart comply with standards of good presentation?
2. Just what is it that they are trying to prove?
3. Are they being fair?
4. What questions does the chart raise (eg about definitions, or structural changes which may have taken place) which it fails to answer?

Chapter 6

PREPARING AN IN-DEPTH REPORT

Chapter 2, and more especially Chapters 3 and 4, assume that the product of your research will be a report. This is useful as a means of recording the results of your investigations and efforts in studying a company's report and accounts and meeting its management. You can thus look back in the light of events and so learn from past mistakes and, hopefully, successes. It is also a way of conveying your thoughts to your peers, and eventually to potential investors.

Preparation of an in-depth report is a two stage process:

1. Gather the facts and form an opinion; and
2. Write up the results.

Essential reference material

Any report which is purely the result of personal observation is likely to lack substance: one needs additional sources of information. Chapter 22 of *Interpreting Company Reports and Accounts* provides a full list of useful sources beyond the report and accounts.

This is fine if you are a member of a largish organisation, with comprehensive, up-to-date library facilities. If you are not, a full set of Extel cards is both expensive and time-consuming to keep up; and DataStream, while invaluable, is far from cheap.

Reuters Textline provides a convenient alternative to taking countless daily and financial papers and keeping a tearsheet cuttings library. It is much more convenient but if used to any extent it is no less expensive.

What then do we regard as the absolute minimum in the way of reference material? Probably:

1. A backfile of the *Investors Chronicle* covering the two previous years.

2. A three month back file of the *Financial Times*, in addition we keep cuttings of significant items likely to be of future use.

3. *Hambro Performance Rankings*, published half-yearly by Hemmington Scott Publishing, is very useful for putting a company into perspective, overall and against other members of its sector, in that it ranks companies in terms of size, market capitalisation, turnover, capital employed, profit margin, earnings per share, earnings growth, dividends per share, liquidity, productivity, and so on.

4. *The Arthur Andersen Corporate Register*, also published half-yearly by Hemmington Scott Publishing, which is a most useful source of contact details (it is probably the fastest way of finding the name of the finance director), and information on directors generally, their other interests, and the company's advisers eg its brokers – inform-ation frequently not to be found in the report and accounts. *The Corporate Register* is now available on computer disk as well as in paperback form.

5. *Hambro Company Guide*, published quaterly by Hemmington Scott, is useful as a source of five year records and details of activities (also available on disk).

6. Crawford's *Directory of City Connections*, which is helpful in tracing company brokers, PR consultants, and auditors.

7. *The Estimate Directory*, published by Edinburgh Financial Publishing Ltd., which shows for major companies how leading analysts (including the company's brokers) compare as regards their view of future profitability, earnings and dividends. *The Estimate Directory* provides a useful check on your

own personal opinions. It also gives other useful company information.

8. Recent brokers' results notes, comment on interims / prelims, share issues and acquisitions; and fuller research reports, especially those produced by the company's own brokers. Since it is in the brokers' interests to promote the company, we find they are often ready to oblige by supplying us with a copy. But never forget: the company's brokers can be expected to show it in a good light. Subject to that caveat, reports produced by a company's broker often provide useful information.

9. A back file of accounts, press announcements, and share price graphs. Companies vary, but we find that shareholder relations departments even of quite small companies will put together a useful folder of recent accounts and releases; and if one expresses real interest in the history of a group will go to the trouble of producing several years back reports (always assuming that they are still available).

Adopt a standard format

It is helpful to develop a standard format for reports. If you work for an organisation which has such standards, you should obviously follow them. Analysts working by themselves have perforce to develop their own methods of working and layout standards. Without them, one report is unlikely to be comparable with another, even that on a company in the same sector with which easy comparison would be useful. Without some standard format, and checklist, important factors and features are likely to be missed.

Structure your reports to suit you and those who will use them. As a minimum, the report should contain:

1. A history of the group.
2. Information on its key products, strengths and weaknesses.
3. Accounting data and numeric information, presented in table or graphical form, covering several years.

This checklist should prove helpful:

1. *Conclusions:*

   Many analysts begin their report with their conclusions and recommendations. They obviously do not *write* these first, they simply place them first because:

   (i) People are more likely to read the beginning of a report than the end
   (ii) If what readers find in the summary of

   conclusions is of no interest to them, they need read no further, but if they are interested, even if they disagree, they may go on.

2. *Historical background:*

   (i) Origins of the company.
   (ii) People in at the start. Their concepts.
   (iii) Past mergers, *major* acquisitions and disposals.
   (iv) Past changes of direction: From? To? When? Why?   The reasons for a major change of direction may not be openly spelled out, but the attempt should certainly be made to obtain answers.
   (v) What strengths was the business built on: Quality? Of product? Of service? Of brands? Are those strengths being maintained?

3. *Basic information:*

   (i) What exactly does the company do (not just the sort of vague statement found in directors' reports)?
   (ii) Where is its UK base?

4. *Principal businesses:*

   (i) How is the group currently organised?
   (ii) What does each division and main company do?
   (iii) Does the group have a presence in other parts of the world. What does it do there? How does it operate (eg through subsidiaries with a 49% local stake)?

5. *The management:*

   (i) Who does what?
   (ii) What are his/her origins; experience?

   A chief executive or chairman is often the public face of a group, but remember: one man cannot do everything; it is the management team as a whole which produces results.

6. *Risk:*

   How is, or would, the group affected by:

   (i) Weather?
   (ii) Fashion and obsolescence risk?
   (iii) Exchange rates?
   (iv) Exchange controls?
   (v) Legislation and potential legislation?
   (vi) Proposed or new EC directives?
   (vii) Nationalisation?
   (viii) Litigation and potential litigation?
   (ix) Loss of major customers?
   (x) Supply problems?
   (xi) Loss of key personnel?

(xii) Labour problems eg at a customer?

7. *Accounting information:*

    (i) Highlight, and seek to explain, significant changes in:

        (a) Profit and lost account;

        (b) Balance sheet;

        (c) Cash flows;

    most especially current year v previous year; but any really significant ones.

    (ii) Accounting policies:

        (a) How do they compare with other companies in the sector?

        (b) Have they changed?

        (c) Are they in any way unusual?

        (d) How lucidly are they explained?

    (iii) Auditors' report: Is there anything significant?

8. *Interim results:*

What do interim figures tell you about:

    (i) The seasonality of turnover and profit?

    (ii) The performance of segments?

    (iii) Borrowings / cash flow? A growing number of companies include a balance sheet and cash flow statement.

    (iv) Where interims represent the latest information available: whether any changes have been made, which will affect future accounts, in activities or structure (eg acquisitions, disposals or closures) or in accounting policies.

    (v) The tax charge?

Include a table showing interim figures where significant.

9. *Growth:*

It is useful to provide six years' figures for year-on-year growth of:

    (i) Sales;

    (ii) Profits;

    (iii) Net cash inflow from operating activities;

    (iv) Earnings per share;

    (v) Dividends per share;

    (vi) Profit margin(s);

    (vii) Shareholders' funds;

    (viii) Cash and cash equivalents;

    (ix) Net asset value per share;

    (x) Borrowings.

10. *Geographical analysis:*

    (i) Where does turnover come from?

    (ii) Where does production take place?

    (iii) Relative profitability?

How does this affect risk?

11. *Segmental analysis:*

    (i) What activities produce what proportion of turnover?

    (ii) What markets does the group sell into?

    (iii) Relative profitability of the various segments?

    (iv) Reasons for abandoning or starting activities?

12. *Stock market information:*

    (i) Current share price;

    (ii) Number of shares in issue;

    (iii) Market capitalisation;

    (iv) Market sector;

    (v) Relative performance of share price:

        (a) to the FT-Actuaries All Share Index; and

        (b) to the sector index.

13. *Recent record:*

For two back years, plus current year forecast and next year forecast, a table showing:

    (i) Turnover;

    (ii) Pre-tax profit;

    (iii) Tax (as a %);

    (iv) Earnings per share;

    (v) Dividend per share;

    (vi) Dividend yield (gross);

    (vii) Net asset value;

    (viii) Cash flow per share.

14. *Capitalisation:*

    (i) Ordinary shareholders' funds;

    (ii) Minority interests;

    (iii) Debt – short term;

    (iv)   – long term.

15. *Major shareholders and directors' shareholdings.*

16. *Your assessment (rating) of:*

    (i) Sector buoyancy;

    (ii) Company's product/service;

    (iii) Management calibre;

    (iv) Eps (in terms of value);

    (v) Assets (in terms of value);

    (vi) Share marketability.

17. *Date of next announcement.*

Why is so much information necessary?

All the above items of information are, we believe, meaningful. Indeed each item has a purpose.

    As an exercise, it would useful to work through the checklist and ask yourself why each item of information matters? Often it will be obvious; sometimes less so. The list of major shareholders: what does that tell us? It may bring back memories of a past, failed, bid. Or it may reflect a stake which was built up, but never developed to the stage of a bid. In either case, there is a possibility that the holding may be dumped when the moment is right (or when the holder is pressed for cash). Alternatively, a stake could represent the threat of a bid which might materialise at any moment.

General institutional support is reassuring. Lack of interest on the part of the institutions tends to be a sign of weakness – but in either case, they can be wrong. And if the institutions desert a company, think twice. Do they know something you don't? Will this institutional lack of interest adversly affect share price long term?

And what about share marketability? A readily marketable security is obviously to be preferred to a less marketable one (since prices are likely to be keener and the 'turn' significantly less) – unless, of course, the rewards are substantially greater.

People tend to believe that a holding is always saleable *at a price*. Experience suggests that this is not always the case. In the Great Crash of 1927, and to a lesser extent in 1987, prices were at times in free fall, and it was difficult if not impossible to sell even blue chip investments. Less marketable investments fared worst of all.

We do not suggest that your report necessarily needs to *contain* all this information. But this is the information you need to have at your finger-tips if you are to understand, and write constructively about, the business. Structure your reports to suit you and those who will use them.

Analyst, a monthly magazine for the serious investor, produces each month several reports of an impressively high standard which will serve as a useful model. It would certainly be instructive:

(i) To research and prepare a report on a company which has been reviewed recently by *Analyst;*

(ii) To compare your report with theirs.

Practice

In Chapter 4, you were asked to select at random a company at the lower end by market capitalisation of the FT-SE Actuaries Non-Financials index, to obtain information about it and to envisage being invited to meet the company by way of a company visit.

1. Continue your exploration of that company. Gather information in every way open to you, using reference material (eg library facilities).

2. Prepare a detailed report on the company. Imagine that your report is specifically directed to the needs of one client, the trustees of the pension fund of a leading pharmaceutical company, which already has a £250,000 stake in the company, and is considering acquiring more. Make a firm recommendation: eg BUY, SELL or HOLD BUT DON'T INCREASE YOUR HOLDING.

Chapter 7

CASH FLOW STATEMENTS AND
THE PROJECTION OF FUTURE CAPITAL NEEDS

How to read a cash flow statement

Like a profit and loss account, a cash flow statement is a historical statement – in this case one detailing the cash flows of a business.

Together with its various explanatory notes, the cash flow statement forms a complex document for which it is advisable to develop a standard method of studying. Essentially, it is a two stage process:

(a) Consider separately each standard heading, together with any relevant notes. Relate the information where necessary to other parts of the accounts in order to put it into perspective;

(b) Consider the document as a whole, and the overall liquidity situation.

It does not matter which of these two comes first, but we will follow that order:

Consider separately each standard heading

FRS 1 on 'Cash Flow Statements' calls for the presentation of cash flows under five standard headings:

1. Operating activities;
2. Returns on investment and servicing of finance;
3. Taxation;
4. Investing activities;
5. Financing.

Working down the statement we find:

1. Operating activities.

The net cash flow from operating activities represents the net increase or decrease in cash and cash equivalents resulting from operations shown in the profit and loss account in arriving at operating profit.

FRS 1 requires a note reconciling the operating profit (for non-financial companies normally the profit before interest) reported in the profit and loss account and the net cash flow from operating activities. This should be studied with care.

The reconciliation can usefully be summarised along the lines of Example 7.1 below.

Example 7.1 Summary of FRS 3 reconciliation

	£	% of Operating Profit
Operating profit		100.0
Depreciation and amortisation		
Changes in working capital		
Other changes		
	———	———
Net cash inflow from operating activities		
	———	———

It is important to have a feel for the relationship between the four components, for that relationship differs greatly from one company to another, and changes even in the same company over its lifetime.

The effect of depreciation, for instance, will be most noticeable in the case of (1) a high fixed cost company, (2) with expensive modern highly automated plant, (3) in time of low activity.

Working capital changes for various reasons:

(i) Changes in the volume of activity eg natural growth or an expansion programme;

(ii) Changes in the mix of activities;

(iii) Changes in relative efficiency of stock control, invoicing, debt collection, and the like;

(iv) Inflation (which necessitates increased investment in working capital to maintain the same volume of activity in real terms);

(v) Changes in the price of specific products/commodities unconnected with inflation

and it is important, where possible, to decide which.

It is the third category, 'Other', which is, perhaps, the most significant and deserving of further enquiry. By its very nature it tends to be unusual and one-off.

Obviously:

(i) If the net cash inflow from operating activities is negative that is a worrying sign.

(ii) If it is less than that the previous year, that again is a disturbing feature which should be followed up.

We find it helps to express the change from year to the next in terms of a ratio:

$$\frac{\text{Net cash inflow from operating activities for the Current Year}}{\text{Net cash inflow from operating activities for the Preceding Year}} \times 100$$

and to compare it with the growth in operating profit year on year.

2. Returns on investment and servicing of finance.

In a simple situation this reflects interest paid, and received, and dividends paid.

It is worth comparing the interest charge in the profit and loss account with the interest paid and received per the cash flow statement – since interest is frequently charged in one period but paid in another ie can represent an adverse future cash flow. Interest is also sometimes capitalised (particularly by property companies or supermarket groups on new developments). The cash flow effect is then often far greater than the profit and loss account charge.

In a complex group one also sees:

(i) The interest element of finance lease payments;

(ii) Dividends received from related companies;

(iii) Dividends paid to minorities.

Without this information it is difficult to tell either:

(i) what was remitted, if anything, by related companies or

(ii) the cash cost of dividends to minorities.

3. Taxation.

It is worth comparing the tax charge in the profit and loss account with the taxation paid (or refunds received) per the cash flow statement – since tax is frequently, indeed normally, charged in one period but paid in another. ACT, in particular, can have substantial effects.

Consider the subtotal (some companies actually show it, most do not):

Net cash flow from operating activities $\pm$ Returns on investments and servicing of finance $-$ Tax paid

This tells us what would have been left had there been no investment (no purchases of tangible fixed assets or businesses) and no sales of either.

If it proves to be negative, there was no money left even to replace essential plant and machinery without dipping into cash reserves (if any) built up in the past It suggests, in the absence of a considerable improvement in trading, the likelihood of: (1) a cut in dividend; and / or (2) an immediate need for further finance.

4. Investing activities.

In studying the cash from investing activities be on the lookout for 'changes in shape' of the group, ie material changes in direction (see Chapters 11 and 12). For example, a move into a new area of operations, or the abandonment of an existing one.

The cash flow statement and the notes to it provide useful information on purchases and sales of businesses.

5. Financing.

The Financing section of the cash flow statement provides a convenient summary of the way in which the group has changed its pattern of finance over the year. To obtain a sense of perspective, relate the amounts involved to the total capital employed and gearing evidenced by the balance sheet. Be especially careful over signs. There are six illustrations to the Standard; four of which are devoted to particular types of company. Illustrations in the first four sections of the cash flow statement are consistent:

	£m
An inflow of cash is shown	123.456
An outflow of cash is shown	(78.901)

Unfortunately, as regards the fifth section the Standard is inconsistent. Of the six illustrations, four use the reverse convention:

	£m
An inflow of cash is shown	(123.456)
An outflow of cash is shown	78.901

and only two the more obvious one.

Consider the document as a whole

Focus on the notes and, in particular, on:

1. The analysis of changes in cash and cash equivalents during the year, and where this shows bank loans and overdrafts, on the effect of any foreign exchange rate changes;
2. The analysis of changes in financing during the year; and
3. The cash flow effects of one off items, whether termed exceptional or extraordinary; eg the provisions made by GENERAL MOTORS in 1992–93 (see page 96) had no cash effects at that time, but very substantial ones later.

A less spectacular, but in its way equally significant, example was KLEEN-E-ZE HOLD-INGS: in 1992 extraordinary items were £265,000 (1991: £675,000), in each case adverse, but because of timing differences the cash flow effect in 1992 was £843,000 (1991: £40,000), outwards in each case, against a net cash inflow from operations in 1992 of £1,039,000.

But don't lose sight of the wood for the trees; never forget it is the overall liquidity which matters.

We stress elsewhere (pages 26 and 112) the importance of knowing just what a company does and not relying on 'personal knowledge'. Take LIBERTY; everyone knows them as a Regent Street store. Actually they do rather more than that. They have shops in most important UK centres, from large cities like Birmingham, Manchester, Glasgow and Edinburgh, to places with a well-heeled clientele like Canterbury, Bath and Cheltenham. The group also has retail organisations in North America and Japan; and a fabric print works in France. The effects of this overseas involvement are greater than one might expect.

LIBERTY *Extract from Notes to the Cash Flow Statement for the year ended 30 January 1993*

2. Analysis of changes in financing during the year

	Share capital and share premium	Loans
	£000	£000
Balance at 1 February 1992	6,552	(1,547)
Receipts from shares issued	155	–
Repayment of loans	–	757
Receipt from loans	–	(50)
Effect of foreign exchange rate changes	–	(325)
Balance at 30 January 1993	6,707	(1,165)

3. Bank loans, overdrafts, cash and cash equivalents

	Brought Forward	Exchange Movement	Repaid/ (Drawn down)	Carried Forward
	£000	£000	£000	£000
Cash and cash equivalents				
Cash in hand	1,411	206	(720)	897
Deposits (under 3 months)	1,078	223	1,054	2,355
Certificates of tax deposit	42	–	(42)	–
Bank overdrafts	–	–	(321)	(321)
Loans (under 3 months)	(489)	(98)	83	(504)
	2,042	331	54	2,427
Financing				
Loans (over 3 months)	(1,547)	(325)	707	(1,165)
Total of net cash and bank balances	495	6	761	1,262

The Financial Review

A growing number of companies now include in their report and accounts a Financial Review; and this always deserves to be studied carefully not least because of the light it sheds on past, present and future cash flows; financing and borrowing policies. The ASB's Statement *Operating and Financial Review* summarises best practice.

AEJO WIGGINS APPLETON Financial Review 1992

Cash flow, borrowings and gearing

Largely as a result of lower operating profit, acquisitions and high levels of capital expenditure, year-end net borrowings increased by £138.4m to £284.9m in 1992, with £27.5m of the increase reflecting the effect on foreign currency borrowings of exchange rate movements during the year.

The gearing ratio of net borrowings as a percentage of shareholders' funds was 23.6%, an increase from the previous year-end ratio of 13.9%. There will be a further increase in gearing in 1993 as capital investment remains high, although management continues to put primary emphasis on working capital control. However, cash levels should benefit from reductions in capital expenditure in 1994, as the focus switches to the achievement of the expected benefits from the investment programme in 1992 and 1993.

To the extent to which it requires borrowings, the Group reduces its foreign currency exposure by denominating borrowings in the currencies of those countries where it has significant exposures, which are, principally, the USA, France and Belgium. The Group's policy is to hedge against exchange risk on foreign currency receivables and payables.

Borrowings equivalent to approximately 30% of the net debt of £284.9m as at 31 December 1992, were at fixed rates of interest, although, over the medium term, the Group will be seeking to increase this proportion to take advantage of lower interest rates and to give more certainty in terms of the interest cover ratio. A total of £136.5m was due after one year, of which £90.5m was due after five years, and the balance was backed by a revolving credit facility maturing in June 1995.

Some of this information could certainly be obtained from the accounts and notes. What the Financial Review does is to put it all into perspective through the eyes of the management.

Centralised banking (and the sweeping up of balances into a single account) is easy in the UK, but rather less so internationally. Traditionally it is rarely mentioned directly. The existence of both large overdrafts and large cash balances in the case of an international organisation may simply reflect this difficulty, but it can be a sign that cash is to some extent locked in (eg as a deposit required to trade in an overseas area; or would suffer tax if brought back to the UK). Or, as was the case with POLLY PECK, is invested to earn high rates of interest in a high risk area such as Turkish Cyprus, where it was to prove difficult to recover.

Future capital requirements

So far we have studied the cash flow statement simply as a historical record. It can also be used both internally and externally:

1. As a diagnostic tool, to answer such questions as: Why did cash generated by operations fall so sharply when profits actually increased? Why did the group need to make a rights issue?
2. As a planning mechanism: How might liquidity be improved? What action should we (they) take?
3. As a means of estimating future capital requirements.

Indeed, one of the advantages claimed (by FRS 1) for cash flow statements over funds flow statements is that they make it easier for analysts and other readers of accounts to project future cash flows, and hence future capital requirements.

Some companies now do, in their chairman's statement or financial review, give an indication of future capital expenditure. But even with the benefit of this and the additional information provided by FRS 1, it is not easy, indeed it is impossible with accuracy, to assess future capital needs. Nevertheless, the analyst needs to try to decide:

1. When the company is likely to approach the market or when it is going to have to talk to its bankers about (a) more money or (b) a continuation or rolling over of facilities.
2. Whether it will face difficulties in doing so?
3. How is it likely to raise the money – by a rights issue or by increasing gearing with an issue of debentures or loan stock? Would it be feasible to issue a convertible?

    If it is seeking to expand or to replace substantial amounts of plant and equipment, would leasing be an answer? If it has substantial debtors, would factoring fit the bill?
4. If it does find it hard to raise the money, what it is likely to do? Sell off subsidiaries, individual assets (like a prestigious headquarters building), investments in related companies, whole divisions? Indeed, can it be saved and, if so, at what cost?

History is littered with companies which got it wrong. We look at some of them in Chapter 9.

Start with the subtotal we recommended (page 30):

| Net cash flow from operating activities | ± | Returns on investments and servicing of finance | – Tax paid |

Adjust this for:

1. The effect of any expected change in profitabilty;
2. Any change possible or neccessary to working capital (compared with the period under review), eg growth in turnover implies a need for increased working capital. Although stocks may be excessive and in theory cuttable, in bad times they may, despite this, continue to increase;
3. Any expected increase / cut in dividend;
4. Taxation payments, which tend to be out of phase with reported profitability;

and so obtain a revised subtotal. From this deduct essential non-operating financial outflows eg payments to vendors, loan redemptions.

The result will be your best estimate of the change in liquidity. We never said it was easy!

Practice: Lucas Case Study

Lucas Industries describes itself as 'a leading international organisation providing advanced technology systems, components and services to the world's aerospace, automotive and other selected markets'. Consider the accounts and extracts from the Notes which follow.

LUCAS *Cash flow statement for the year ended 31 July 1992*

	Notes	1992 £m	1991 £m
Net cash flow from operating activities [A]	29	181.8	107.2
Returns on investment and servicing of finance			
Interest received [E]		27.3	17.8
Interest paid [F]		(45.2)	(42.2)
Interest element of finance lease payments		(6.4)	(4.7)
Dividends from related companies		0.5	0.6
Dividends paid (including minorities) [G]		(49.9)	(49.8)
Net cash flow from returns on investment and servicing of finance		(73.7)	(78.3)
Taxation			
UK corporation tax paid		(17.7)	(21.2)
Overseas tax paid		(11.2)	(17.9)
Tax paid		(28.9)	(39.1)
Investing activities			
Purchase of tangible fixed assets [H]		(89.3)	(107.2)
Disposal of tangible fixed assets		11.6	8.9
Proceeds from sale of investments		–	1.5
Purchase of subsidiary companies (net of cash equivalents) [I]		–	(30.6)
Investment in related companies		(0.6)	(4.3)
Net cash outflow from investing activities		(78.3)	(131.7)
Net cash flow before financing [J]		0.9	(141.9)
Financing			
Issue of ordinary share capital		4.0	14.6
Increase in secured loans		2.1	0.9
Increase in unsecured loans [K]		177.2	31.5
(Decrease)/Increase in commercial paper [L]		(70.6)	42.9
(Increase)/Decrease in short term deposits [M]		(23.3)	2.4
Capital element of finance lease rental payments		(9.9)	(10.1)
Minority interest		–	2.0
Net cash flow from financing	32	79.5	84.2
Increase/(Decrease) in cash and cash equivalents	30	80.4	(57.7)

NOTES TO THE ACCOUNTS:

Note 4: Interest payable (extract)

	1992 £m	1991 £m
Interest on bank overdrafts and loans repayable within 5 years	41.2	28.8
Premium on convertible bonds	0.7	0.8
Interest on bank loans over 5 years	1.4	0.1
Interest on loans over 5 years	13.4	14.2
Interest on finance leases	7.5	4.7
	64.2	48.6

Note 5: Taxation (extracts)

	1992 £m	1991 £m
United Kingdom: Corporation tax at 33% (1991 33.7%)	11.0	7.0
Deferred taxation	(1.6)	3.5
Double taxation relief	(9.0)	(5.0)
Adjustment in respect of prior years	(1.9)	–
Advance corporation tax written off	14.7	13.7
Net United Kingdom tax	13.2	19.2
Overseas tax – current	14.4	12.6
– deferred	–	(2.4)
Related companies tax	0.4	2.1
	28.0	31.5

Losses for the year in a United Kingdom subsidiary have been carried back against prior year profits resulting in a net credit of £3.4m after taking into account an effective write off of Advance Corporation Tax previously utilised.

Note 9: Tangible assets (extracts)

	Group Land & Buildings £m	Group Plant & Equipment £m
Cost or valuation at 1 August 1991	359.6	865.7
...		
Additions	18.4	104.8
...		

Note 13: Creditors
Amounts falling due within one year (extracts)

Group	1992 £m	1991 £m
Trade creditors	11.5	7.1
Finance lease obligations	18.6	26.4
Social security and other taxes	53.6	59.3
Accruals and deferred income	152.1	176.8

Note 14: Creditors
Amounts falling due beyond one year (extracts)

	Group 1992 £m	Group 1991 £m
...		
Finance lease obligations	56.7	46.7
Accruals and deferred income	11.1	19.5

Note 29: Net cash flow from operating activities

	1992 £m	1991 £m
Profit before interest and tax including distribution from pension fund surplus	59.9	113.5
Share of losses (less profits) of related companies	2.6	(6.0)
	62.5	107.5
Depreciation [B]	82.3	81.5
Net profit on sale of tangible fixed assets	(0.6)	(2.0)
Provision for restructuring [C]	72.2	–
Other non-cash items	0.9	(0.3)
Decrease/(Increase) in stocks	26.4	(33.6)
Decrease in creditors [D]	(75.0)	(33.5)
Exchange adjustments on opening working capital	(16.8)	(8.6)
	181.8	107.2

Note 30: Analysis of changes in cash and cash equivalents during the year

	1992 £m	1991 £m
Balance at beginning of year	(62.7)	(2.9)
Net cash inflow/(outflow) before adjustments for the effect of foreign exchange rate changes	80.4	(57.7)
Effect of foreign exchange rate changes	9.1	(2.1)
Balance at end of year	26.8	(62.7)

Note 31: Analysis of the balances of cash and cash equivalents as shown in the balance sheet (extract)

	1992 £m	1991 £m
Cash at bank and in hand	161.1	121.1
Short term deposits	–	14.3
Loans and acceptances	(74.1)	(106.0)
Bank overdrafts	(60.2)	(92.1)
	26.8	(62.7)

Note 32: Analysis of changes in financing during the year

	Share Capital and Share Premium A/c 1992 £m	Net Loans and Finance Leases 1992 £m	Share Capital and Share Premium Account 1991 £m	Net Loans and Finance Leases 1991 £m
Balance at beginning of year	466.1	264.6	451.5	172.9
Cash inflow from financing	4.0	75.5	14.6	67.6
New finance lease commitments		23.4		20.3
Exchange movements		(8.0)		3.8
Balance at end of year	470.1	355.5	466.1	264.6

EXTRACT FROM 5 YEAR SUMMARY

	1992 £m	1991 £m	1990 £m	1989 £m	1988 £m
Group turnover	2,370.1	2,488.2	2,334.1	2,187.3	1,972.1
Group operating profit	58.3	113.5	207.4	195.5	169.2
Dividends per share	7.00p	7.00p	7.00p	6.25p	5.25p

Now try your hand at preparing a commentary.

Commentary

1. Operating activities

At first sight [A] there has been a dramatic improvement in cash generated by operations (from £107.2m to £181.8m, an increase of 69.6%). An analysis on the lines suggested shows:

	£m	% of Operating Profit
Operating profit	62.5	100.0
Depreciation and amortisation	82.3	131.7
Changes in working capital	(35.5)	(56.8)
Other changes	72.5	116.0
	181.8	290.9

which, for a start, is totally different in balance from 1991:

	£m	% of Operating Profit
Operating profit	107.5	100.0
Depreciation and amortisation	81.5	75.8
Changes in working capital	(79.5)	(74.0)
Other changes	(2.3)	(2.1)
	107.2	99.7

Note in particular:

(a) The high dependence upon depreciation, the effect of which in 1992 was 31% greater than that of operating profits. This is typical of the highly automated company suffering if not a downturn a plateau in turnover [B]. The 5 year summary showed how this has come about. [There is a minor unexplained difference in operating profit for 1992]

(b) The provision for restructuring (1992) of £72.2m. This has been charged to profit and loss account but not so far spent. In other words substantial adverse cash flows lie ahead [C].

(c) The substantial decrease in creditors in each year (which has a major effect on the working capital change). Is this, one at first wonders due to falling production; or the reluctance of creditors to offer long-term credit [D]? It is difficult to reconcile with notes 13 and 14, but they make it clear that the cause is far more complex than this.

2. Returns on investment and servicing of finance
It is apparent that:

(a) Dividends have been held [G] (study of the 5 year summary shows that they rose to 7.00p in 1990 and have remained at that level since).

(b) Interest received is growing [E] – a good sign

(c) Interest paid looks as though it is reasonably well contained [F] though it is almost equal in amount to the ordinary dividends. But study of Note 4 shows that this is an illusion. There has in fact been a substantial increase in overdraft interest. Interest has accrued but not so far been paid.

3. Taxation
It is difficult to interpret this in conjunction with Note 5, but it seems that UK profits were insufficient to allow full recovery of ACT.

4. Investing activities
One thing stands out: the high level of investment in fixed assets [H]. Additions to plant and equipment in 1991-92 were £104.8m. Which does not suggest any reluctance to invest.

Any other changes are insignificant. There were no acquisitions or disposals of subsidiaries in the year [I].

The net cash flow before financing was £0.9m in 1992 compared with £(141.9m) in 1991 [J].

5. Financing.
In each year increasing use has been made of unsecured loans [K]. Increased use of commercial paper was made in 1990–91, but that use fell away sharply in 1991–92 [L], and the group was able place money on short term deposit [M].

6. Overall picture.
Notes 30 and 31 show an improvement in net liquid funds from £(62.7)m to £26.8m. But the £72.2m provision for restructuring has yet to be spent.

Somewhat cynically, in *White Knights and Poison Pills*, David Olive and Paul Stevenson define restructuring as:
'An attempt at self-redemption, in which everyone and everything is moved up, down or sideways, and then given a new name to see if the firm works better that way.'

The implication being that it possibly won't.
This case study demonstrates just why competing analysts may form diametrically opposing views. No one, even the board, can tell just how well restructuring will work out in a particular case. The one thing we do know is that it will absorb a considerable amount of cash.

Foresight

By early 1993, City talk was all of the steps Lucas was having to take to defend itself against predators. It mounted a major advertising campaign in quality journals stressing its merits in an apparently successful attempt to defend its position.

Takeover specialists are always on the look out for companies like LUCAS, the profits of which are down because of restructuring, and whose share price reflects the disappointment and dissatisfaction of shareholders – and which thus come cheap and are an easy prey.

Those with long memories may recall the TRAFALGAR HOUSE takeover of CUNARD, just as things were coming right. More recently, in 1992 HONGKONG LAND was able to return the complement by acquiring a substantial stake in TRAFALGAR HOUSE when *its* share price was low.

Chapter 8

FINDING THE MONEY

At the drop of a hat

A wise finance director, like a boy scout, needs to 'Be prepared'. Most especially, to be prepared for the need to raise money urgently. Since one of the most obvious activities of the finance man is the preparation of budgets, their presentation, and monitoring, that may seem an odd suggestion, but it is not.

Why is money sometimes needed on the spur of the moment? By way of background, here are just seven possibilities of many:

1. In business, there are few certainties. One may plan to replace a key machine next year rather than this, but a breakdown, followed by the discovery that repairs are impossible, may change things. The budget will go by the board and money for the replacement will have to be found.

2. A dock strike may prevent shipment of a major contract, meaning that payment will be deferred. Or, it may result in a shortage of supply, delay production, and hence restrict sales.

3. The opportunity to purchase the ideal site may bring forward plans for development in a new area.

4. Directors, who do not always live by their own rules (budgets), may seize the opportunity, and make a major acquisition.

5. Because they handle the debtors of a range of companies, factors are among the first to spot trouble. So a company which factors its debtors may find to its distress that the factor refuses to accept sales to one of its major customers. It is said that in 1971 when Rolls-Royce went to the wall, leading factors refused to accept sales to Rolls-Royce, and thus ensured its collapse.

6. The group's bankers may find themselves over-exposed to a particular sector (and / or be told by the Bank of England to reduce their exposure); or they may have bad experience with customers in a similar line of business which shakes their confidence. As a result, they may reduce a group's facilities for reasons unconnected with its particular strengths.

7. Exchange controls may be imposed at home or abroad, making it impossible to remit needed funds from one part of a group to another.

Internal sources versus external

Where time is of the essence, external sources of finance are frequently faster. It is easy to draw down a loan already arranged; and comparatively easy to finance a new asset purchase by leasing. It takes rather more time to arrange a syndicated loan or a public issue of shares or debentures, because of the legal formalities involved. But most businesses have a cheaper, if less immediate source, available to them: internally generated funds.

We look at profit improvement in Chapter 10 and, in the long term at least, improved profitability tends to mean improved cash generation from operations (though beware, this is not always the case in the short term).

But the good finance director is continually looking for ways of improving cash flow eg by more efficient invoicing, credit control and debt collection; or by improved stock control, by better systems of cash transfer to the centre; and by persuading his board to sell off unused or underperforming assets.

Desirable though these measures are, they often cost money in the short term and in an emergency it is usually quicker to turn to the bank.

Relations with banks

There is an old saying about bank managers: 'A bank manager is a man who will offer you an umbrella when it is not raining' – and by implication, won't when you really need it.

The wise finance director maintains good relations with his company's bankers at all times; endeavours to keep them in his confidence; does not make promises he cannot keep; and seeks to have in place all the facilities he is going to need *before* the need becomes apparent. If the going gets tough, he talks to the bank at an early stage. This instils confidence:

1. That he knows what he is doing.
2. In his integrity.

Some FDs employ several bankers, arguing that if one will not help, another will; and possibly deliberately play one off against another. This may, sometimes, work, but it does not please. And for a bank to discover at a late stage that it is one of thirty or more, as some banks did with Polly Peck is, rightly, disquieting.

Cases arise, of course, where the use of more than one bank is legitimate, even necessary; for example, where a foreign bank is used to handle specialised business such as collections for an overseas subsidiary, or a connection was inherited because of acquisitions. But it can also be the cause of disputes, as Queens Moat Houses found in 1993, when a standstill agreement had to be negotiated with the hotel group's 65 bankers.

A banker is in a privileged position, vis à vis other creditors, investors and analysts. He can, if he is the sole banker, keep day-by-day tabs on liquidity. Indeed a perceptive banker can read a great deal into a study of a company's detailed bank statements, particularly in the case of the smaller business:

1. Is the average balance rising, or falling?
2. Are peaks and, more especially, troughs changing in extent, and/or timing?
3. Has lending which previously was seasonal become hard-core?
4. Have major former suppliers disappeared (suggesting that they have doubts about the customer's financial stability)?
5. Have significant previously regular customers disappeared (suggesting competition, a fall-off in trade or, suspect quality, performance or delivery)?
6. Have requests been made to the bank to meet cheques which take the account over limit – if so, have they become more frequent?

A banker who is one of many is blind to much of this information and is far more likely:

1. To run into trouble.
2. To find out too late.
3. To be more accommodating than he would have been had he possessed all the facts

– as many bankers found to their cost in 1990–91.

Since this is a second-stage work the reader is assumed to be familiar with the basics of bank loans, overdrafts and other financial instruments. In this book we will build on that knowledge.

In deciding what form bank borrowings should take, the FD of an international group considers:

1. Where to borrow?
2. In what currency?
3. Over what period?
4. On a fixed or floating rate basis?
5. Whether as a loan (or the facility to draw down in the form of loans) or by way an overdraft?
6. What security is available (and what the company is willing to provide)?

This is not, of course, entirely his choice. At a particular time, he may not be able to borrow in certain markets, or stated currencies, or over a particular period. Or the rates quoted may be prohibitive. Or it may be unwise to borrow in a particular country because of the foreign currency and exchange risk (something we consider more fully in Chapter 15).

He is likely to take the advice of the company's financial advisers (merchant bank) who, if the issue is substantial, may arrange an international consortium of lending bankers and institutions.

A smaller company operating solely in the UK has many of the same problems but tends to have fewer options.

Shares or loan capital: the choice

Companies in practice finance themselves through various forms of capital such as shares, debentures, convertibles and unsecured loan stocks. The extent to which they rely on loans and borroings rather than equity will depend on the type of business and the special circumstances of the time.

In an ideal world, the finance director in need of funds has a choice of financing method – between a rights issue or placing of equity; the issue of preference shares, debentures or loan stocks, or the raising of a bank loan or overdraft. But this is not an ideal world. Sources dry up – the equity market collapses, making an issue of ordinary shares both problematical and expensive (in historical terms). Interest rates may rise, making any sort of borrowing prohibitive. And, once he has made a rights issue, it is difficult to make another for a couple of years. That is why many companies (like oil com panies working in partnership or joint venture with others) get the capital in place well up front, lest market conditions deteriorate.

Lenders, in general, and bankers, trustees for debenture holders, and institutional holders of loan stocks, tend to set:

1. A minimum income cover;
2. A maximum gearing;
3. Covenants providing additional disclosures

without which they either:

1. Will not lend in the first place; or
2. Having done so, would have the right to appoint a receiver.

FDs seek to maintain a capital structure which, as far as can reasonably be foreseen, keeps well clear of such limits. Furthermore, while an FD will go along with *reasonable* demands from the board for unbudgeted funds, he tends to dig in his heels if there is any danger that borrowing limits could be exceeded.

The effects of gearing

The general effect of gearing in (1) a down-turn with high interest rates; and (2) an up-turn with lower rates, is obvious; but the effects of gearing on a particular company at a particular time are more complex, and less well understood. The analyst needs to dig.

First we will take a general look at the phenomenon (see Example 8.1).

Example 8.1 The effect of gearing on WRONGFOOTED

PROFIT AND LOSS ACCOUNT		Year 1	Year 2
		£m	£m
Turnover		10.000	8.000
Operating profit	[O]	1.100	0.720
Interest paid		0.480	0.840
Profit after interest	[P]	0.620	(0.120)
Rate of interest	[I]	8%	14%
BALANCE SHEET			
Equity shareholders' funds	[E]	6.000	6.000
Bank Loan	[L]	6.000	6.000
Capital employed	[C]	12.000	12.000

As will be seen, Wrongfooted has a capital employed of £12m of which 50% was raised by means of a bank loan. In year 1 this bears interest at 8%. In year 2, a recession strikes. The bank raises the rate of interest to 14%. This alone would have been sufficient to reduce profit after interest by 58%. Unfortunately, the operating margin was also squeezed (from 11% to 9%), which taken by itself would have cut the profit after interest by £0.200m, ie 18%. Turnover also fell somewhat (from £10m to £8m) – sufficient by itself also to have reduced the operating profit by £0.200m .

Each effect on its own was bearable, but because they all occurred together, profit was wiped out altogether, and a loss of £0.120m sustained, a swing of £0.740m.

In year 1, the effect of gearing had been favourable. Shareholders' funds of £6m earned £0.620m ie 10.33%. Without it the profits available for equity would have been £1.100m on £12m ie 9.16%. So gearing improved earnings for equity by 1.17%.

In year 2 the gearing effect was disastrous. Without it the profits available for equity would have been £0.720m on £12m, ie 6.00%. So gearing reduced earnings for equity from 6.00% to – 1.00% ie by 7.00%.

In mathematical terms, the increase in return to equity because of gearing, the *gearing effect* [G], is built up of two components, so:

$$G = A \times B$$

where :

A is the difference between the rate of return on the capital employed and the rate of interest paid; and

B is the relationship between equity and loan capital.

$$A = (O \div E) - I$$

where:

O is operating profit
E is equity shareholder's funds
I is the rate of interest

$$B = (L \div E)$$

where:

L is debentures and loans.

Another way of expressing this is:

$$G = \{(O \div E) - I\} \times (L \div E)$$

Using the figures in Example 8.1:

$$G = \{(1.100 \div 12.000) - 0.08\} \times (6.000 \div 6.000)$$
$$= \{0.0917 - 0.08\} \times 1 = 0.0117 \text{ or } 1.17\%$$

In a recession, both components of A change, normally adversely; which has the effect of magnifying the problem. Ratios which move in this way (ie are doubly 'hit' by change) are, in fact, quite common; and you should look out for them.

Just how hurtful the effect is also depends upon the relationship between equity and loan capital, ie the gearing, represented by the multiplier [B]. If this is high, or *as a* result of recession *becomes high*, the problems are magnified.

In difficult times, B often does become higher, for a variety of reasons. For example:

1. Fixed costs continue, but depend for support on falling sales (ie the company suffers also from the effects of *operational gearing*).
2. Losses erode equity shareholders' funds.
3. Cash flow suffers not only because of 1 and 2 but because debtors refuse or are unable to pay; and because unsold stocks build up. So borrowings rise.

That is the simple bit. To fully understand the effects of gearing on a particular business in a changing economy one needs to know:

1. Where the money has been borrowed? Interest rates in different countries tend to be different and to behave quite differently.
2. In what currency? Exchange rate considerations may be involved.
3. How the interest rate is determined? Money borrowed on a debenture will normally bear a rate fixed at the outcome, so subsequent interest rate changes have no effect on the borrower until such time a refinancing is necessary, when they may be disastrous.
4. How permanent the arrangement is? Borrowing at 1% over LIBOR may sound fine, but if the arrangement is a temporary one, and another source at LIBOR + 5% might need to be found in a matter of weeks, that is a different kettle of fish.

Some of this information will be found in notes to the accounts, but it is sometimes necessary to make an educated guess.

Cost of capital

Academic texts on finance place a great deal of stress on a company's cost of capital; comparing on a mathematical basis the relative cost of equity, preference and loan capital and other borrowings, taking into account tax, and discounting future payments (eg of a premium on redemption) back to the present.

While some major organisations certainly do adopt this approach, the majority, in terms of number, even of listed companies, almost certainly do not. Nor, where it is adopted, can the analyst normally tell; and it most certainly should not be assumed either that a group thinks this way or without good reason, that it is its primary consideration.

One always needs to take into account:

1. Interest cover;
2. Gearing;
3. Flexibility (ie the possibility of raising money, particularly in any future emergency);
4. The effect of the transaction on the published accounts.

Decisions made on the basis of cost of capital eg those based on present value theory (See Appendix 2 of *Interpreting Company Reports and Accounts*), or DCF techniques, take a substantially longer-term view than that presented by accounts for a single year. What looks good in present value terms often has unfavourable repercussions in the short term eg on earnings per share.

Some people suggest that Britain's poor performance industrially is in part due (1) to historically high interest rates (compared with Germany and Japan); and (2) to the use by British companies of such rates in discounting future cash flows when assessing capital projects.

Example 8.2 Effect of cost of capital

Imagine a British oil company (cost of capital 12 per cent) and a Japanese company (cost of capital 5 per cent) looking at a project requiring the expenditure of £100m now to receive £90m net in each of years 8, 9 and 10:

	British	Japanese
Present value factors:	12%	5%
Year 8	0.4039	0.6768
Year 9	0.3606	0.6446
Year 10	0.3220	0.6139

	British	Japanese
Present value of an annuity of 1 at the end of years 8, 9, 10	1.0865	1.9353
Present value of £90m net at the end of each of the years 8, 9, 10	£97.785m	£174.177m
Present value of cost	100.000m	100.000m
Net present value of the project	(£2.215m)	£74.177m

The project would be rejected by a British company but entirely acceptable to its Japanese counterpart.

Unusual capital instruments

When studying accounts, be on the look out for unusual capital raising schemes. Such schemes have often in the past been very complex, involving overseas financing subsidiaries incorporated in countries with (1) lower rates of tax; and (2) significantly less full disclosure requirements than those found in the UK.

To understand fully their consequences it is necessary to have a detailed knowledge both of UK and overseas tax far beyond that likely to be possessed by a reader of this book. Such schemes are the realm of the merchant bank, City solicitor or international accountancy firm with bright (possibly untried) ideas, seeking ways to attract business, and to make money – money for those companies who take their advice (always assuming that the scheme works), but most especially substantial fees for themselves. Frequently, open disclosure of what is afoot is the last thing they have tended to seek. But the informed reader should at least make the attempt to understand.

This is changing. The Accounting Standards Board is taking a tough line and we need to be on the look out for changes in presentation as the new Standard is implemented, some of which will sharply effect the look of the balance sheet from one year to the next.

So far as investors, and lenders looking at borrowing limits, are concerned it is the accounts and accounting ratios that seem to carry most importance. So far as the treasurer, and the bank manager, are concerned it is the cash flows that matter. Difficulties arise if either view prevails at the expense of the other.

Always remember that:

1. Propositions (and forms of capital structure) which look good in cost of capital (or present value) terms, do not necessarily produce the best result when measured in eps or profit terms in the short term; and vice versa.
2. The income, cost and profit consequences of a transaction do not necessarily match (and are often quite out of phase with) the cash flows.

The distinction between loan stocks or bonds and share capital has over the past few years become less clear, resulting in accounts the truth, if not the fairness, of which could be questioned. By removing some of the supposed attractions of such instruments, accounting standards (FRS 4 on 'Capital Instruments'), are likely to have made them less attractive, but one still needs to be on the look out for them. Some 'clever' accountant, solicitor or merchant bank will certainly try to find a way round the rules.

Among the less common capital instruments currently found are:

1. *AMPS* ('auction market preferred shares') are preference shares which are entitled to dividends determined in accordance with an auction in which a panel of investors participate, the shares being transferred at a fixed price to the investor who will accept the lowest dividend. AMPS are usually issued in the US.

2. *Convertible capital bonds* are debt instruments on which interest is payable periodically, issued by a special purpose subsidiary outside the UK. Prior to maturity they may be exchanged for shares of the subsidiary which, at the option of the bond holder are immediately redeemed or exchanged for shares of the parent.
3. *Convertible debt with a premium put option* contains an option for the holder to demand redemption (either at maturity of the debt or at some earlier date) for an amount which is in excess of the amount originally received for the debt.
4. *Convertible debt with enhanced interest.* Instead of a premium option, the convertible debt may contain an undertaking that interest will be increased at a date in the future.
5. *Debt issued with warrants for ordinary shares.*
6. *Deep discount bonds* are bonds which carry a low nominal rate of interest and are issued at a discount to the value at which they will be redeemed.
7. *Zero coupon bonds* are deep discount bonds which carry no interest.
8. *Income bonds* pay interest only where the issuer has sufficient reported profits.
9. *Index linked loans* do not state a specific amount for the payments. Instead they include a formula eg LIBOR + 2%. They may be redeemed at the principal amount multiplied by an index.
10. *Limited recourse debt* is debt where the lender's recourse is limited to specific security.
11. *Perpetual debt* is debt where the issuer has neither the right nor the duty to repay. Interest is usually expressed as a fixed margin over LIBOR or at a fixed rate..
12. *Stepped interest bonds* are debt where the interest rate increases by steps over the period of issue.
13. *Subordinated debt* is debt where the rights of the lender are not as great as those of other creditors of the issuer.

Accounting for capital instruments

Current best practice, ie generally accepted accounting principles, can be summarised (post FRS 4):

1. All capital instruments are accounted for in the balance sheet under one of three categories:
    (i) liabilities;
    (ii) shareholders' funds;
    (iii) minority interests.

2. They are classified as *liabilities* if they contain 'an obligation to transfer economic benefits (including a contingent obligation)'. Otherwise, with one minor exception referred to in 11, they are reported within *shareholders' funds*.

3. Convertible debt is reported within liabilities, on the face of the balance sheet and stated separately, and the finance cost computed as though it will never be converted. In other words, conversion of debt is no longer anticipated.

4. When convertible debt is converted, the amount recognised in respect of the shares issued is the amount of the liability for the debt at the date of conversion.

5. Immediately after issue, debt is stated at the amount of the net proceeds. (Traditionally, it was stated at the amount due on redemption).

Example 8.3

A 12 year £10m deep discounted bond (coupon 2%) is issued at 45, the proceeds of issue after deducting commission and expenses being £4.300m.

The bond will appear in a balance sheet at that time:

	£m
2% Bond (19xx)	4.300

rather than as:

	£m
2% Bond (19xx)	10.000

Without consulting the terms of issue it is impossible to say what the liability would be in the event of receivership or liquidation.

---

6. The finance costs of debt are allocated to periods over the term of the debt at a constant rate on the carrying amount. All finance costs are charged in the profit and loss account, except in the case of investment companies where special rules apply.

Example 8.4

The finance cost of the 2% bond referred to in Example 8.3 is computed as follows:

	£m
Nominal amount	10.000
Proceeds of issue	4.300
	5.700
Interest: 12 years at £200,000	2.400
	8.100
Nominal amount	10.000
Total payments/repayments over 12 years	18.100

The constant rate that needs to be applied is calculated using a spread sheet program or annuity tables as 10.622%. The charge in the first year is £456,743, of which interest paid represented £200,000. That in year 12 is £979,383, of which, again, £200,000 represents interest actually paid.

---

7. The carrying amount of the debt is increased by the finance cost in respect of the period less any payments made in respect of the debt in that period.

Example 8.5

The carrying amount of the 2% bond referred to in Example 8.3 is £4,556,743 at the end of year 1, ie £4,300,000 + £456,743 – £200,000. It increases year by year, so that at the end of year 12 it is £10,000,000.

---

8. In the balance sheet the total amount of shareholders' funds is analysed between equity interests and non-equity interests.

9. The net proceeds from the issue of share capital or warrants for equity shares is credited directly to shareholders' funds and not subsequently adjusted to reflect changes in the value of shares or warrants.

10. An issue of non-equity shares is treated rather like an issue of debt: it is the net proceeds of issue which are credited to non-equity shareholders' funds. This amount is increased by the finance cost in respect of the period and reduced by dividends or other payments.

11. Shares issued by subsidiaries other than those held by companies within the group (which disappear in the consolidation) are accounted for as liabilities, ie debt, if any member of the group has an obligation to transfer economic benefits in connection with the shares. In any other case they are reported as *minority interests*.

Yellow Book requirements

The Stock Exchange's Yellow Book requires as regards bank loans and overdrafts and other borrowings an analysis between:

1. Debt due in one year or less, or on demand;
2. Debt due between one and two years;
3. Debt due between two and five years;
4. Debt due in five years or more.

This analysis deserves careful study.

Off balance sheet finance

Off balance sheet finance may be defined as 'the funding or refinancing of a company's operations in such a way that, under existing legal require ments and accounting conventions, some or all of the finance may not appear in its balance sheet'. Defined in this way, however undesirable it may be, it is both lawful and permissible.

That is not to say, however, that transactions do not exist off balance sheet which *are* outside the law either here or where they are executed, and which other auditors, possibly but not necessarily at another time, might not countenance. Opinions differ and it is up to statute law and accounting standards to plug any loopholes; and they do.

Although termed *off balance sheet*, off balance sheet transactions often affect both the profit and loss account and the cash flow statement too. They are, in any case, or were closely related to ways of keeping transactions out of current operating profits/losses. For example, provision would be made as an extraordinary item for the discontinuance of certain activities, and losses incurred later charged against that provision and not against profits from continuing operations – a practice which should disappear as a result of FRS 3.

Various reasons were advanced by supporters of off balance sheet finance for its existence, eg that where a group of companies were reasonably similar as to activity, but one, say a finance subsidiary, was markedly different, with very different operating and balance sheet ratios, it would confuse bankers and analysts to aggregate them.

Indeed, the reasons generally advanced for off-balance sheet finance tended to have one thing in common: they assumed that the reader of accounts was unable to understand the background to financial ratios, and, in particular, why those of one company should be different from those of another, even though the nature and background of the companies were different. Those who suggested this could have been right. There may not, in fact, have been enough information available for the outsider to make a reasoned comparison.

The Companies Act 1985 (as amended by the 1989 Act) and FRS 2 ('Accounting for Subsidiary Undertakings') tightened the rules on subsidiaries and largely prevent this form of off balance finance. FRED 4 ('Reporting the Substance of Transactions'), the latest attempt to overcome the problem of off balance sheet items, takes this further. FRED 4 adopts the principle that 'A reporting entity's financial statements should report the substance of the transactions into which it has entered. Where the entity has a quasi subsidiary, the substance of the transactions entered into by the quasi subsidiary should be reported in the consolidated accounts.'

For this purpose a quasi subsidiary is a company, trust, partnership or other vehicle which, though not fulfilling the definition of a subsidiary,

is directly or indirectly controlled by the reporting entity and represents a source of benefit. Inflows or outflows for that entity are in no substance different from those that would arise were the vehicle a subsidiary.

FRED 4 is complex, since its purpose is to avoid manoeuvres which do not reflect the substance of transactions. It is concerned with the recognition of assets and liabilities; and when it is appropriate to cease to recognise assets. It introduces to standards the concept of linked presentation for certain non-recourse financial arrangements subject to a long list of criteria being met.

Offset is only permissible to net debit and credit balance which do not constitute separate assets and liabilities.

FRED 4 considers a number of specific financing schemes / arrangements for which the analyst should be on the look out:

1. Consignment stock: commonly found in the case of motor manufactureres / dealers. Stock is held by the dealer but owned by the manufacturer on terms which give the dealer the right to sell the stock in the normal course of business or, at its option, to return it unsold to the legal owner.
2. Sale and repurchase agreements are arrangements under which assets are sold by one party to another on terms that provide for the seller to repurchase the asset in certain circumstances.
3. Factoring of debts.
4. Securitised assets, eg household mortgages.
5. Loan transfer.

A definitive Standard is imminent. Until it appears, because these arrangements are so complex, it is worth studying the Appendix to FRED 4 by way of background.

Factoring

Factoring is a perfectly legitimate form of off-balance sheet finance (See Chapter 9 of *Interpreting Company Reports and Accounts*). The factoring of some, but not all, debtors (allowed by some factors, but not all, but always possible as regards the group as a whole by factoring debts of some companies but not others) made it difficult to discover from a study of the accounts whether factors were being used; though one's suspicions could be raised either by an unusually short collection period – or one which showed a sudden fall.

FRED 4 envisages three presentations:

1. *Derecognition*: where the seller has retained no significant benefits and risks in respect of the debts and has no obligation to repay amounts received from the factor. The debts are re

moved from the balance sheet and no liability is shown.

2. *Linked presentation*: where the conditions are met for link presentation, the proceeds received, to the extent that they are non-returnable, should be shown deducted from the gross amount of the factored debts (after providing for credit protection charges) on the face of the balance sheet.

3. *Separate presentation*: where neither 1 or 2 is appropriate, the gross amount of the debts should appear as an asset; and a corresponding liability in respect of proceeds shown within liabilities.

Until recently, derecognition was the norm.

Leases and hire purchase contracts

Admirable though the battle for disclosure may be, previous attempts to put off balance sheet finance onto the balance sheet, although they may enlighten the initiated, serve to confuse the layman.

For example: GRAND METROPOLITAN, acquires assets subject to *finance leases* (the capital value of the asset appears among fixed assets, and is shown by way of note; depreciation on the value of the asset is charged to profit and loss account, and the notional interest appears in the note explaining the interest charge; and the present value of future lease payments is shown in the balance sheet in the note on other creditors).

The group also *owns* plant which it leases out under *operating leases*, and which therefore also appears among its fixed assets, and is duly depreciated. It also has *finance lease* receivables (where it owns assets, eg plant and machinery, vehicles or aircraft, which it leases, and which do not appear among fixed assets).

The amounts involved are perhaps, in the context of a group of this size, immaterial (£100m or so) but the subtleties of all this will almost certainly be lost on the average reader.

Despite their relatively high cost, and the accounting complications they bring, leasing and hire purchase may nevertheless be attractive ways of acquiring assets, most especially when a company is somewhat strapped for cash. But in studying accounts, do not forget that:

1. The accountant, when he follows SSAP 21, 'Accounting for Leases and Hire Purchase Contracts', is applying the doctrine of 'substance over form', which freely translated means 'I don't care a damn what the law says, I believe that this is simply a way of the lessee acquiring assets, and that is how I am going to reflect it in the accounts'.

2. Nevertheless, the legal position of a company with machinery which is leased, or on hire purchase, is very different from that of a company which actually owns its plant. Assets which a business owns can be sold or rented to someone else; or given in security, but assets which are leased under a finance lease cannot – without payment of at least the discounted value of future rentals. Just as if you sell a car which is subject to a hire purchase agreement (and thus does not belong to you), you will be in trouble; so would a company.

Practice: Asda Case Study

Study the financial results of Asda Group for the years 1987–91 provided below, together with the statement of cash flow and share price graph for the three years 1989, 1990 and 1991 on page 44.

FINANCIAL RESULTS (Extracts)

	1987 £m	1988 £m	1989 £m	1990 £m	1991 £m
Turnover, excluding VAT	2,667	2,728	2,708	3,550	4,468
Operating profit	188.6	188.5	199.4	225.1	262.4
Interest receivable/ (payable)	6.9	23.3	34.5	(29.9)	(85.5)
Profit on ordinary activities before taxation	191.3	210.8	242.1	175.8	168.3
Earnings per ordinary share (p):					
Basic	11.36	12..38	14.22	10.23	10.09
Fully diluted	11.21	12.10	13.82	10.13	10.01
Net dividends per ordinary share	3.50	4.10	4.80	4.80	4.80
Net borrowing as a % of capital and reserves	31.9%	–	10.4%	80.4%	72.1%

FINANCING	1987 £m	1988 £m	1989 £m	1990 £m	1991 £m
Financed by:					
Capital and reserves	512.6	854.3	934.3	1074.3	1209.9
Long term loans	225.2	209.6	340.9	555.3	496.9
Minority interests	–	–	–	4.3	0.2
	737.8	1063.9	1275.2	1633.9	1707.0
Net cash (Short term borrowings)	61.8	391.5	244.0	(308.5)	(375.4)

CASH FLOW

	1987 £m	1988 £m	1989 £m	1990 £m	1991 £m
Funds generated from operations	230.2	246.3	271.5	233.7	250.7
Extraordinary items	–	482.8	–	174.7	–
Shares issued by the company	5.7	17.8	8.7	15.6	0.6
Convertible capital bond issued by a subsidiary undertaking	–	–	–	–	73.0
Shares issue by subsidiary undertaking to minority interests	–	–	–	4.3	–
Total funds generated	235.9	746.9	280.2	428.3	324.3
Net purchase of fixed assets	256.7	270.7	451.7	154.3	143.2
Purchase of businesses	–	–	–	771.8	–
Utilisation of acquisition provisions	–	–	–	58.0	28.2
Investment in associated undertakings	–	–	–	117.2	1.4
Working capital changes	(1.8)	21.4	23.8	(79.1)	36.1
Taxation	49.7	56.8	29.3	116.7	63.1
Dividends	37.4	43.1	50.6	56.1	56.4
Dividends paid to minority interests	–	–	–	0.2	0.3
Bond and preference share conversion and redemption	6.3	14.7	3.6	–	4.1
Total funds applied	348.3	406.7	559.0	1,195.2	332.8
Funds generated/ applied	(112.4)	340.2	(278.8)	(766.9)	(8.5)
Net cash funds/ borrowings	(163.4)	181.9	(96.9)	(863.8)	(872.3)

Shortly after that statement was published Asda sought to make a 9 for 10 rights issue at 35p a share to raise £369m.

The chairman reported that 'Since the beginning of the year, growth in Asda's food sales has continued below the industry average'. He wrote of an industry-wide 2 per cent volume decline in food and of 'no sign of any upturn' in home furnishing.

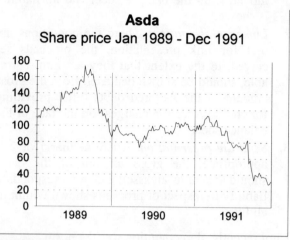

Asda
Share price Jan 1989 - Dec 1991

Assignment

1. Explain why a rights issue was necessary.
2. Comment on the group's financing policy from 1987 to 1991.
3. The issue clearly was not well received. Why do you think that was?

Abbreviated solution

1. The issue was necessary because of:

   (i) The sharp deterioration of liquid resources (net cash of £391.5m in 1988 became short-term borrowings in 1991 of £375.4m.

   (ii) The severe swing in interest (net) from a peak of £34.5m net receivable in 1989 to £85.5m payable in 1991, so that in the latter year it absorbed 32.6% of operating profit).

   (iii) The £771.8m purchase of businesses (including 62 superstores from Gateway) in 1990 was not covered by long-term finance.

2. (i) In hindsight, the failure to get long-term finance in respect of the 1990 acquisition of superstores from Gateway in place at that time is regrettable.

   (ii) There does not seem to be a consistent policy on gearing. Consider:

1987	31.9%
1988	nil
1989	10.4%
1990	80.4%
1991	72.1%

   but the latter figure regards as equity £73m of capital bonds which many would regard as borrowings.

   Both of which suggest weak financial planning and control.

3. The issue was not well received because:

(i)   It was exceedingly heavy (9 for 10).

(ii) It came at the wrong time (at a point when substantial rights issues generally were meeting trouble).

(iii) It came at the end of three years of falling earnings (down almost 30% since 1989).

(iv) It came at the end of three years of static dividends.

(v)   Financial management looks suspect. Note the massive extraordinary write-offs in 1988 and 1990; the failure to get finance in position at the time of the acquisition; the poor performance (turnover in the year to 27 April 1991 was £4,468m against £3,550m in 1990 (up 25.9%) but operating profit rose only £37.3m, ie 16.57% despite £771.8m of acquisitions in 1990 – and £55.6m more in interest).

Follow through

As an exercise it is worth following up the story of ASDA:

1. The appointment, after the rights issue, of Archie Norman (formerly FD at Kingfisher) as chief executive;

2. The marked improvement in 1992, both in profitability and market performance; and

3. The successful rights issue in January 1993.

Chapter 9

IMPENDING DISASTER AND HOW TO SPOT IT

Just as the medical profession learns from pathology, so investors can learn from the analysis and study of companies that have failed. History provides useful information not only on the causes of death but the symptoms of impending disaster.

One useful source is an analysis of the 45 listed, USM and 3rd Market companies that went into receivership in 1989 and 1990 as the UK was hit by recession, published as a briefing paper by County NatWest (now NatWest Securities) under the title 'Company Pathology' – a paper from which we draw morals in the first part of this Chapter.

Failure: size and age are a factor

The companies which failed can be analysed:

	Failures	Out of	%
Full listing	26	1,725	1.5
USM	14	379	3.7
3rd Market	5	49	10.2
	45	2,153	2.1

The fully listed companies that failed included four that had graduated from the USM; and 19 of the 45 companies that failed had been listed or on the USM less than five years.

Moral: Allow for the increased risk of failure if a company is small and / or newly listed.

Companies can grow *too* fast

A striking feature was the speed at which many companies had grown. The chairman of ROCKWOOD, in what proved to be his last report, said: 'The bare statistical facts are that last year, Rock-wood delivered a 452% increase in turnover from £19.9m to £109.8m ...'.

That is an extreme example, but the average annual compound rate of growth in turnover of the County NatWest companies was more than 50%, and 18% had grown at over 100% per annum, whereas only 6% of companies that survived had grown at that rate.

There are two ways of achieving such growth:

1. Acquisitions; or
2. A major expansion of existing business (or both)

– and they each proved disastrous.

Overambitious ill-timed acquisitions

A major contribution to the demise of BRITISH & COMMONWEALTH was the acquisition of Atlantic Computers; while COLOROLL went under after the overambitious and ill-timed acquisition of John Crowther.

An equally disastrous, if smaller, acquisition was civil and electric engineering services group OAKWOOD'S £29m takeover of ailing branded textile garment manufacturer Coxmore in August 1988. This trebled the size of Oakwood. In the first six months of the following year the group reported an operating loss of £1.49m arising entirely from the textile operations; and adverse exceptional items of £2.4m and adverse extraordinary items of £2.9m both related to Coxmore. This is a classic example of the risk of making a large takeover of a totally unrelated business. A receiver was appointed before the end of 1989.

Earnouts that had not been prefinanced also featured as a cause of death. Take marketing services company FKB, whose last report and accounts showed shareholders' funds of only £4.7m (net of all the goodwill arising on acquisitions), while additional future payments on earnouts amounted to a maximum of £58.8m.

Moral: Beware overambitious people and over-ambitious companies.

Expanding too fast

Several instances were found of companies failing to weather the expenses and disruption of moving to larger premises. Others simply undertook too much at the same time. Aerosol manufacturer TALBEX, for instance, opened a new 100,000 sq ft purpose-built aerosol plant, resulting in chronic overcapacity – and at the same time acquired a medical equipment company in the United States – and expanded its development and construction divisions, also by acquisition.

Property developer and contractor RUSH & TOMKINS took on a £750m development programme, largely through joint ventures, at a time when it had shareholders' funds of only £35m.

Advertising agency YELLOWHAMMER opened up in Europe but simultaneously invested in a series of major new ventures in London. As the chairman/chief executive wrote in his 1989 report: 'We are currently embarked on the most ambitious investment programme ever undertaken by the Group'.

But, in the words of the administrative receivers appointed not long after:

'Most of the Group's ambitious plans were funded by overdraft, attracting high interest rates. Attempts to refinance into longer term debt were unsuccessful. Furthermore, the group recently set up representative offices in Madrid and Paris, requiring material capital injections. Neither [proved] ... successful and both investments had to be written off.'

Moral: Major expansion brings stress; and stress brings increased risk.

Excessive and short-term borrowings

Very high borrowings (ie gearing), and an increase in borrowings from the previous year, were a feature of companies that failed.

Gearing	Number of companies final year	Number of companies previous year
50–100%	6	10
100–200%	10	6
200–400%	9	8
Over 400%	12	6

– but this was affected in some cases by the immediate write off of goodwill.

Borrowings of failed companies tended to be skewed towards the short term:

Borrowings due within 1 year as a % of total borrowings	Number of companies final year
0–20%	3
20–40%	6
40–60%	10
60–80 %	8
80–100%	18

Moral: Keep a watchful eye on the level of short-term borrowings.

Dominant characters and a resigning board

Over 60% of failed companies in the County Nat-West research had a combined chairman and chief executive – compared with 45% of USM / 3rd Market companies, and 35% of Listed companies, that did not go bust.

In most of these cases there was evidence that the company had been run by a single dominant character – indeed if one adds those companies where the role of chairman and chief executive was split, the proportion of failed companies run by a single dominant character rises to 70%.

Non-executive directors did not necessarily provide the protection one might hope. Only 5 companies in the 45 in the sample had no non-executive directors; though a further 17 only had one. But it is impossible to say whether these directors could fairly be classed as *independent* non-executive directors – they could well have been former executive directors, ex-employees or family. But, as the report shows, well-known names amongst the non-executive directors do not necessarily provide any safeguard.

Resignation appears to be something to be on the look out for. More than half the companies in the sample showed resignations from the board in the accounting period immediately before collapse:

Number of resignations	Number of companies	Notes
1	5	
2	4	
3	6	
4	4	
5	1	BRITISH & COMMONWEALTHH
6	1	COLOROLL
8	1	CHARTERHALL

In a number of cases, resignations at the company's last AGM (ie not included in the table above) gave warning that all was not well. For example, the two directors who ran the main operating divisions of PARKFIELD left, one nine months before the end, the other three months later.

Moral: Be on the lookout for internal strife.

Other warning signs

There was widespread use of joint ventures to keep finance for property off balance sheet; the borrowings being secured on the developments. An illustration showing: (a) how important it is to read the notes to accounts; and (b) how fast a position can deteriorate, is provided by RUSH & TOMKINS. Their last accounts showed a net investment in joint venture developments of £7.78m, and the provision of an additional £17m for working capital. But the notes disclosed:

'The joint venture companies have entered into a number of non-recourse and limited recourse banking arrangements ... which amounted to approximately £89m.'

At the time group borrowings were around £25m, but when the company went into receivership just over a year later it was reported as owing about £300m and to have been involved in 40 joint venture developments valued together at about £600m.

A less reputable example of off-balance sheet finance was discovered by the *Mail on Sunday* some time after PARKFIELD collapsed. It concerned the sale of video tapes to a related company, with a written agreement that the videos could be sold back to Parkfield after the year end. The scheme removed a quarter of the video stockpile from the balance sheet, and boosted profits by showing the transaction as a sale. It is this sort of thing which FRED 4 wants to highlight.

In assessing the strength of a group, it is also worth considering the financial advisers. The County NatWest survey showed that the failure rate amongst companies with no specified financial adviser was 2.2%, compared with 1.4% for those with financial advisers.

The disappearance of the names of well-known financial advisers is a warning signal. Both Samuel Montagu and Panmure Gordon appeared in LEADING LEISURE'S 1988 report, but neither was there in the 1989 report.

Most of the 45 companies which failed gave the name of their principal bank or banks, but the five that did not included BRITISH & COMMONWEALTH and POLLY PECK, the two largest borrowers. Often this is a sign that a number of banks are used. Even they may not know who else is involved.

A company which uses a whole raft of banks is extremely vulnerable. Take PARKFIELD, on the day administrators were appointed, the group's borrowings were £227.2m from 16 banks of which 10 were foreign. It took only one of these to withdraw its support to bring collapse.

Other warning signs highlighted by County NatWest are to be found in the annual report. If it is over lavish, look out (Parkfield changed in its last year to paper so shiny that one could not write on it even with a highlighter pen). A report which is both over-lavish and non-standard in size (ie above A4) like POLLY PECK'S does not augur well.

Accounts which blow the trumpet too hard (as LOWNDES QUEENSWAY'S did) or which 'name drop' like those of Newcastle-based STANLEY MILLER (with a portrait by Lord Snowdon of the chief executive, and a photograph of the company's 94 Mount Street Mayfair offices reflected in the bonnet of a gleaming Rolls Royce) should give rise reservations rather than overawe.

Learning from inspectors' reports

Under the Companies Acts, the Department of Trade and Industry may appoint inspectors to enquire into the affairs of a company or group of companies. It may do this at the request of the company, a group of shareholders, or a financial regulator such as the SIB, or off its own bat.

Typically there are a hundred or more investigations a year. Almost invariably in the case of major investigations, two inspectors are appointed, a QC and an eminent accountant. They are required to report to the Secretary of State, and frequently, but not universally, their report is published.

Inspectors' reports represent rewarding reading. They demonstrate just how complicated business affairs and company structures often are, and why it is difficult for a jury to understand the evidence in a complex fraud trial. More than that they shed light on human frailty.

The precise situation differs, but certain factors repeat themselves time and again:

1. Greed;
2. A willingness to believe what looks, and is, too good to be true;
3. Over-weaning ambition;
4. Dishonesty, theft, and fraud;
5. Incompetence, neglect, not to say negligence (of directors, managers, bankers and professional advisors including auditors).

Moral: Investors, analysts, and bankers, need to learn by experience (and from the experience of others). They do not seem good at this.

Scientific methods of predicting failure

Various attempts have been made to assess the likelihood of failure scientifically. Among them was the 'Z' score, developed in the United States by Edward Altman in the late 1960s, which combines key ratios to give a single number:

$$Z = 1.2a + 1.4b + 3.3c + 0.6d + 0.99e$$

where:

a = working capital / total assets;
b = retained earnings / total assets;
c = earnings before interest and tax / total assets;
d = market value of equity / book value of total liabilities;
e = sales / total assets.

A score in excess of 3 is said to indicate a safe company, and one below 1.8 a candidate for failure. But some companies with a low score survive. Maybe some companies read the warning signs for themselves, are able and have time to put things right.

What goes up ...

Fortunes are made, to mix metaphors, by hanging on to the coat tails of those who are going places, but knowing just when to parachute to the ground. What one is trying to do is to sort out the sheep from the goats.

How does one recognise companies about to take off – and do so *before* everyone else has hitched a ride? According to Judi Bevan and John Jay in *The New Tycoons – Becoming seriously rich at 40* they are: 'Young, lean and fit, the modern heads of growing businesses work punishing hours, turning themselves and others into millionaires. Obsessive, visionary and ruthless, they fire the imagination of investors, staff and customers.'

This is an exciting, illuminating book which tells what people like Anita Roddick (BODY SHOP), George Davies (NEXT), Sophie Mirman (SOCK SHOP), Gerald Ratner (ratners, now SIGNET), Martin Sorrell (WPP), Alan Sugar (AMSTRAD) and John Ashcroft (COLOROLL), to name just seven, did right, which made each of them millionaires – and occasionally it shows where they went wrong. Some have learned very hard lessons; Gerald Ratner, for example, has learned that truth is not necessarily the best policy. It is a book well worth studying, and which provides an introduction to the world of the high-flying stock.

Funds flow into institutions such as insurance companies and pension funds in vast amounts, and fund managers do not like to waste opportunities by keeping it in the bank (though that is sometimes the best course). Instead they are constantly on the look out for investments which will beat the index. The recognition by the institutions of a small, but growing company, as having investment potential is often a self-fulfilling prophecy: interest on the part of the institutions brings a re-rating, and spectacular share price growth.

The press, tip sheets, brokers' circulars, and even major individual punters play a part too.

POLLY PECK *Effect of a press announcement*

In June 1982, first half-year results were announced: profits of £3m up from £18,000 the previous year. Asil Nadir chose this moment to announce that Polly Peck was planning an electronics venture to build TV plants in Turkey and Egypt – a very different business from citrus exports. In a press announcement Brian Handicott (ex Thorn-EMI, who became Polly Peck's commercial director) explained that Polly Peck were to be licensees: Thorn-EMI were providing both the technology and the know-how.

Despite widespread fear that there would need to be a rights issue, Polly Peck's share price shot up from £1.75 to £16.78.

Equally, when institutions lose interest or faith and withdraw their stake (or tip sheets suggest the ride is over), collapse is just as spectacular. A classic case was the Australian company POSEIDON, shares of which in the 1970s started at 25p, peaked at £124 and then crashed right back again.

Moral: Beware of shooting stars.

Danger signals

So far we have looked at signs of imminent collapse to be found from a study of the report and accounts. But what does one find when one arrives at the offices and plant as a receiver or liquidator? What distinguishes a company about to fail?

A number of people involved in corporate reconstruction and insolvency have, over the years, listed their own personal danger signals. In no particular order they include:

1. No accountant on the board;
2. Elderly or unqualified accountants;
3. Too many auditors;
4. Too many bankers;
5. A pre-occupation with tax avoidance;
6. A combined chairman/chief executive;
7. Too many board papers, too few, or too late;
8. Personalised number plates on company Rolls;
9. Impressive new offices opened by prime minister;
10. Company flagpole, fountain in the forecourt, fish tank in the boardroom, founder's statue in reception;
11. Chairman/chief executive president of CBI or BIM;
12. Chief executive's office full of sporting etc trophies and mementoes;
13. Company yacht / company aircraft.

We are not saying that in all cases a particular item is unjustified, eg companies need offices; and, if they expand, new offices, even relatively impressive new offices, may be justified. Companies where immediate worldwide response is essential may find a need for their own aircraft. It is not one of these which raises doubts so much as a combination of, say five or more, status symbols in a smallish organisation which together suggest that the day to day running of the company may not be getting the attention it needs.

Moral: Ask yourself – does management appear on the ball, or is it over-anxious to seek the trappings of power?

Down but not out

There comes a point of no return, when banks, investors, and even customers lose faith to such an extent that recovery is impossible. But until that point is reached, all is not lost.

It is worth reading *The Phoenix Factor* by David Clutterbuch and Sue Kernaghan, which includes case studies of a number of well-known companies (like Dunlop, Raleigh, Alfred Herbert, Sinclair and Rolls-Royce) which rose from the ashes.

Everything depends, it seems, upon changing attitudes:

1. To controls;
2. To customers;
3. To investors;
4. To the team.

It is worth seeking out and identifying such companies for oneself.

Moral: There is money to be made in spotting a potentially successful turnaround before the rest of the market does.

Practice

Try to find, assemble accounting information and other salient details of:

1. A company which is being widely tipped, whose shares may well rise;
2. A shooting-star, likely to fizzle out;
3. A company which could rise from the ashes.

After some months have elapsed, follow up your selections. If with hindsight they prove to have been wrong; ask youself what you missed; and why.

Chapter 10

PROFIT IMPROVEMENT

Some companies have it – others don't

Statements of corporate objectives which appeal to ideals like motherhood and apple pie, often suggest that a group's main aim is customer satisfaction, a stable and contented work force, brands with an international reputation, and so on; all of which may be true.

Even where the statement is more direct, it does not always help much. Consider, for example HANSON.

HANSON *Company profile, inside cover 1992 report*

Over the next decade Hanson aims to enhance shareholder value by increasing earnings per share and dividends generated through profitable internal growth and selective acquisitions.

But the bottom line is profit and the name of the game is profit improvement: ever larger profits, earnings per share and dividends. On this rest share price and the company's ability to raise money. And it is this ability for which an investor, acquirer or analyst must look in studying a company.

Some companies have it; others don't. Why? How does one come by it? Where does one find it? Can one buy it? Are consultants, perhaps, the answer?

Using consultants

Management consultancies come in all shapes and sizes, and spring from a number of different disciplines. There are, for instance, numerous consultancies representing the business arms of firms of chartered accountants, others from a public relations, design, print, legal or marketing background. While most employ specialists from a range of disciplines, the origins and ownership of a consultancy do, in many ways, determine its specialisation.

Consultants are expensive; and they do not always bring an expertise, or special knowledge, which is superior to that of management on the ground. What they bring is breadth of experience – people on the job can be too close to see alternative approaches which are obvious to an outsider.

Because they are expensive, they tend to be appointed by and their views listened to by senior management, often that at board level. Why pay someone if you are not going to take notice of what they say?

One great advantage of consultants is that they are given, or, if they are not, they demand, clear instructions – a brief. This compels managers to take time to consider the situation, to discuss with one another the way they see the problem, and to agree as to what it is – something which surprisingly they may not have done previously.

Another advantage is that they are prepared to listen to people at all levels; to talk to the man on the shop floor, to retailers and even their customers. And when they do, those people are prepared to talk to them in a way that they might not talk to a director.

Sometimes consultants are used by middle management, or a faction of the board, to persuade an autocratic chief executive to change his mind – the views expressed may still be those of middle management, but because they are voiced by consultants, to whom the company is paying the earth, they are listened to.

But the function of management is to manage, not to be told what to do. For a company with a world-wide reputation and presence in an area, like oil-exploration or pharmaceuticals, to employ consultants to tell it where to drill or what drug to aim for, would be rather like the Institute of Chartered Accountants employing consultants to tell it how to set up a system of general ledger codes as part of its internal accounting system: ludicrous.

It is also the function of management to assess and where necessary accept risk; and not to try find someone else, some consultant, to share or even take the blame.

Useful though management consultants may be, their existence is rarely mentioned in a report and accounts. Reference may, however, be made to their existence in a works visit or interview. Where it is, if it is as a crutch or aunt sally, it should be viewed as such.

We are speaking here of management consultants in a profit improvement context. Specialists, who may broadly be termed consultants, are quite properly used in other ways to support and advise management in areas in which it cannot be expected to possess expertise eg actuaries advising on pension fund contribution levels, investment, and the like; and surveyors advising a landlord on rental levels, or valuations.

Normally, profit improvement (to use our catch phrase) and business improvement (to use a more general but possibly less exciting phrase) is a primary responsibility of management at all levels.

Just as a physician and surgeon work together to improve the health of a human being, we view the problem of profit improvement in two parts. In this chapter we consider ways of improving the existing business. In Chapters 12 and 13 we turn to surgery, to cutting out the dead wood and / or implanting something healthier.

Improving the existing business

It is sometimes said of an accountant that he is tight-fisted, that 'he would cut a halfpenny in half'. Such stringency has a place in profit improvement, particularly where the business has reached an almost terminal state and an administrative receiver (what used to be termed a receiver and manager) has been appointed and is endeavouring to keep the business running, probably with a view to sale.

Perhaps twenty years ago, the concept of zero-based budgeting was imported from the US, the idea being that every expense needed to be justified, otherwise the budget was zero.

Although the concept did not catch on generally, it does make the point: if nobody can demonstrate that incurring a cost produces anything of value, why incur it?

At the simplest level, we can consider profit to be the result of these three calculations:

1. Turnover – Cost of Sales = Gross Profit

2. Gross Profit – Other Operating Costs = Operating Profit

3. Operating Profit – (Administration etc Costs + Interest (Net)) = Net Profit

Looked at in this way, profit improvement breaks into three parts:

1. Increasing gross profit;
2. Reducing other Operating costs;
3. Reducing administration etc costs and interest (net).

'Margins are king' we are told; and there is a lot of truth in that. BTR is an example of a company which, first under Sir Owen Green amd more recently under Alan Jackson, has always paid very close attention to improving margins from its industrial manufacturing. For net profit is largely determined by the gross profit. Nevertheless, gross profit is more than just a matter of margins:

Gross profit = Turnover × Gross Profit Margin

and can be improved by improving either (and holding the other constant) or both. It is even possible, where the market allows, to improve it by reducing one and more than compensating for the effect of this by increasing the other eg to cut prices but more than compensate for the effect by selling vastly more.

In other words, one cannot, maximise profitability (even at the gross profit level) by focusing on margins alone.

Changes in margin are easy to see in the case of a retail business. If the cost of sales is not stated on the face of the profit and loss account, and the gross profit specifically shown, cost of sales will appear in the note on operating costs or operating profit, and the gross profit can be calculated.

Gross margin usually is not shown as such in the case of other types of business (eg organisations engaged in construction or manufacturing) and it is necessary to have regard instead to the ratio of operating profit to turnover. But it is then much more difficult to understand any change because:

1. Companies differ somewhat in the way in which they define operating profit.
2. Whereas cost of sales in the case of a retail organisation is directly related to turnover, many operating costs (like rent, rates and salaries) tend to be relatively fixed in nature.
3. Operating costs often include apportionments of head office or central administration costs and even an interest charge.

The interpretation of margins is even more difficult in the case of a group with international operations because of the effects of transfer pricing (the price set by one part of a group when it supplies another). Where do profits arise: at the point of manufacture or the point of sale – if, as seems reasonable, they should be shared: in what proportions? And what if tax is saved by charging a low transfer price (and hence producing a low level of manufacturing profit in a country with high levels of taxation); or by charging a high transfer price (and hence producing a high level of manufacturing profit in a country with low levels of taxation). Is that fair, and to be expected, or reprehensible? It certainly occurs where international groups are able to get away with it.

Despite these difficulties:

1. Most companies say something about margins in their chairman's statement or review of operations; and the analyst should study this with especial care noting every nuance.
2. Most are well aware of the importance of maintaining and, if possible, increasing margins in their efforts to improve profits overall; and when they are successful are likely to tell you so with pride.

They may even tell you how they have done it but most do not.

Food retailers, like SAINSBURY, TESCO and ARGYLL represent an exception. In the past decade they have all strived hard to improve both margins and overall profitability, and they have not been reticent about telling people how. Although many of the things they have done are of special application to the food retailing industry, others are equally applicable to stores, or to businesses generally.

SAINSBURY AND TESCO *How they improve margins*

In the 24 years 1969–93, Sainsbury's sales rose from £166m to £10,270m (representing almost 19% pa compound). Profits grew over the same period from £4.3m before tax to £732m (just under 24% compound).

How did they achieve this?

In 1981 Sainsbury's UK operating margin was 3.67%. It rose steadily, year by year. By 1986 it was 5.30%. A year later, 5.75%, and so on until in 1993 it reached 8.35%.

They achieved this in part by developing bigger stores. In 1986, for instance, the average store size was 16,760 sq feet, but the new stores added in that year averaged 27,430 sq feet. By 1992, the new stores added in that year averaged 34,900 sq feet – and the largest, Hedge End, near Southampton, was 48,000 sq feet. It fell marginally in 1993 to 32,710 sq feet.

This same emphasis on store size and modernity is exhibited by Tesco. In its year 1992–93 Tesco created 859,000 sq feet of new sales area, the average sales area

of stores opened in the year was 34,400, down to the 1989–90 level) and the overall average was 25,100 sq feet against 21,700 5 years earlier. At the end of the year 1990–91 23% of total selling space had been opened within the previous three years. Pleasant, modern, spacious stores are another feature. Store size enables supermarkets to broaden their product range. Tesco added over 900 new lines in 1992–93.

Own label products have been developed to provide economy and consistent product quality to the customer and, at the same time, higher profit margins to the store. Of Sainsbury's 17,000 product lines, 8,000 are own label, over 1,400 of which were added in 1992–93.

Most of the major food retailing organisations have, from time to time, proclaimed massive price reductions with a view to attracting custom. Careful study suggests that any reductions are very selective and that margins generally are maintained.

The supermarket groups have spent in the last few years hundreds of millions on installing EPOS (electronic point of sale) and EFTPOS (electronic funds transfer and point of sale) equipment, building distribution centres (fewer and larger depots), computerised stock control, ordering and despatch systems and data links together allow just-in-time supply.

Just-in-time supply brings lower stocks, and hence a lower investment in stocks, fewer stock losses and less deterioration, but it imposes tight disciplines both on the supplier and the store.

EPOS makes it possible both to measure and reduce shrinkage and to largely eliminate undercharging (which it seems always outweighed overcharging), and together with branch computing allows merchandising systems and technology to become scanner driven.

Tesco has set up an advanced sales based ordering (SBO) system which automatically calculates store replenishment requirements based on item sales and generates orders for delivery to stores within 24–48 hours. Stock levels and wastage are reduced, productivity is improved, and even fewer products go out of stock in the stores. By 1992 SBO for grocery products was operating in 247 stores.

Tesco has set up electronic data interchange (EDI) links with over 900 suppliers, and more are to follow.

Sainsbury and Tesco now seek to build, or where necessary lease, only stores which meet defined criteria: a minimum size, ease of access both internal and external, availability of parking, and so on. But falling property values and a newly accepted need to provide depreciation have dampened their enthusiasm.

Observe that while the focus may have been firmly on margins: sales volume, customer service, overall efficiency, and asset management all play their part. This is typical of profit improvement.

Both Tesco and Sainsbury are seeking to expand overeas (Tesco in France, and Sainsbury in the US).

There is an old Scottish saying: 'Many a mickle maks a muckle' – a lot of little things make a lot. And profit improvement is like that. But margins are currently under pressure because of low inflation and competition from discount chains.

Other ways of improving profitability

Earlier we said that profit improvement could be broken into parts. We have already discussed:

1. Increasing gross profit.

We now look at:

2   Reducing other operating costs;
3. Reducing administration etc costs and interest (net).

Other operating costs, administration costs and the like are a mixed bag, some of which vary directly with turnover (or with sales volume), and others move broadly with it. Many are fixed in nature but vary in line with inflation, or are market, local authority or central government determined, like rent and the business rate.

Some (like the costs associated with a prestigious headquarters building) are easier to avoid in the first place than to contain after the event, though Hanson make a point of cutting out head office expenses in companies acquired.

Larger groups frequently end up with too many layers of administration and spend a great deal of money in rationalising (not always successfully).

There is generally a degree of pain associated with cost cutting (whether it be a requirement that senior staff travelling by air do so business class, or by rail at standard rate, rather than first class; a dictat that lunch time entertaining of customers is out, that executive secretaries be shared, that paper towels replace real ones in the directors' loo, or that the chairman's car be sold).

Experience suggests that costs are very resilient: the post that is cut one day all too frequently reappears under another guise a few weeks later.

Companies, faced with static or declining sales, are forced to cut costs, and often this means reducing employee numbers. Pruning and cost cutting is sometimes mentioned by a chairman's report, but rarely in sufficient detail to be meaningful to an analyst. More and more companies since the recession (from BT, to BP and BURTON), have publicly announced redundancies. Some, like Burton plan to make greater use of part-time staff. Where companies do they often state the effect on numbers employed, wage and salary costs, and possible pension costs.

Ratios to watch

What the analyst can do is to watch carefully three key ratios to be found from the profit and loss account and notes:

1. Other operating costs / Sales;
2. Selling and distribution costs / Sales;
3. Administrative expenses / Sales;

– or their equivalents.

If they rise, it is a warning sign. If these costs rise faster than inflation, when turnover is static or falling: beware.

The better the business is doing, the lower these ratios should become (because fixed costs are spread more thinly).

In poor trading conditions, they tend to rise. They also tend to rise ahead of an expansion of activities. Effective management tries to ensure that any such rise is as small as possible. Business death (receivership or liquidation) is often the price of failure to contain these costs.

Case study: Abbey Crest

Our case study, which shows how one small group, ABBEY CREST, who design, manufacture and distribute gold and silver jewellery, faced the 1989–90 recession, is something of a model.

ABBEY CREST *Extract from profit and loss account and Notes for the year to 31 December 1990*

		1990	1989
		£000	£000
Turnover		60,171	59,187
Cost of sales		48,981	47,479
Gross profit		11,190	11,708
Other operating expenses	3	5,881	4,208
Operating profit		5,309	7,500

Note 3:	£000	£000
Distribution costs	98	111
Selling and marketing costs	906	789
Administration expenses	5,024	3,317
Other operating income	(147)	(9)

In ratio terms:

	1990	1991
	%	%
Gross profit margin	18.60	19.78
Distribution costs / Sales	0.16	0.18
Selling and marketing costs / Sales	1.51	1.33
Administration expenses / Sales	8.35	5.60
Other operating income / Sales	0.24	0.02

Year on year:	%
Turnover	+1.66
Cost of sales	+3.16
Gross profit	– 4.42
Other operating expenses	+39.76
Operating profit	– 29.21

An unhappy year, with margins falling; sales growing, but far below the rate of inflation (about 10%); and costs rising far ahead of inflation.

The chairman explains why:

'Business volumes increased to new record levels in 1990 as the group achieved further penetration in a difficult market. However, with the prices of the majority of the group's products linked to the price of gold, and with gold trading at the lowest levels for a decade, only a marginal increase in turnover resulted.

'We had markedly different experiences in the various sectors of the market which we serve. The onset of the consumer recession coincided with jewellery multiple retailers, in particular, placing much greater emphasis on stock control. They de-stocked throughout 1990 and our business with them suffered commensurably, although the number of lines we supplied was similar to the previous year. The resulting shortfall was made up by increased penetration of independent retail and export markets, and a small step forward with the home shopping sector.

'Group margins were impaired by the highly competitive nature of the market place. With major customers cutting back on business very late in the season there was a large scale over-supply problem in the industry, the effects of which are still being felt. Production efficiency at Gallery was also adversely affected as production batch sizes were reduced.

'Previously planned group expenditure proved out of proportion to the levels of business achieved. There was significant feed-through from the additions to the infrastructure of our businesses which we made in 1989. In 1990 we bore the full year effect of these enhancements and made further improvements in anticipation of continuing business development.' A reasonable explanation of the problem.

He goes on: 'Cost cutting measures were implemented in the early autumn, as it became apparent that this extra business would not materialise, but it was too late in the year to make significant inroads'.

Points to note:

1. Growth plans often involve costs up front and cannot easily be cancelled once they are under way.
2. Seasonal businesses usually fix their accounting year so that it ends just after their seasonal peak. If the expected level of business at that seasonal peak fails to materialise, it is too late to cut costs and affect materially that year's results.
3. The importance of Christmas to stores groups.
4. Journalists and analysts often think that they are very clever, and have spotted trends which a group itself has not spotted. Occasionally this is true. But a group with a sound accounting system should detect trends as they develop – often in a matter of days – and will already have acted upon them long before they are visible in annual accounts.

A year on:

Things did not immediately get better. In 1991 the chairman reported: 'The year under review was the most challenging that the group has ever experienced. Whilst extensive discounting in the retail jewellery sector over the peak Christmas season stimulated volumes, our market still contracted by more than 20%. I mentioned in my commentary on the interim results that many competitors were foundering or cutting back. As we were often able to capitalise on those misfortunes and continued our business development activity where others curtailed theirs, sales did not fall in line with the market and we were able to increase our market share to record levels. We acquired Erics Jewellers, the largest cash and carry unit in the Birmingham jewellery quarter ...'

They were hit by bad debts 'when several retail customers failed' (the profit and loss charge for bad debts was £494,000 compared with £41,000 in 1990). The dividend was cut slightly. Earnings per share were down from 12.1p to 9.8p, but there is something to be said for a company which succeeds where others fail, and which survives without allowing itself to be blown off course.

Reducing net interest payable

In a period of recession like the early 1990s, induced in part by high interest rates, interest costs rise. They do so for two reasons:

1. Shortage of cash;
2. Higher interest rates.

Finance directors seek by various means to reduce so far as possible the impact of higher rates (by borrowing for a term at a low, fixed rate when this is possible), by borrowing overseas (see Chapter 15), by rate caps and swaps. They also seek by central banking arrangements, and the sweeping of all spare cash into interest bearing accounts or overnight money to maximise any interest receivable and minimise any overdraft.

Such arrangements may be mentioned to analysts at the time of a company visit (as an indication that management is on the ball) and they may be mentioned in the finance director's review.

General satisfaction that the net interest charge is low, or falling, is reasonable; but one cannot fairly compute an interest rate (by taking interest paid / bank overdraft) from annual accounts, because the bank balance on any one day, and most especially that on the last day of the accounting year, is probably untypical and not the average balance.

More questionable improvements

Most listed companies seem to prune out less profitable businesses, most especially in a recession. But it is important to distinguish profit improvements which are 'genuine' *and* maintainable from those which are one-off or questionable.

Improvements in apparent profits (or a masking of a deterioration) have in the past been achieved by questionable, not to say dishonest means, by flouting the law and by bending accounting standards and conventions. FRS 3, on which we focus in Chapter 11, seeks to prevent this.

Let it suffice here to say that over the years, countless cases have occurred, and been widely reported, of banks, merchant banks, professional advisers and investors being cheated – taken in by schemes and companies in ways which, with hindsight, suggest surprising gullibility. A fair general rule is: 'If it looks too good to be true, it probably is' – but one still has to find out why.

FRS 3 alone will not make people less gullible.

Cash flow effects of profit improvement

Profit improvement cannot be considered in isolation. Back to back with any profit improvement plan must be considered:

1. Its short term effects on profitabilty;
2. Its overall cash flow effects.

Profit improvement plans frequently have adverse short term effects on profitability; for example:

1. A major advertising campaign may produce profitable sales growth in the longer term, but the costs of planning, design and the placing of the advertisements, have to be borne up front;
2. Overhauling and modernising a production line not only costs a great deal of money, it tends to bring lost time and lost production as it is being carried out;
3. Expanding overseas frequently incurs planning and set up costs long before any facilities exist;
4. Research into a potentially valuable drug may be carried out for years before any profits appear – assuming they ever do.

The cash flow effects are, if anything, more important. There is, for a start, and this is obvious, the expenditure needed to put the plan itself into effect (the cost of planning, designing and placing the advertisement in (1); the cost of the overhault, the modernisation and the staff time lost in (2), and so on.

Less obvious, and often forgotten by managers who should know better, are the working capital effects. If sales are expanded, debtors will increase. If production is expanded, there is likely to be need for additional stocks of raw materials, more work in progress, bigger stocks of finished goods, and, assuming the production is sold, increased debtors. The same is true if the company expands into an overseas market. Research into a new drug, will, if successful, have similar effects.

Probably *the* most common mistake made by small businesses, when they approach the bank with an expansion plan, is to forget they will need more working capital. If they do, it is an obvious black mark. But the error is not confined to small businesses.

Practice

Growth can be measured in a number of different ways; each of which has its uses.

Imagine you are:

1. Investment manager of the pension fund of a leading chemicals group;
2. Marketing director of a pharmaceutical company;
3. Financial adviser to a substantial private investor, who has no other income; and
4. Chairman of a major international integrated oil company.

Which of these would you regard as the best indicator of growth:

(i) turnover;
(ii) share price;
(iii) earnings per share;
(iv) earnings per share before exceptional items (or normalised eps);
(v) dividend per share;
(vi) profit from continuing operations;
(vii) profit before, or after, tax;
(viii) equity shareholders' funds;
(ix) total assets;
(x) cash generated by operations;
(xi) net asset value per share?

– and why?

Abbreviated solution

1. The investment manager of the pension fund of a leading chemicals group will look for several things: growth in the overall value of his holding (ie in share price) in order to meet future pensions; growth in dividends (in order to meet increasing demands for current pensions); a reasonable level of risk. Risk cannot be avoided altogether but if it 'hits' causes a pensions fund manager great pain.
2. The success of the marketing director of a pharmaceutical company is likely to be measured in turnover terms; though profit growth is what really matters.
3. The financial adviser to a substantial private investor, who has no other income, will tend to focus on dividend growth, and earnings growth without which it cannot continue.
4. The chairman of a major international integrated oil company really needs to be watching all these measures. But cash flow and earnings may well top his list.

Chapter 11

REPORTING FINANCIAL PERFORMANCE

We devote this entire chapter to FRS 3, 'Reporting Financial Performance', for four reasons:

1. FRS 3 represents probably the most important single change so far introduced by the Accounting Standards Board.
2. FRS 3 fundamentally redefined: (a) profit; and (b) earnings per share.
3. Unless accounts and historical summaries for earlier periods are restated, they will not be comparable with those currently produced.
4. There will undoubtedly be some resistance to the new rules, but the future credibility of the ASB depends upon its ability to make them stick.

SSAP 6, 'Extraordinary Items and Prior Year Adjustments', introduced in April 1974, though sound in intention, failed largely because of a refusal on the part of the Accounting Standards Committee to provide interpretations of standards. As a consequence large companies in particular pushed hard against the limits, and pressured their auditors to allow treatments which are today seen as questionable. As one auditor succumbed to a particular treatment, so the position of the rest became more difficult. This did not happen in the US, where interpretations of standards are published.

FRS 3 summarised

1. FRS 3 introduced two new statements:

   (i) A statement of total recognised gains and losses;
   (ii) A reconciliation of movements in shareholders' funds.

2. All gains and losses recognised in the period are to appear in the profit and loss account or the statement of recognised gains and losses.

3. Gains and losses may be excluded from the profit and loss account only if they are specifically permitted or required by accounting standards or, in their absence, by law to be taken to reserves.

4. There is a new focus on continuing activities. The aggregate results of:

   (i) Acquisitions (as a component of continuing operations); and
   (ii) Discontinued operations;

   are to be disclosed separately. We expand on acquisitions, disposals and discontinuations in Chapters 12 and 13.

5. Exceptional items, subject to the exceptions in 6, are credited or charged in arriving at the profit or loss on ordinary activities being included under the statutory format headings to which they relate. The amount of the item, either individually or an aggregate of items of a similar type, should be disclosed separately by way of note, or, if that degree of prominence is necessary in order to give a true and fair view, on the face of the profit and loss account.

6. Certain items, including provisions in respect of them, namely:

   (i) profits or losses on the sale or termination of an operation;
   (ii) costs of a fundamental reorganisation or restructuring having a material effect on the nature and focus of the reporting entity's operations;
   (iii) profits or losses on the disposal of fixed assets;

   are shown separately on the face of the profit and loss account after operating profit and before interest, and included under the appropriate heading of continuing or discontinued operations.

7. The profit or loss on the disposal of an asset is the difference between the net sale proceeds and the net carrying amount (ie historical cost less any provisions made, or valuation, as appropriate), and should be accounted for in the profit and loss account of the period in which the disposal occurs.

8. Extraordinary items are defined as 'Material items possessing a high degree of abnormality which arise from events or transactions that fall outside the ordinary activities of the reporting entity and which are not expected to recur. They do not include exceptional items nor do they include prior period items merely because they relate to a prior period.' Explanatory notes make it clear that:

'Extraordinary items are extremely rare as they relate to highly abnormal events or transactions that fall outside the ordinary activities of a reporting entity and which are not expected to recur. In view of the extreme rarity of such items no examples are provided.'

By definition, an item which the Standard requires to be treated as exceptional cannot be extraordinary. It is this which gives FRS 3 much of its force.

9. Any extraordinary profit or loss is shown separately on the face of the profit and loss account, after the profit or loss on ordinary activities after taxation and minority interests but before appropriations such as dividends. Any subsequent adjustment to the tax on extraordinary items is also to be treated as extraordinary.

10. Any special circumstances that affect the overall tax charge or credit for the period , or that may affect those of future periods, should be disclosed by way of note to the profit and loss account and their individual effects quantified.

11. Paragraph 10 of SSAP 3 on earnings per share has been superseded. Earnings are to be based on the profit (in the case of a group on the consolidated profit) of the period after tax, minority interests *and extraordinary items* and after deducting preference dividends.

The overall effects of the change are difficult to predict, but frequently they are substantial. Consider KINGFISHER, (alongside) which, because in 1993 it showed both old and new presentations, brought out very clearly the effects of FRS 3.

KINGFISHER *Extracts from accounts to 30 January 1993*

Consolidated Profit and Loss Account

	1993 £m	1992 £m
Turnover	3,547.9	3,388.8
Operating profit	208.7	218.9
Loss on disposal of properties used by Kingfisher retail businesses	(3.2)	(11.4)
Profit on ordinary activities before interest	205.5	207.5
Net interest payable	(0.7)	(11.8)
Profit on ordinary activities before taxation	204.8	195.7
Tax on profit on ordinary activities	(56.9)	(61.5)
Profit on ordinary activities after taxation	147.9	134.2
Dividends	(75.1)	(63.4)
Retained profit for the year	72.8	70.8
Earnings per share	30.1	28.5
Fully diluted earnings per share	29.0	26.9

Note 29
Proforma Consolidated Profit and Loss Account
The following proforma consolidated profit and loss account of Kingfisher plc and its subsidiaries is prepared on a basis consistent with previous years. ...

	1993 £m	1992 £m
Turnover	3,547.9	3,388.8
Profit before interest	235.1	233.6
Net interest payable	(0.7)	(11.8)
Profit before exceptional items	234.4	221.8
Exceptional items		
Development work in progress write down	(26.4)	–
Profit on disposal of group occupied properties	2.9	20.6
Restructuring costs	–	(14.7)
Profit on ordinary activities before taxation	210.9	227.7
Tax on profit on ordinary activities	(56.9)	(61.5)
Profit on ordinary activities after taxation	154.0	166.2
Dividends	(75.1)	(63.4)
Retained profit for the year	78.9	102.8

	1993	1992
Earnings per share	31.3p	35.2p
Fully diluted earnings per share	30.1p	33.0p

The differences between the profit on ordinary activities before taxation shown above and that shown in the consolidated profit and loss account on page 36 are:

	1993 £m	1992 £m
Profit on ordinary activities before taxation shown above	210.9	227.7
Prior year property revaluation surplus realised during the year	(6.1)	(32.0)
Profit on ordinary activities before taxation shown on page 36	204.8	195.7

Extract from Financial Review

The shape of the Group's accounts has changed this year, driven by early adoption of Financial Reporting Standard FRS 3. The most significant impact on the accounts is the treatment of exceptional items and the profit or loss on the disposal of Group occupied properties.

Most exceptional items are no longer disclosed as a separate category but are now accounted for in arriving at operating profit. Thus the operating profit in 1992–93 includes the effect of the write down of the property development portfolio, and in the previous year the effect of the restructuring provisions at Comet and Titles.

The profit or loss on the sale of group properties is now calculated as the difference between proceeds and net carrying amount rather than depreciated historical cost. Thus in this year's accounts we have a small loss reflecting the decline in the property since the last valuation.

We feel that the Financial Review commentary would prove helpful to the average shareholder. Indeed, analysts should look carefully at the two sets of figures.

Given 1992 basis figures they might well have written:

1. Profit before interest is marginally up (up 0.64%) at £235.1m; and that before exceptional items improved (by 5.68%) to £234.4m as a result of a fall in net interest payable.
2. As a result of exceptional items (a write down of development work in progress, and restructuring costs) profit after tax fell 7.34% to £154.0m.
3. Earnings per share fell from 35.2p to 31.3p (down 11.08%).
4. A disappointing year.

Whereas, given 1993 basis (FRS 3) figures they might well have written:

1. Operating profit fell somewhat against 1992 (down 4.66%) at £208.7m; and that on ordinary activities by marginally less (because of smaller losses on disposal of properties used by Kingfisher retail businesses) (ie by 0.96%).
2. As a result of a reduced net interest charge profit before tax improved slightly (up 4.65%) to £204.8m and that after tax rather more (by 10.21%) to £147.9m.
3. Earnings per share rose from 28.5p to 30.1p (up 5.61%).
4. A satisfactory year in which Kingfisher weathered the recession well.

But which was 'right'?

Statement of total recognised gains and losses

The profit and loss account and the statement of total recognised gains and losses are together intended to present all an entity's gains and losses recognised in a period. The statement of total recognised gains and losses includes the following components:

1. Profit or loss before the deduction of dividends;
2. Adjustments to the valuation of assets;
3. Difference in the net investment in foreign enterprises arising from changes in foreign exchange rates.

Until such time as the ASB changes the present rules regarding goodwill on consolidation, goodwill written off directly to reserves falls under 2,

---

BOC GROUP *Extract from the 1992 accounts*

Total Recognised Gains and Losses

	1992 £m	1991 £m
Parent	109.9	165.7
Subsidiary undertakings	96.2	21.7
Related undertakings	2.4	6.1
Goodwill written off	(117.1)	–
Profit for the financial year	91.4	193.5
Unrealised surplus / deficit on revaluations	1.0	(2.0)
Exchange translation effect on		
– results for the year	1.5	0.6
– foreign currency net investments	20.3	38.7
Total recognised gains and losses for the year	114.2	230.8

In this case the goodwill write off was not a write off against reserves but represented an exceptional item:

	£m
Goodwill write-off on disposal of operations	(117.1)

Reconciliation of movements in shareholders' funds

Traditionally, accountants have expressed little interest either in net asset value or shareholders' funds – probably because they have felt little confidence in balance sheet valuations.

Analysts, for their part, have focused on asset value in certain cases (eg investment trusts and property companies), but rarely stopped to consider *why* equity shareholders' funds changed between the beginning and end of a period.

The new reconciliation may well persuade both accountants and analysts to think again.

The following illustration shows (a) just how complicated the adjustments are where a substantial acquisition is made (Dowty); (b) how substantial their effects may be; and (c) the effect of foreign exchange on goodwill.

TI GROUP *Extract from Note 1 to 1992 accounts*

Movements in Shareholders' Funds

The group	Called up Share Capital £m	Share Premium Account £m	Capital Reserve £m	Retained Earnings £m	Total £m
At 31 December 1991	80.4	48.9	143.1	443.1	715.5
Total recognised gains and losses	–	(12.5)	–	70.3	57.8
Dividends	–	–	–	(49.6)	(49.6)
Issues of shares					
Dowty Group plc	35.0	–	453.5	–	488.5
For cash	0.3	1.6	–	–	1.9
Scrip dividends	0.1	1.6	–	–	1.7
TI Shareholders' Funds – gross at 31 December 1992	115.8	39.6	596.6	463.8	1,215.8
Less: Goodwill written off (below)					(947.1)
TI Shareholders' Funds – net at 31 December 1992					268.7

Goodwill written off	£m
At 31 December 1991	470.4
Written off in current year (note 3 – not reproduced)	392.0
Written back on disposal of discontinued operations	(33.0)
Exchange translation	117.7
	947.1

Transitional problems

FRS 3 is standard as regards accounting periods ending on or after 22 June 1993, but the ASB recommended that it be adopted 'as soon as possible'. A number of companies have done this. Some, like KINGFISHER (illustrated on page 58) have both restated figures for the preceding year and shown those figures and what the current figures would have looked like pre-FRS 3 by way of note. Many have just restated figures for the preceding year.

Some produced their interim results on the pre-FRS 3 basis while commenting that they would adopt FRS 3 in their annual accounts. Some like FORTE have revised their historical summary to split continuing and other operations. UNITED BISCUITS have adjusted their five year additional information to an FRS 3 basis.

This makes it difficult without careful study to decide which accounts are the first in a historical summary which adopt FRS 3 principles. This makes comparisons of performance difficult.

One company which made a virtue out necessity and restated 1991 figures is TRAFALGAR HOUSE.

TRAFALGAR HOUSE *Extract from Chairman's and Chief Executive's Report 1992*

Financial Reporting

In February 1992 the Financial Reporting Review Panel notified the company that it was considering certain matters in connection with the company's accounts for the year ended 30 September 1991. The Panel's principal concerns related to the reclassification of certain properties from current assets to fixed assets and the amount of ACT carried forward in the balance sheet.

On the basis of independent legal and accounting advice, your Board's view of the treatment of those matters in the 1991 accounts was in accordance with accounting standards and complied with the Companies Acts. However, the Panel continued to express concern and, after due consideration, and in order to avoid the delays and uncertainties which would have resulted from prolonged litigation, your Board agreed to make certain changes and adjustments in the 1992 accounts and to the comparative figures for 1991 in these accounts. The Panel did not require the 1991 accounts to be reissued.

We agreed to adopt, early, the requirement of Urgent Issues Task Force Abstract 5, issued on 22 July 1992,in our 1992 accounts. Consequently, the 1991 comparative figures show deficits on revaluations of property of £102.7m as a charge to the profit and loss account rather than to reserves. We also agreed to write off £20.0m of ACT to the prior period.

Other changes, which have been made to reflect developments in current accounting practice, include the adoption of Urgent Issues Task Force Abstract 3 (treatment of goodwill on disposal of businesses) and Financial Reporting Standard 1 (cash flow statements), The Board also decided to present the 1992 accounts in accordance with Financial Reporting Standard 3 ...

Now look alongside to see the effects of the change.
Rather a difference!

Earnings per share

Earnings per share have two key uses:

1. As a measure of performance during a period;
2. As a starting point in the estimation of future profitabily, earnings per share, and prospective price / earnings ratios.

As a measure of performance during a period, earnings per share come as close to fact as any accounting data.

In simple terms earnings per share may be viewed as the after tax profits available to ordinary shareholders.

Dividend cover is then: $\dfrac{\text{Earnings per share}}{\text{Ordinary dividend}}$

TRAFALGAR HOUSE *Extract from Note 1:*

Comparative figures have been restated to reflect these changes in the basis of preparation of the accounts. This can be summarised as follows:

	Shareholders' Funds at 30 September 1991 £m
September 1991 published accounts	704.6
ACT write off as described above	(20.0)
September 1992 accounts – comparatives	684.6

	Year ended 30 September 1991 Profit / (loss) £m
September 1991 published accounts – (before dividends)	44.9
Property write downs previously charged to revaluation reserve, now reflected in the profit and loss account in accordance with UITF 5	(102.7)
ACT write off as described above	(20.0)
Goodwill reflected in loss on disposal of discontinued operations in accordance with UITF 3	(21.6)
September 1992 accounts – comparatives	(99.4)

But this assumes that the profit after tax which forms the basis of the earnings per share calculation is synonymous with profits legally available for distribution by way of dividend. In our view, under SSAP 6 as it has been applied in recent years, it clearly was not. Many items which fell below the line in the earnings per share calculation (ie were not deducted in computing earnings) would have been deductible in arriving at profits available for distribution.

FRS 3 basis earnings per share are much nearer to the legal definition of distributable profits; and cover computed on the basis of them, much more realistic. This is not a point pursued by FRS 3, which takes the view that: 'It is not possible to distil the performance of a complex organisation into a single measure. ... To assess the performance of a reporting entity during a period all components of its activities must be considered. For this reason and to provide a starting point for analysis, the FRS requires earnings per share to be calculated on profit attributable to equity shareholders of the reporting entity. If preparers wish to highlight any other version of earnings per share, they are required to provide an explanation of the particular significance they are attaching to that version and to itemise and quantify the adjustments they are making to the earnings per share required by the FRS.'

The second use of earnings per share is as a starting point in the estimation of future profitability, prospective earnings per share, and prospective price / earnings ratios.

For this purpose, a reasonable starting point is the earnings from continuing operations exclusive of any non-operating items such as profits and losses on the sale of businesses. We look in Chapters 12 and 13 at more complex situations in which businesses are acquired, sold, rationalised and closed down, and at the estimation of future earnings of such a business.

The Institute of Investment Management and Research (formerly the Society of Investment Analysts) has produced a statement of investment practice, 'The Definition of Headline Earnings', to delineate the trading outcome under FRS 3. Excluded from the headline earnings are profits and losses on capital items such as fixed assets and subsidiaries. However it includes all trading items no matter how unusual or large, although in the case of large items an explanatory note may be necessary.

The *Financial Times,* Extel, Datastream, and many City research organisations are using this headline earnings figure to calculate price earnings ratios. Moreover, a growing number of companies appear to be showing the headline earnings figure in addition to the FRS 3 one when they publish their interim and full year results.

Meanwhile, one group which attempts to provide a suitable starting point is PEARSON (alongside).

Other companies, like TI GROUP and INCHCAPE, show what they term *normalised earnings,* ie earnings per share excluding exceptional profits and losses on disposals.

Normal, or underlying, earnings

A number of leading brokers adopt the concept of 'normal' or 'underlying' earnings per share. In moving from eps reported under FRS 3 to their version of normal earnings, James Capel generally exclude costs incurred in closure or withdrawal from a business segment; gains or losses on disposal of properties, substantial assets or businesses; and, in some cases, other specified unusual items. Ongoing redundancy or rationalisation costs are not excluded.

FRS 1 has caused brokers to redefine cash flow. Net cash flow was a simple yardstick which predated funds flow statements, when it meant profits after tax plus depreciation less dividends. James Capel now take cash flow as being net cash flow from operations excluding movements in working capital; plus / less returns on investment / servicing of finance, excluding dividends paid other than to minority or preference shareholders; less tax paid. The main differences from their previous approach are the complete exclusion asset disposal proceeds, the adjustment for timing differences between provisions charged and cash utilisation of provisions, and the adjustment for timing differences in interest paid.

Cash flow is sometimes expressed on a per share basis as cash flow per share.

PEARSON *Earnings per share note in the 1992 accounts*

	1992 £m	1991 £m
Profit for the financial year	105.3	134.1
Adjustments for non-operating items		
Continuing operations		
Profit on sale of fixed assets	(8.8)	(16.2)
Loss on sale of businesses	–	25.2
Discontinued operations		
Profit on sale of associate	–	(33.2)
Tax on the above	3.8	(0.2)
Adjusted earnings	100.3	109.7

	1992 pence per share	1991[*] pence per share
Earnings per ordinary share	**19.3**	**24.7**
Adjustments		
Non-operating items shown above	(1.6)	(4.5)
Tax	0.7	–
Adjusted earnings per ordinary share	18.4	20.2
Weighted average number of ordinary shares issued	545.5m	543.6m

The adjusted earnings per ordinary share has been calculated to eliminate the distortions caused by including non-operating items. These are profits or losses on sales or terminations of businesses and profits or losses on the sale of fixed assets.

[*] Restated, where appropriate, to reflect the one-for-one capitalisation issue in June 1992.

Practice

Endeavour to find five companies which in their 1992–93 report explained the impact of FRS 3 on their accounts (eg in their Financial Review):

Compare: (1) the degree of support for FRS 3 apparent; and (2) the explanations given.

Form, and explain, your personal opinion of the treatment(s) adopted.

Chapter 12

ACQUISITIONS AND MERGERS

The reader is assumed to have a basic knowledge of group accounts. If there is need for revision, Chapters 15–17 of *Interpreting Company Reports and Accounts* (Holmes and Sugden) cover in detail accounting for acquisitions and mergers; subsidiaries and group accounts; and associated undertakings.

Few listed companies operate without subsidiaries and all but the smallest groups regularly set out to acquire other businesses. In this chapter we look, beyond accounting, to ask:

1. Why companies make acquisitions; and
2. What the analyst can and should learn about a group from its reports and accounts?

Why companies make acquisitions

One obvious reason to make an acquisition (or to divest (something we look at in detail in Chapter 13) is to improve the business in some way. Often the focus is on earnings per share. But whatever the precise focus, the improvement may be immediate, or in the short term (possibly to bolster falling profits elsewhere), but hopefully in the long term also.

Companies make *acquisitions for cash* where the acquisition represents the most profitable use of surplus funds, that is to say, where the attractions of the acquisition exceed those of:

1. Direct expansion;
2. Paying higher dividends (remembering that it is difficult to reduce them once shareholders and the market become used to a particular level of payout); or
3. Investment in the existing business.

Companies tend to make *acquisitions for shares* when they see themselves as having a share price advantage ie when their shares trade at a higher price / earnings ratio than those of the company they are seeking to acquire. Consider Example 11.1.

Example 11.1

Predatory plc 50p ordinary shares stand at 250p, on a price / earnings ratio of 20. The £1 ordinary shares of Minnow plc stand at 200p, on a p/e of 10.

	Predatory	Minnow
Shares in issue	200,000,000	10,000,000
Earnings	£25,000,000	£2,000,000
Earnings per share	12.5p	20.0p
Market price	250p	200p
p/e	20	10
Market capitalisation	£500,000,000	£20,000,000

If Predatory acquires all the shares in Minnow in exchange for the issue of 10m ordinary shares of 50p (representing a premium of 25% on their existing value), the effect would appear to be:

	Predatory
Shares in issue	210,000,000
Earnings increase to	£27,000.000
Earnings per share	12.857p

an improvement in eps of 2.86%. And if the existing price / earnings ratio is maintained, the share price of Predatory could well rise (to 20 × 12.857p = 257p).

So goes the theory, but the questions we have to ask ourselves are:

1. Will the profitability of Minnow really remain unaffected by the change of ownership (or will, say, the loss of independence, the weight of paper and controls, reduce effort, enthusiasm and hence profitability; or will Predatory, with ample financial resources,

effective control and support systems, find ways to increase the earnings of Minnow?). It is difficult to tell (impossible from the information we have given), but in real life analysts have to form a view.

2. Will the market view Predatory as basically unchanged, or will it see the strength of the earnings as somewhat reduced – and hence worthy of a lower p/e? The amounts involved are, in this illustration, small enough not to affect the market. Had Minnow been ten times as big the answer could well be different as is shown in Example 11.2.

Example 11.2

	Predatory
Shares in issue	300,000,000
Earnings	£45,000.000
Earnings per share	15.00p

If the p/e of 20 was maintained, this would mean a share price of 300p.

But would the market in this case really see the risks of Predatory as being unchanged?

3. If this was a contested bid, would shareholders of Minnow accept? Study Example 11.3.

Example 11.3

Consider dividends per share. Imagine these were:

	Predatory	Minnow
Dividend per share	5p	10p

Since the bid represents one share in Predatory for every share in Minnow, the dividends received by a shareholder in Minnow would halve.

Would he accept? No. That is why companies normally seek the advice of their brokers and merchant bank in structuring any bid. They do not like egg on their face.

In the 1980s, takeovers were encouraged by the banks which, with plenty of money to lend after the ending of credit controls, thought this was safer than lending to Third World countries (see page 147).

Lowish interest rates, have at times allowed companies to make a substantial number of acquisitions where the consideration was a mixture of various kinds of paper eg a small number of ordinary shares and a much larger part in debt, usually unsecured and non-convertible, or preference shares.

This has the advantage to the acquirer of obtaining an equity interest in another company with little dilution of his own equity. It often gave the short-term advantage to the shareholder in the acquired company of a higher income, at the cost

of the long term disadvantage of largely losing his hedge against inflation.

The owners of a business, wishing to retire, may, on the other hand, be only too happy to sell in exchange for loan notes maturing over several tax years as part of their CGT planning.

Between these two extremes of: (1) acquisitions representing the most profitable use of surplus funds; and (2) companies which acquire for shares to take advantage of the fact that their shares trade at a higher p/e than those of the company they are seeking to acquire, lie a number of other reasons for acquisition which can broadly be classed as *visionary / opportunistic.*

Visionary / opportunistic acquisitions

What we term visionary / opportunistic acquisitions cover a spectrum, lying between two extremes: desirable and undesirable; those made for sound, honest, fair reasons, and those which are not.

Some are socially and in other ways entirely desirable, for example, the agreed takeover of a successful retail business in the same trade in a nearby town, the owner of which wants to retire.

At the other extreme (though the law at times seeks to prevent those which achieve sufficient prominence) are acquisitions in restraint of trade ie whose main aim is achieve a monopoly position not for the public benefit but for the business advantage of the acquirer.

Between these extremes lie a variety of other possible reasons:

1. The vision on the part of the acquirer to recognise that a business which can be bought relatively cheaply can be improved (eg by changing its image or that of its products, repositioning them in the market) or redeveloped (eg that an unprofitable old printing works could be demolished, appropriate planning permission obtained, and the area redeveloped as a leisure complex or shopping mall, this being either retained as an investment or sold on at a profit).

2. The foreseeing by a trader or manufacturer of potential shortages or interruptions in supply, where the acquired company provides continuity of supply.

3. Recognition of production life cycles eg that an existing division specialising in, say, the manufacture of furs and trimmings, is in rapid decline, and that the acquisition of a suitable business in, say, fashion could fill the gap and provide a means of developing in a new but related area.

4. It often appears cheaper to buy an existing business (and possibly its key management)

than to set up a green field operation. This is particularly the case where there is a need to establish business overseas (possibly in the EC to take advantage of the single market).

5. The ability to see a relatively unprofitable business as a series of component parts, some more viable than others, and to purchase it with the intention of keeping the good and throwing out the dross.

    Several whiz-kid take-over artists were specialists (not least Hanson, and Jim Slater of Slater–Walker) in seeing situations in which one part of an organisation or group was dragging the rest down.

    Sometimes existing management did not even know – it took better accounting to demonstrate the fact. There is no reason why this should be the preserve of take-over artists and it is not. To cut out dead-wood, or to turn round the inefficient, can be expensive not merely in time and effort but in closures and redundancies. But it is not always necessary. If you can find someone else who actually wants your problem company or division and is willing to pay for it, you can have the best of both worlds.

Example 11.4

Results of Sadd plc for 1992 can be summarised as follows:

	£m
Sales	40
Net profit	1
Capital employed	60

An entirely unsatisfactory position.

But imagine that careful study shows that the business consists of two discrete bits:

	UK	Germany
	£m	£m
Sales	25	15
Net profit (loss)	7	(6)
Capital employed	40	20

and that it is possible to off-load the German end, to a German company which wants the site, for £12m.

A once-and-for-all write-off of £8m (ie £20m – £12m – which in the past would have been treated as an extraordinary item, and might still be in the acquisition fair value calculations) will bring an improvement in profit from £1m to £7m pa, and would almost certainly be far easier to achieve than any profit improvement exercise either in Germany or in the UK.

It is important, where this sort of thing takes place, for the analyst:

(i) To understand what happened;
(ii) To recognise that while the profit improvement is entirely valid, and should be maintainable, the *rate* of apparent

profit growth (600% in the case of Sadd) almost certainly won't. The 'growth' is once-and-for-all.

6. In times of tight financial controls in which bank lending and the raising of new capital were both restricted, groups sometimes sought *cash shells* (companies with little in the way of assets apart from cash), or investment trusts selling well below asset value, and, by means of a share exchange, obtained an injection of cash for themselves while at the same time avoiding an immediate CGT liability on shareholders of the acquired company. They also looked for *cash cows*, that is to say dying companies which, while generating little in the way of profit, required no new investment, so any depreciation charges tended to be reflected in cash useful to the rest of the group. Cash flow statements, because they show the overall group position do not highlight this; and the ASB missed a trick when it failed to require either segmental cash flow statements or wholly owned subsidiaries to publish their cash flows. This may make it difficult to see why a particular company has attractions and is not just disposed of.

7. Personal aggrandisement of the chairman / chief executive: empire building; or even spite. This is easier to suspect than to prove.

8. Management can be egged on by merchant banks and professional advisers eager for fees. Morgan Grenfell were noted for this in the 1980s.

It is always worth while trying to decide which was the key factor in any particular case.

Keys to success

The effect of acquisitions is crucial to an understanding of a group. It is vital, therefore, to:

1. Read carefully and critically any documentation produced by the company, whether to its own shareholders or those of the acquiree company.

2. Try to form a view of the group's acquisition strategy: why is it making this particular acquisition (and its real reasons are not necessarily those given most prominence) and what its policy is generally.

3. Try to detect whether the acquisition is the product of central, group management, or stems from a proposal made by divisional management (groups differ greatly in their approach to acquisition search/appraisal).

4. Ask yourself whether the bid is an agreed bid (in which case the bidder is likely to be well-informed on problems and prospects) or a contested one (in which case he is likely to be fencing somewhat in the dark).

5. Follow through: study carefully press material, interim statements and annual reports for indications of whether the expressed objectives of earlier acquisitions were fulfilled.

6. Distinguish whether the acquired company is a private one or listed.

7. Consider the financial effects: borrowings, eps, possible dividend payout.

8. Consider the accounting effects:

   (i) Where an acquisition is of a high growth company the market value of the shares acquired may bear little relation either to their nominal value or to net asset value - the 'goodwill' element represents the value placed by the acquirer on growth potential. The practice of writing off goodwill either against reserves or to a negative reserve does not mean it can be forgotten: whether the shares acquired are paid for in cash or by an issue of shares, goodwill represents 'money' paid out by the acquirer.

   (ii) The accounting method adopted (merger accounting or acquisition accounting) and the treatment of goodwill (immediate write off to reserve or amortisation over a period) affect many of the key ratios (return on equity, return on net assets, earnings per share, p/e ratio, and net asset value, in particular) – indeed, the present position is far from satisfactory. Pressure is mounting to allow merger accounting only where there is a true merger (see FRED 6 'Acquisitions and Mergers').

Post-acquisition audit

Well-managed groups perform a post-acquisition audit; asking themselves:

1. Whether their assumptions, ie the basis of their acquisition decision, were well founded, and, if not, why not? That is, they learn by their mistakes.

2. Whether information with which they were provided by the acquiree was fair and honest, and, if not, whether warranties given by the acquired company provide any redress?

3. What action needs to be taken:

   (i) To strengthen the acquired company's business, ie what additional finance, equipment, management skills are needed?

   (ii) To bring the new subsidiary into line with the rest of the group, ie what changes need to be made to its accounting policies and reporting structure?

4. Whether, had they their time to come again, they would make the acquisition?

The results of this audit are not usually published but one can sometimes gain an insight.

LINCOLN HOUSE *Extracts from Notes 1 and 14 to the accounts for 1991*

1. Basis of presentation

On 19 April 1990 the group acquired Troika Limited. The company was placed in administrative receivership on 16 April 1991. The company's loss of £33,000 for the period of ownership to 31 December 1990 has been consolidated using acquisition accounting, and a provision of £800,000 has been made for the residual liability of the group. See Note 14.

2. Subsidiary in Administrative Receivership

Troika Limited has not been included in the consolidated balance sheet at 31 December 1990 as it was placed in receivership on 16 April 1991. The directors believe that a fair presentation of the group's balance sheet is provided by including a provision for the anticipated shortfall arising from receivership. The trading results of Troika Limited for the period of ownership to 31 December 1990 are included in the consolidated profit and loss account.

Anticipated shortfall arising from the closure of Troika Limited

	£000
Non-Group net assets at 31st December 1990	115
Provision for non-realisation of Net Assets above	685
Extraordinary loss (Note 9)	800

The company is pursuing claims against the vendors under the warranties given in the purchase and sale agreement.

Deferred consideration

Note carefully any liability in respect of deferred consideration, particularly where it is contingent upon the earning of a stated level of profit ie earn-outs. Because payment is due after the profits have been earned, and possibly when they have already turned down, it may fall due at an inconvenient time.

It is not always clear whether the acquired company will meet earnout targets which vary widely in 'hopefulness'.

Most companies disclose possible earn-outs as contingent liabilities, but they may appear in a separate note, and not be referred to elsewhere in the accounts. This makes the point: it is not safe to study the accounts, and to trace down from the accounts to the appropriate note. Some notes are never referred to in the accounts themselves. Nor are all potential earn-outs necessarily fully spelled out in the documentation of acquisitions (although FRED 7 will require more detail). They may be the result of a less formal understanding.

SUTHERLAND *Extract from the Directors' Report for the year ended 28 April 1990*

Saint Martin Food Products Limited
Under the terms of an agreement dated 10th April 1987, and an exchange of letters between Mr D. G. Giusti and the company in February and March 1988, regarding the establishment of a second production facility at Saint Martin Food Products Limited, additional consideration became payable by the company in respect of the acquisition of this subsidiary.

On 3 July 1990, the final additional consideration, based on earnings up to 31 March 1990, was determined at £5,400,000.

This came at a somewhat unfortunate time: profit attributable to shareholders fell away from £1,676,000 in the 69 weeks to 24 April 1989 to a loss of £1,420,000 in 1989–90.

Because earn-outs normally involve a multiplier factor applied to what may be termed 'super-profits', disputes can prove expensive to resolve.

AITKEN HUME INTERNATIONAL *Extracts from Notes 6 and 21 to the 1991 accounts*

Extraordinary items	1991
	£000
Professional fees in respect of the determination of further consideration payable to the vendors of The Bachman Group	302

Contingent liabilities

...
Under the terms of the agreement for the acquisition of The Bachman Group Ltd further consideration may become payable to the vendors calculated by applying a multiple of ten to the increase in the adjusted profits after tax of Bachman & Co Bankers Ltd, over an initial base of £800,000 in each of the five years to 31 March 1993 subject to a maximum further consideration of £23 million of which £6,858,371 in respect of the years up to and including 31 March 1990 has been settled. The consideration for these payments is expected to be provided through the issue of additional ordinary shares but in certain circumstances any or all payments may be satisfied, or may be required to be satisfied, in cash. To date the parties have been unable to agree the amount of further consideration payable in respect of the year ended 31 March 1991. The current estimate of the amount calculated by Aitken Hume International plc to be payable is £2,253,140. The vendors and their advisors have calculated the amount payable to be £4,253,140. As referred to in note 15 provision has been made ... of £2,253,140. In the event that the parties are unable to reach agreement ... the agreement provides for the matter

to be referred to an independent firm of chartered accountants whose determination, when known, shall be conclusive and binding on the parties.

Fair value adjustments

SSAP 14 on 'Group Accounts' requires the allocation of purchase consideration between the underlying net tangible and intangible assets on the basis of the fair value to the acquiring company and SSAP 22 'Accounting for Goodwill' suggests that 'when ascribing values at the time of an acquisition, a provision may be needed in respect of items which were taken into account in arriving at the purchase price, that is, anticipated future losses or costs of reorganisation.'

There has been concern about some features of current practice, in particular the creation at the time of acquisition of provisions in respect of anticipated future losses or post-acquisition expenditure, the effect of which is to avoid charging such items against future profits.

'Fair Values in Acquisition Accounting', FRED 7, produced by the ASB in December 1993, proposes that:

1. Provisions for future losses in acquired businesses and for reorganisation costs following an acquisition should not be accounted for as liabilities of the acquired business but as post-acquisition items in the consolidated profit and loss account of the acquirer. Post-acquisition reorganisation and integratation costs should, where material, be reported as exceptional items.

2. When determining fair values of assets and liabilities (including any goodwill) acquired, the assets and liabilities that may be recognised should be restricted to those that existed at the acquisition date and should not anticipate the acquirer's plans for making changes to the acquired company's activities or, as a result of the acquisition, to the acquirer' own activities.

3. The principles of valuation should generally follow the 'value to the business' principle outlined in the Board's Discussion Draft of Chapter 5 of Statement of Principles, 'Measurement in Financial Statements' issued on 25 March 1993.

Provisions for merger expenses or group restructuring were, until recently, made as extraordinary items. FRS 3 and 'Fair Values in Acquisition Accounting' mean that in future they should be treated as exceptional items. Not only have such provisions at times been very pessimistic (see COURTAULDS, page 68), but sometimes they have been enormous; and often extremely difficult to evaluate (see SMITHKLINE BEECHAM below).

COURTAULDS *Note 14 to 1990–91 accounts (extract)*

14. Acquisitions

The effect of fair value adjustments on the balance sheets of major acquisitions during the year is shown below:

	Unaudited acquisition balance sheet	Adjust to Courtaulds accounting policy	Fair value adjust ments	Fair Value to the Group
	£m	£m	£m	£m
Fixed assets				
Tangible assets	10.0	–	(3.4)	6.6
Current assets less current liabilities	4.8	(1.1)	(3.7)	–
Provisions for liabilities and charges	–	–	(5.2)	(5.2)
Net assets acquired	14.8	(1.1)	(12.3)	1.4
Cash consideration				26.0
Goodwill written off to reserves				(24.6)
				1.4

SMITHKLINE BEECHAM *Extract from Note 6 to the 1990 accounts*

6. Extraordinary items

	1990 £m	1989 £m
Merger transaction expenses	–	(77)
Group restructuring and rationalisation costs arising from the merger	–	(500)
Net profits on disposal of businesses	319	143
Taxation (net)		
United Kingdom Corporation Tax	(5)	30
Overseas tax	(11)	58
	303	(346)

Where to look for information on acquisitions and mergers

The analyst needs to understand the importance of group 'shape' and, in particular, 'changes in shape'. This information tends to be widely spread, so it is a good idea to follow a planned order:

1. FRS 3 requires the aggregate results of acquisitions to be shown as a component of continuing operations. The consolidated profit and loss account gives an indication of the effect of acquisitions on turnover and on profit of the current period.

INCHCAPE *Extracts from report and accounts for 1992*

Consolidated profit and loss account

for the year ended 31 December 1992

	1992 £m	1991 £m
Turnover		
Continuing operations	4,002.4	3,461.5
Acquisitions	956.1	82.8
	4,958.5	3,544.3
Discontinued operations	78.2	80.6
	5,036.7	3,624.9
Cost of sales	(3,911.8)	(2,793.5)
Gross profit	1,124.9	831.4
Net operating expenses	(915.2)	(672.2)
Operating profit	209.7	159.2
Share of profits of associates	51.4	28.0
Operating profit plus share of associates		
Continuing operations	201.4	183.4
Acquisitions	61.5	3.2
Discontinued operations	(1.8)	0.6
	261.1	187.2
Profit on sale of properties and investments of continuing operations	3.2	4.9
Profit on disposal of discontinued businesses	–	12.9
Provisions for loss on sale or termination of discontinued businesses	(2.1)	(2.3)
Profit on ordinary activities before interest	262.2	202.7

2. If an acquisition has a material impact on a major business segment, FRS 3 requires that impact to be disclosed and explained – so look at the segmental analysis.

3. FRS 1 requires payments to acquire investments in subsidiary undertakings to be shown as cash outflows from investing activities. Acquisitions may appear either there or as major non-cash transactions. Material effects on the amounts reported under each of the standard FRS 1 headings reflecting the cash flows of a subsidiary acquired in the period are disclosed by way of a Note. So the cash flow statement and supporting notes are a useful source.

4. Companies normally include a balance sheet note on subsidiaries - which deserves careful study - and sometimes pro forma balance sheet showing the effect of acquisitions subsequent to the balance sheet date.

5. The chairman's statement, financial review and directors' report will also contain valuable information.

Note 2 Analysis of Turnover, Profit and Net Assets

	TURNOVER BY ORIGINS		OPERATING PROFIT PLUS SHARE OF ASSOCIATES		YEAR END NET OPERATING ASSETS		CONTRIBUTION TO PROFIT	
	1992 £m	1991 £m	1992 £m	1991 £m	1992 £m	1991 £m	1992 £m	1991 £m
By class of business:								
Motors	3,350.3	2,145.2	177.3	110.5	693.6	390.6	60.4	49.9
...								
Discontinued operations*	78.2	80.6	(1.8)	0.6	19.4	18.1	(0.6)	0.3
	5,036.7	3,624.9	293.2	221.4	1,227.1	781.3	100.0	100.0
Central charges			(14.5)		(14.3)			
			278.7		207.1			

...
*Discontinued operations relate mainly to Timber (1992 and 1991) and to Tea in 1991.

Contribution from material acquisitions

Tozer Kemsley & Millbourn from 2 March 1992 included in Motors	£m
– turnover	908.6
– operating profit plus share of associates	48.3

...

Note 34 Goodwill on Acquisitions

During the year the Group made several acquisitions for cash, only one of which was individually material. The following table analyses the fair value of each major category of businesses acquired and the goodwill arising therefrom.

	As acquired Company's Accounting Records £m	Revaluation £m	Provision for Reorganisation Costs £m	Other Provisions £m	Accounting Policy Adjustment £m	Fair Value to the Group £m
Motor businesses						
Tozer Kemsley & Millbourn						
Fixed assets – tangible assets	195.8	(66.1)	–	–	28.5	158.2
– investments	21.3	(0.6)	–	–	2.3	23.0
Stocks	145.8	–	–	–	(8.1)	137.7
Debtors	128.9	–	–	(2.2)	37.1	163.8
Cash at Bank	4.0	–	–	–	–	4.0
Borrowings	(97.4)	–	–	–	(52.9)	(150.3)
Other creditors and provisions	(199.8)	–	(15.0)	(6.9)	7.4	(214.3)
Minority interests in existing subsidiaries	(3.1)	–	–	–	–	(3.1)
	195.5	(66.7)	(15.0)	(9.1)	14.3	119.0
Fair value of consideration						394.1
Goodwill						275.1

... [In all the Note runs to two A4 pages]

Case Study: Inchcape

Inchcape (see pages 68–70) provides a model of what good presentation today involves. But it does demonstrate just how much work an analyst who wants to get to grips with a group and estimate its prospective earnings needs to put in.

Note 35 Acquisition of Tozer Kemsley & Millbourn (TKM)

On 2 March 1992 the Group acquired IEP (Automotive) Ltd and Tozer Kemsley & Millbourn (Holdings) plc, its subsidiary undertakings and its interests in associated companies for a total consideration of £388.9m, including interest of £6.4m calculated from 1 January 1992. Additional costs of the acquisition amounted to £5.2m.

The results of TKM for the period 2 March to 31 December 1992 are included in Note 2 under Motors.

The fair value adjustments and goodwill ... are described in Note 34. The principal fair value adjustments were in respect of the revaluation of properties, the recognition of a surplus in the TKM pension scheme and provisions for reorganisation costs reflecting the rationalisation of the TKM and Mann Egerton organisations.

Results of TKM prior to 2 March 1992 which are required to be disclosed by the Companies Act 1985 are as follows: Profit before taxation for the financial year 1991 was £62.5m and for the period 1 January to 1 March 1992 was £6.8m. Operating profit plus share of associates excluding property profits for the financial year 1991 was £69.4m and for the period 1 January to 1 March 1992 was £9.4m

Cash Flow Statement

There were detailed notes on acquisitions and disposals in the Cash Flow Statement, which we do not reproduce.

Financial Review (Extract)

Fair value adjustments totalling £76.5m have been made in relation to the TKM acquisition which is in line with our expectations. These were mainly in respect of properties, last valued in May 1990, for which writedowns totalling £66.1m have been required. In addition, restructuring provisions of £15.0m have been made.

Review of Activities

A substantial section of the Review of Activities was devoted to TKM, the background to the acquisition, and to the way in which TKM was being incorporated into Inchcape (which we do not reproduce).

Note in particular:

1. The information on turnover and profits of the acquired companies;
2. The separate treatment of the major acquisition; and
3. The comment in the Financial Review that the fair value adjustments made in relation to the TKM acquisition were in line with expectations.

We found the Review of Activities (which for space considerations we do not reproduce) gave a valuable insight into Group strategy.

FRED 6

FRED 6, 'Accounting for Acquisitions and Mergers', issued on 27 May 1993, seeks to confine the use of merger accounting to the relatively small number of cases which are true mergers of two companies and not the takeover of one company by another. Apart from such exceptions, the intention is that acquisition accounting will be used.

The two methods, merger accounting and acquisition accounting, produce radically different reported profits and group balance sheets, both in the year the transaction occurs and for several years afterwards. Currently a company can often choose which accounting method it adopts. Merger accounting has sometimes been used artificially to boost reported earnings by including the full year's profit of a subsidiary acquired late in the year. It is right that this device should be prevented.

Practice

Obtain the annual report and accounts of Grand Metropolitan; if possible, from 1988 to date.

Consider the changes of 'shape' which have taken place. Evaluate the repositioning in terms of:

1. Brands;
2. Profitability;
3. Geographical spread of operations;
4. Assets employed;
5. Degree of risk.

Using the cash flow statement(s), explain how the major changes were financed.

Chapter 13

DISCONTINUED OPERATIONS AND DISPOSALS

Why groups dispose of subsidiaries

'Half of all mergers and acquisitions fail' according to a study published in May 1993 by accountants Coopers & Lybrand. The study, compiled from interviews with 100 top companies covered 50 acquisitions worth a total of £13 billion. It should come as no surprise: earlier studies, conducted in 1973 and 1988, showed very similar results.

Other research suggests that some 50% of all businesses acquired are sold or closed within 10 years.

There are a number of possible reasons:

1. The acquiring company:

   (i) Did not do its homework;
   (ii) Saw the acquisition through rose-tinted spectacles; or
   (iii) Was misled;

   so profits from the acquisition never matched expectations. According to Coopers & Lybrand, the 'due diligence' verification (that they were buying what they thought they were buying) was left too late, and came only after companies had decided to buy.
2. The acquisition did not fit the group's culture. Failure was most often blamed on management attitudes, differences in style and resistance to change in the acquired company.
3. It was always known that there were problems, but they proved greater than anyone realised.
4. Disposal of all or part of the company was part of the plan.
5. Part of the business was sold (hopefully at a profit) to finance purchase of the part that the group needed.

There are a number of more general reasons for sale which apply to acquired businesses and home-grown ones alike:

1. Companies change their strategic aims, and the way they see their central purposes – this often happens when a new chairman / chief executive takes power.
2. Finances of the subsidiary which was sold (we use the term subsidiary to include businesses which are not separately incorporated) having deteriorated, either: (1) the group is unable or unwilling to provide the further funds needed; or (2) bank finance is not available without guarantees from the holding company which it is not prepared to give (preferring to retain the option of allowing the subsidiary to fall into receivership / liquidation without further group involvement).
3. The subsidiary sold may have failed to meet group financial (ie profitability and return) targets and group may see a more profitable use for funds.
4. Trading conditions may have deteriorated. Re-cent acquisitions by TSB (of Hill Samuel), Dixons (of the US Silo chain), Ratners, WPP, Berisford and Saatchi brought considerable pain and raised the question of their sale.
5. A purchaser may have been found prepared to pay more for the business than the group (knowing all the circumstances and problems) feels it is worth.

Why companies resort to closure

Where a group wants to be rid of a subsidiary, it will normally sell it; always assuming that it can find someone willing to buy.

One exception is where the group is seeking to rid itself of excess capacity. It would not wish to see some purchaser flood the market. Straight closure is then the only sensible course.

Apart from that, businesses are closed down, rather than sold, because they won't sell, when:

1. They are intrinsically unprofitable; for example:

    (i) The product on which they are based (ie which is manufactured, imported or distributed) has been superseded (as jute largely was by plastic forty years ago);

    (ii) Costs are too high (eg shop and public house rents rose so sharply in the late 1980s that it became impossible for the tenant to operate at a profit);

    (iii) Demand has fallen in a recession to a level which generates losses rather than profit (eg as was found in the early 1990s with some motor distributors).

2. They are unduly capital intensive, and seen by group and outsiders as requiring a bottomless purse.

3. They are unduly risky eg in a war-torn or inflation-ravaged unstable overseas territory.

4. Cheaper production facilities exist elsewhere in the group (eg in some other part of the EC or simply in a more highly automated plant in the UK).

5. It is cheaper to purchase the goods they manufacture from an outside supplier.

We are not saying that any one of these factors is sufficient, or that it will inevitably result in closure, or even that it could not and should not have been avoided – simply that there are many reasons for closure. It is always worth asking: Why?

Changes in 'shape'

Be on the look out for disposals which form such a significant part of the assets and liabilities of the group, or are such a major source of profits (losses) that they change entirely or significantly the nature of the business (what we term the 'shape' of the organisation) .

CHLORIDE *Extracts from the Directors' Report and Profit and Loss Account for the year to 31 March 1991*

Divestments

On 27 March 1991, the disposal was completed of Chloride's Industrial battery division, based in Manchester, together with its sales and distribution operations in Western Europe and North America for a consideration of £43.5 million in cash, subject to adjustment ...

The sale of the Group's entire shareholding in Chloride Eastern Industries Ltd ... for £14.0 million ... In January 1991, Chloride Ferrostatics Limited, the group's

small precision engineering subsidiary in the UK, was sold ...

Consolidated profit and loss account for the year ended 31 March 1991

Notes		1991	1990
1	TURNOVER	£m	£m
	Continuing operations	117.7	134.6
	Discontinued operations	97.9	164.2
		215.6	298.8
	Cost of sales	151.4	211.9
	GROSS PROFIT	64.2	86.9
2.	Net operating costs	48.3	66.3
	OPERATING PROFIT BEFORE EXCEPTIONAL ITEMS		
	Continuing operations	2.6	7.1
	Discontinued operations	13.3	13.5
		15.9	20.6

FRS 3, *Reporting Financial Performance*, calls for the results of continuing operations, acquisitions (as a component of continuing operations) and discontinued operations to be reported separately. This provides an opportunity to assess the significance and effect of activities which have ceased or been disposed of; that is to say, of the change in shape.

Reporting discontinued operations

Not all closures and sales of business result in 'discontinued operations' for the purposes of FRS 3:

1. A sale or termination undertaken primarily in order to achieve productivity improvements and / or cost savings is included under 'continuing operations'.

2. To be included in the category 'discontinued operations' the sale or termination must have a material effect on the nature and focus of the reporting entity's operation.

3. To be classified as a discontinuation a sale or termination must be the result of a strategic decision by the group either:

    (i) To withdraw from a particular market (whether class of business or geographical) or

    (ii) To curtail materially its presence (ie materially reduce its turnover) in a continuing market.

Narrowing the definition still further, FRS 3 provides that operations are to be classified as 'discontinued' only when the sale or termination is *completed* either: (1) in the period; or (2) before the earlier of: (a) three months after the commencement of the subsequent period; and (b) the date the financial statements are signed.

Future costs cannot be included; only the results of operations up to the balance sheet date are included; operations in the subsequent period are included in the results of that period.

Income and costs associated with a sale or termination that has not been completed are included as 'continuing operations'.

If the results of operations that are in the process of discontinuing are shown separately, they are not to be termed 'discontinued operations'.

There are several ways of showing the results of discontinued operations. We saw one in Chapter 12 (page 69). Here is another. FORTE sold Gardner Merchant and associated businesses on 6 January 1993 and its sales are shown in the accounts to 31 January 1993 on a discontinued basis.

FORTE *Consolidated Profit and Loss Account for the year ended 31 January 1993*

	Before exceptional items	Exceptional items	Total	Total as restated
			1993	1992
	£m	£m	£m	£m
Sales				
Continuing operations	1,936	–	1,936	1,845
Discontinued operations	785	–	785	817
	2,721	–	2,721	2,662
Operating costs	(2,424)	(61)	(2,485)	(2,397)
Gross trading profit	297	(61)	236	265
Depreciation	(97)	(12)	(109)	(88)
Trading profit				
Continuing operations	169	(73)	96	144
Discontinued operations	31	–	31	33
	200	(73)	127	177
Share of (losses) / profits of The Savoy Hotel plc	(1)	–	(1)	2
Net deficit on property and other disposals of continuing operations	–	(91)	(91)	(13)
Profit on disposal of discontinued operations	–	257	257	–
Profit on ordinary activities before interest	199	93	292	166

Note 2 provided a breakdown of turnover showing the discontinued operations as entirely contract catering.

Note 3 broke down operating costs and depreciation before exceptional items, showing the make up of the £2,424m as £1,677m continuing operations and £747m discontinued; and that of depreciation £90m and £7m, respectively.

Note 8 explained that: The group disposed of the Gardner Merchant contract catering companies and businesses on 6 January 1993. As part of the consideration, the group has taken an investment in the new holding company, details of which are described in Note 14. Purchased goodwill has been realised and deducted to arrive at the gain arising on disposal.

Note 14 explained that the company now holds 23.65% of the voting equity of Gardner Merchant Services Group Ltd. This comprises:

	£m
Ordinary shares of 1p each	–
Convertible redeemable preferred ordinary shares of 1p each (net dividend 6% per annum)	2
Redeemable preference shares of 1p each (net dividend 6% per annum)	29
Deep discount bonds 2001 (yield to redemption 21% per annum)	29
	60

We do not reproduce the rest of the note which relates to voting restrictions and conversion rights.

Note 34 showed the assets disposed of, and that the total consideration of £402m was satisfied £342m in cash and £60m by investments.

The *Financial Review* commented: 'The profit of £257m from the disposal of Gardner Merchant represents largely the realisation of goodwill, because the amount of net tangible assets was relatively low. We have confidence in the further development of that business and have retained a stake of just under 25%.'

The *Review of Operations* told of the sale of Gardner Merchant, continuing: 'The figures include 49 weeks in the year covered by this report'.

The *Chairman's Statement* told us of: 'The fall off in international travel since the Gulf War ... The operational gearing of our business is such that loss of top line income cannot be fully compensated by reductions in costs and therefore has a significant impact on the bottom line profit. The extent of this fall off in sales has to some degree been obscured by the additional businesses we have acquired over the last three years.' ...

He went on: 'Trading conditions have also caused the returns on moneys invested over the last three years to be lower than had been anticipated ...'.

'The considerable sums invested over the past few years have resulted in an increase in our debt. Lower trading profits cause this to be a greater problem than would otherwise have been the case....'.

'Clearly this situation had to be addressed. Therefore our priorities over the next eighteen months to two years are a reduction of the debt, maximisation of the profitability of existing assets and the disposal of those assets which are underperforming or do not form part of the core business of the group.'

'As part of this process we sold Gardner Merchant ... realising an exceptional profit of £257m. This shows our ability to sell non-core businesses at a premium price ...'.

Read these extracts from Forte's accounts carefully and note, in particular:

1. How much information is provided about the discontinuation (and there is more, in the cash flow statement, for instance, which we have not space to reproduce);
2. The way one builds up bit by bit a clear picture of what happened and why;
3. The substantial refocussing by Forte;
4. The way they arrive at profit on ordinary activities, making it clear that £199m is the result of continuing activities and £93m that of exceptional items. Other companies may not bring this out so clearly.

Turning to earnings per share: Forte show three figures for earnings:

	1993	1992
		as restated
	pence	pence
Earnings per share		
Net	14.1	4.3
Nil distribution	17.4	5.7
Cash earnings per share		
(before exceptional items)	16.8	10.5

Cash earnings per share are defined as the net cash inflow from operating activities before exceptional items attributable to shareholders (ie after interest paid and received, dividends etc to minorities and tax paid) divided by the weighted average of ordinary and trust shares.

Note, in particular, the marked difference in 1992 between the net and cash earnings per share.

Management buyouts

Be on the look out for management buyouts, which are sometimes used to remove unprofitable areas of operation – which is entirely reasonable; sometimes to get rid of activities which no longer fit (and perhaps never did) – which is also reasonable; and sometimes, one suspects, to encourage managers to perform for themselves in a way they could not when subject to the rules of group or, less straightforwardly, chose not to do for other people. Do not be too surprised if there is a loss on such a sale; with luck it will result in improved future profitability.

Companies sometimes themselves take a stake in the buyout (eg Forte in Gardner Merchant). It may be then be difficult to tell whether this represents an act of faith, ie trust in the future

profitability of the venture (as Forte suggest), or one of desperation, as the only way to get rid of a burden (Olives Property and Continental Paper spring to mind).

Demergers

Be on the look out also for demergers. In the three years 1989–91, Courtaulds became 'an international industrial materials company spanning five broad business areas linked by their common reliance on polymer technology and surface science'. The wood-pulp business was sold, Textiles demerged (by allotting one fully paid ordinary share in Courtaulds Textiles for every four ordinary shares in Courtaulds, paid up out of reserves) and Products Research Chemical Corporation was acquired. Courtaulds helpfully provided proforma accounts for 1990 on a demerged basis.

More recently ICI demerged its bioscience operations into ZENECA.

Keeping track

Keeping track of the acquisitions and disposals of a major international group, their effect upon the scope of the business and its profitability, is difficult, in some cases virtually impossible.

The Stock Exchange requires shareholder approval of major deals, but a number of cases have arisen where companies have pressed ahead with a major deal before getting shareholders' approval. In 1988, for instance, Grand Metropolitan agreed to buy 105 pubs from USM-quoted Gibbs Mew. Grand Met insisted on a confidentiality agreement, so the Quotations Department was not consulted. Once the tender was accepted, the Stock Exchange was told and sought to persuade Grand Met to make the contract conditional on acceptance by Gibbs Mew's shareholders. It would not. So the emergency meeting the Stock Exchange insisted be called of Gibbs Mew's to rubber-stamp the deal was largely cosmetic. But it is easy to understand the reluctance of companies to disclose a potential transaction if disclosure will compromise the agreement.

Acquisitions for shares generally require, if not shareholder consent, formal announcements and documentation to shareholders. Information provided in this documentation needs to be studied with care if a full picture is to be gained, since this level of detail is not normally repeated in either annual accounts or interim statements.

Treatment of goodwill on disposal of a business

Urgent Issues Task Force Abstract 3 addressed the question of the treatment of goodwill on disposal of a business. It took the case of a subsidiary purchased for £500m, of which £150m was attributed to the net assets acquired and £350m taken against reserves as goodwill.

If in a subsequent accounting period when, for simplicity, net assets are still £150m it is sold for £400m, is the result of the sale, they asked, themselves:

1. A loss of £100m (proceeds of £400m less cost of the business sold £500m); or
2. A gain of £250m (proceeds of £400m less carrying value £150m)?

UITF Abstract 3 requires the former presentation; and this principle applies equally to:

(i) negative goodwill;
(ii) closures of business.

Thus, were the above business closed, on the date used previously, when the net assets realised £145m, the net loss would be £355m (ie £500m less £145m).

This will make it hard for companies to hide losses on disposal of a business. Companies, of course, stress that goodwill does not affect cash flows as it has already been written off. But there is no getting round the fact: the cash effect (or diminution of equity) of a bad acquisition occurred at the time of purchase – but it still occurred.

Practice

Find an example of a group which has closed facilities or companies but which did not report them as 'discontinued activities' but did show the effect upon earnings elsewhere in the accounts (one example was the disposal of Chesterman Home Furnishers' stores by Argos in 1992).

Chapter 14

GROUP PHILOSOPHY;
METHODS OF CONTROLLING A LARGE GROUP

Five key factors to consider

When considering a company and its board of directors, look for evidence on five key factors:

1. Independence;
2. Transparency;
3. Succession;
4. Rationale, for the group's existence;
5. A blend of skills among top management.

More particularly look for any suggestion that one of these is lacking.

Practice tends to be well ahead of the legal requirement when it comes to directors. Recommendations in the Cadbury Report, for instance, were being widely applied well before they became a Yellow Book requirement (periods ending after 30 June 1993); but they still have not been incorporated in law.

At a more basic level, someone has to take the chair at meetings of shareholders and of directors, but that duty can rotate or be decided in any way the directors decide. In law the chairman has no other duties – he is simply a director and (apart from possibly having a casting vote) has exactly the same rights and duties as any other director.

Nothing in law requires a company to appoint any one to the *office* of chairman, but all listed companies do.

Similarly, special articles apart (and they are comparatively rare), nothing requires a company to have a managing director or chief executive, or specifies the duties of one if he is appointed – they tend to be spelled out in a service contract.

In fact, most companies have both a chairman and a chief executive – and, in the light of Chapter 9, do not combine the roles one individual.

But the danger lies less, in their combination than in the company's being dominated by a single individual, be they chairman, chief executive or both.

Independence

There is nothing intrinsically wrong with powerful leadership. What one needs to be on the lookout for is any evidence, be it in the chairman's statement, the review of operations, financial review, press briefings or company visits, of an autocrat who will brook no dissent; or a bully sufficiently powerful to stifle criticism, internal or external.

Independence is something to look for in top management generally, but the respected invitee who is known to have declined a non-executive directorship, and the director (be he executive or non-executive) who leaves mid-term without apparent cause, speak volumes.

No auditor resigns unexpectedly without very good reason, though he may not spell it out. It is not unknown, however, for auditors to write direct to shareholders (in 1993 Touche Ross wrote to shareholders of Trafalgar House, for instance).

Ideally, if these people know something is wrong, they will speak out publicly. But that is easier said than done. If as an auditor or non-executive director your suspicions are aroused, if you get the feeling 'I wouldn't touch him (or that company) with a barge-pole' or that 'There is a nasty smell – I cannot quite put my finger on it but ...', the sensible course is to resign. But without concrete evidence, the laws of libel make it difficult to explain why one has done so; and can be and are used to ensure that it is.

Companies with both a chairman and a chief executive differ in the way they see these roles; and as it is the chairman and chief executive who, between them, give an organisation its own special stamp, it is useful to glean from reports and accounts, from company visits and the press, just how they work together and who is responsible for what.

Often the division is that the chairman is responsible for development of long-term strategic plans; and the chief executive for the implementation of that strategy and for day-to-day operations, but that need not be the case. Some are much more forthcoming on strategy than others. An example of best practice was the pharmaceutical company MEDEVA, for which 1990 represented a year of not inconsiderable change.

MEDEVA *Extract from chairman's report 1990*

I am very pleased to be able to report a group net profit of £4,013,000 compared with a loss for the previous year of £2,623,000 ...

The encouraging results were achieved in a environment of rapid and fundamental change. We began the year as Medirace, a small research-based company with sales of less than £1 million per annum, operating at a loss, and with a net worth of £425,000. We ended the year with profits, no borrowings, and shareholders' funds of £44.6 million, having become the UK's largest manufacturer and distributor of generic pharmaceuticals. Additionally ... Medeva is now the principal supplier of human vaccines to the NHS.

The interim report to shareholders provided the first opportunity to outline the Group's strategy. In that report I described the two sectors of our business which would form the basis of our future growth – Branded Pharmaceuticals and Generic Pharmaceuticals. The former sector offers the greatest potential for profitable growth, both in the UK and overseas markets, and it is in this sector of our business where development will be focused. I previously defined our Branded Pharmaceuticals as those products not patent-protected but with sufficient advantages of competitors to warrant identification by brand names and the investment required to promote those brands directly to general practitioners and hospital doctors. This sector of our business will be handled by Evans Medical Ltd which is now assembling a portfolio of products from internal and third-party sources. For historical reasons, some of these products fall outside the 'branded' definition, but our objective will be to change this balance to branded in the medium term through acquisition. ...

[The managing director then reported separately on the group's two main divisions]. Subsequently, there was a change of strategy, involving withdrawal from UK basic generic drug distrbution, but that is another story.

In many companies, the chairman is strictly non-executive. Often, as he nears retirement, the chief executive becomes chairman, in harness with a newly appointed chief executive. This can be a mixed blessing: a tired chief executive does not necessarily have the thrust and grasp of new processes and ideas needed by a strategic planner; and a powerful former chief executive may seek to dominate his successor.

Promotion from within has its advantages, for example it offers a promotion ladder and so helps to retain good people who would otherwise leave, but suffers from the disadvantage of in-breeding in that little new blood is introduced and adds to the difficulties a chief executive serving with a dominant chairman who was himself formerly chief executive.

We have, in fact, said a lot about dominant leaders. Chairmen and chief executives come in all shapes and sizes, but they do not rise to that position without a well-developed leadership ability; and without being able to take decisions and accept the responsibility for them.

Although City opinion is now against this, many companies seem for many years to have operated successfully with a combined chairman / chief executive. Examples were Grand Met, Barclays, Argyll, T&N, Bass, Sainsbury, Kingfisher and Reed International – but there have been notable failures.

It is all a matter of degree. What one is trying to spot is the man who is *so* determined, and *so* self-contained, that he pays scant regard to the advice of others even when he is wrong, and is likely to bend the rules in an attempt to get himself off the hook. History abounds with men like that. Whether they are caught or not it is generally the investor who has to pick up the bill.

Some directors are very successful at projecting themselves to analysts, journalists and a wider public, but may be less good at running their companies than more reticent directors. What one is trying to do is to spot this.

The role of the Finance Director

Just as nothing requires a company to have a designated chief executive (though most do), nothing in company law compels it to have a finance director, though the Stock Exchange now requires one director of a listed company to be responsible for finances.

The finance director plays a number of key roles. He is responsible for the existence of:

1. Effective reporting procedures (this will involve daily, weekly, monthly, quarterly, half-yearly and yearly figures to many different levels of management). By effective we mean: accurate, prompt, and relevant.
2. Budgeting and budgetary control ie proper financial planning.
3. Financial controls and internal audit. For example: if the group has a treasury function engaged in foreign exchange market operations,

swaps and the like, it is the FD's job to ensure that operational rules, procedures and limits are laid down and observed.

4. Effective cash handling and banking procedures, including short as well as long term cash forecasts.

5. Planning any needed capital raising or borrowing needed.

6. A taxation strategy.

The finance director also plays a key role in ensuring the independence of the Board in the face of a dominant chairman / chief executive, who tries to bend the rules.

Cases have arisen of finance directors who have blown the whistle and / or resigned, but by then it is usually too late. Often it is the pressure that a finance director (and possibly the auditor) exerts behind the scenes that is important. Pushed to the limit, he (they) will threaten to resign. That often has the desired effect. But as a last resort, he (they) will be forced to fulfil their threat. Unfortunately, the law on confidentiality, and once again that of libel, ensure that a finance director stands very much on his own.

The Institutes of Chartered Accountants are rarely able to help a finance director seeking to blow the whistle, and he runs the risk of dismissal or possible legal action if he goes to the police, the Serious Fraud Office, or the Department of Trade and Industry.

That is why it is important as Cadbury suggests, for companies, and certainly any major listed company, to have an audit committee chaired by a non-executive director to whom the auditor and finance director, in particular, can express any disquiet.

Non-executive directors

For some years, non-executive directors have been viewed as an important safeguard; and provided that they are truly independent, people of stature, possess a sufficiently determined character, and are not only able but prepared to devote the time, they probably are.

But if the executive top-management can be taken by surprise (as that of Allied-Lyons was, see page 82), can outsiders who devote a day a month, and possibly less, be expected to be better informed?

There are still plenty of yes men around who are happy to enjoy a monthly lunch, and not ungenerous fees. And, surprisingly, there is no evidence to suggest that companies like Maxwell Communication, Brent Walker and Polly Peck had any trouble finding non-executive directors who, by no stretch of imagination, would be classified as yes men. But that did not keep them out of trouble.

Transparency

Another thing we look for when considering a company and its board of directors is what we term 'transparency'. More particularly we look for any suggestion that transparency is lacking.

By transparency we mean the ability of an outsider to see clearly what a company is about:

1. What it does, where and why; and
2. Where ultimate ownership lies.

There may be perfectly good (tax and estate duty) reasons for a key shareholding (eg of a founder chairman) being held by a Jersey family trust. A loan may be raised through a finance subsidiary incorporated in the Cayman Islands because that offers tax advantages or confidentiality sought by an overseas lending institution. But a host of interlocking Jersey or Panama companies whose affairs are controlled in a way which would be illegal under UK law; and family trusts in Andorra, controlling companies in the Netherlands' Antilles, the Isle of Man, Sark ... leave one, often rightly, suspecting the worst.

Succession

Not only do some founder chairmen / chief executives (and it is often the people who built a business from nothing) see themselves as omniscient, some assume immortality. It is important, therefore, in examining a company to ask about succession. Is the climate at Amstrad, for instance, such that, were anything to happen to Alan Sugar (chairman and managing director), the group would continue to flourish, or that Sainsbury will do as well under David Sainsbury as it did under Lord Sainsbury his predecessor? Or Forte under Rocco Forte?

Rationale

We looked in Chapter 12 at the many reasons companies offer for forming or acquiring subsidiaries. Here we turn this on its head, asking ourselves:

1. What is the rationale offered for the group's existence?
2. Does it hold water?
3. Is there evidence of a clear purpose (a strategy) or did the group just grow like Topsy? In other words, which came first: the group or the supposed strategic rationale?

A group which lacks any real rationale is a group which is difficult both for group management to control (especially if it covers a diverse range of specialist activities), and for investors and analysts to understand. It is also likely to be unstable; with subsidiaries coming and going at a whim.

Controlling the larger group

In this section we look at larger groups:

1. Those big enough to group their activities into divisions *(divisionalised companies)*;
2. Those where little or no logical relationship exists between the companies in a group (even if they are grouped into 'divisions') – which we refer to as *conglomerates.*

Let us begin by examining the difference between a segment and a division.

A *segment* is simply an accounting device; in effect, an analysis column. In many cases it has no separate physical existence whatever, sharing staff and facilities with other segments. This means that many costs have to be allocated or apportioned, and that it is quite difficult to arrive at the capital employed in the segment. Such a segment is not necessarily either localised or insignificant. A group like W. H. Smith will, for internal management purposes, subdivide its retail activities into newspapers and magazines, books, records and tapes and stationery, by analysing the results of every retail store. It would be difficult to dispose separately of a segment of this sort; and study of the accounts of individual subsidiaries will not provide the analyst with much help.

But a segment can be organised as a separate legal entity (as a subsidiary or intermediate holding company plus subsidiaries), and a *division* usually is.

The difference between a division and a segment is largely an organisational one. Responsibility for a division is generally vested in a divisional board with very considerable delegated powers, powers which normally stop short of the power to raise capital. This generally means that the division represents some form of intermediate holding company and its subsidiaries. Such a company is likely to be wholly-owned. It will not therefore present group accounts generally – so there is no easily obtainable information – but it is quite easy to dispose of as a distinct unit.

To add to the confusion:

1. The published segmental analysis often does not represent the activities of a single division;
2. The results of a single division often fall in several segments

– something which has to be borne in mind when studying the review of operations.

What kind of group is it?

It is possible to identify extremes of corporate detachment and involvement in strategy decisions, which we will term:

1. *Holding companies*, the approach of which is to minimise the strategic role of the centre. Corporate management intervenes little to influence strategy at the business unit level, allowing each business or division to develop and pursue its own strategy. Businesses tend to reinvest their own funds, and where there are bids for investment that exceed a business's own funds, the choice of proposals to fund becomes a political one. Where budgets and planning processes are found, they are regarded by the units as a paper exercise and there is little control of achievement against plan.
Symptoms to look for: lack of focus in resource allocation; inability to turn round or dispose of non-performing businesses; lack of any attempt to manage interdependencies or to develop synergy.
Many listed companies are still in this category.

2. *Centralised companies* are the very opposite. Corporate managers play an active role, themselves determining strategy for each business and allocating the resources to support those strategies. Units can be held responsible only for the execution of strategy; and the centre is left with the difficult task of controlling itself strategically.
Symptoms: Responsibility is removed from front line management which is closest to the business; because the centre takes the decisions, business unit managers do not feel so responsible, and are less committed to implementing the strategy; indeed it inhibits strategic thinking on the part of those who must put decisions into practice.
This makes it difficult to develop general management experience, capability and judgment down the line. By failing to create and encourage multiple views of strategy, such groups run the risk of tunnel vision and the development of inflexible strategic plans.

Most companies fall somewhere in between.

Styles of strategic management

It is possible to identify three main styles of strategic management, examples of all of which are to be found in top UK groups:

1. *Strategic planning:* in which the centre works with business unit managers to develop strategy. Group establishes extensive planning processes, makes substantial contributions to strategic thinking, and may have a corporate strategy (or mission) guiding and co-ordinating developments across business units.

Less attention is paid to the control process and to annual targets; performance targets being set in broad strategic terms (eg 'To be the world's leading car hire group'.
Examples: BOC and Cadbury Schweppes.

2. *Strategic control:* in which the centre prefers to leave the initiative in the development of plans to business unit managers. The centre then reviews and criticises the plans more as a check on the quality of business unit managers than as an opportunity to give direction. But the control process is an important influence mechanism. Targets are set for both strategic objectives like market share and for financial performance; and managers are expected to meet these targets.
Examples: ICI and Hanson.

3. *Financial control:* where the centre's influence is exercised mainly through the budget process. The centre focuses on a close review of the annual budget. Profit targets are set when the budget is approved, and careers are at stake if they are missed. On the other hand, the centre plays a limited strategic role, leaving long term plans largely to individual business units.
Examples: GEC and Tarmac.

These are the main styles, though it is possible to identify others like strategic venturing, where the centre delegates the development of strategy to the business units, makes few attempts to challenge their proposals, and like a venture capitalist only intervenes if serious problems seem to be emerging.

That such distinct, diverse, incompatible management styles should exist at all is surprising; and that they should all continue to be found among leading companies is perhaps more so. They are the result of very different philosophies on how to develop a winning team all of which seem to work in the right circumstances, with the right management group.

The analyst's concern with style

The analyst's task is first of all to decide, on the evidence available:

1. What kind of management exists in a particular group;
2. Whether anything suggests that it is inappropriate (or is becoming so);
3. Whether a planned succession is 'working out'. To succeed a powerful and successful

man is not easy; particularly if he becomes chairman. Do nothing and you are seen as weak and ineffective. Change the shape of the business too fast or kill off his 'pet projects' and you are in trouble. Consider the case of Dr Ernest Mario who was brought in to be chief executive of Glaxo. When he ceased to be chief executive a couple of years later (11 March 1993) the supposition was that chairman and previous chief executive, Sir Paul Girolami, did not like the way he was running the group. What ever the reason, the share price tumbled.

The analyst should then ask himself whether the group is falling into any other of the more obvious pitfalls and areas of tension:

1. Tradition: 'It's always been done that way.'
2. Bureaucracy: 'If there are problems, add another layer of management' or 'let's introduce a specialist function'.
3. Arbitrary and unpredictable intervention from above.
4. Across-the-board, possibly inappropriate, instructions.
5. Moving the goal-posts ie changing strategic aims and measure of success without telling the people at the coal-face.
6. Retention of non-core businesses, for historical or sentimental reasons; often outside the mainstream planning, and probably little understood by either managers in other divisions or companies, or group.

These pitfalls are quite difficult to spot from outside. But the company visit offers opportunities, if one is on the look out; and the report of activities or chief executive's report may provide clues.

Practice

Take the latest accounts of Hanson.

1. Seek out evidence of independence; transparency; and provision for succession.
2. What is the rationale for the group's existence?
3. How would you categorise the group's management style?
4. How do you view the future of the group; will it continue as in the past or are changes likely?

Chapter 15

FOREIGN OPERATIONS AND CURRENCY RISK

UK companies are involved with foreign operations and foreign currency transactions in a variety of ways. In the simplest terms this may represent purchases from overseas, or sales to customers abroad. At the other extreme, a UK registered company may buy, sell, manufacture, distribute, raise finance, and have stock exchange quotes overseas to such an extent that it sees itself, and is seen by others, no longer as a UK company but as a worldwide group with cross border loyalties.

Examples of almost every possible combination between these extremes are to be found. We stress this because it adds substantially to the difficulty of (1) interpreting results; (2) audit.

UK COMPANIES TRADING ABROAD

Why companies buy and sell overseas

Companies purchase overseas:

1. Where there is no UK supplier of the goods required;
2. To obtain goods of a particular quality, performance or style;
3. To obtain a keen price; or simply
4. To cut out the middleman.

In the case of capital equipment, an overseas supplier may, often because of government subsidies or financing arrangements, but sometimes simply because of lower interest rates than in the UK, be able to offer favourable deferred terms, eg hire purchase or leasing arrangements at low effective rates of interest.

UK companies sell overseas:

1. As a way of expanding, or protecting, their market; or even
2. Because it is more profitable; but sometimes
3. As a result of government exhortation in the light of the balance of payments, because they are conscious of its desirability.

In each case, the relative attraction of trading overseas is affected by exchange rates, but it is unlikely that the annual accounts will shed much light on this aspect. Nevertheless, it is important to glean what one can.

A UK trader selling to an overseas customer has the choice of fixing his price in sterling or doing so in foreign currency. If he expresses it in sterling, the risks of foreign exchange, and the conversion costs fall on the purchaser. If he expresses it in the foreign currency, he may find it easier to sell but the risks of foreign exchange, and the conversion costs fall on him. The same applies, in the reverse direction, with purchases from overseas.

If the risks and conversion costs fall upon the overseas customer or supplier, the transaction is recorded at the UK end just as it would be with a UK customer or supplier.

If the UK supplier or customer bears exchange risks or costs, there are, essentially, two ways of handling overseas trading transactions in the accounts. At the simplest, the UK trader merely records the net sterling proceeds of the sale (or overall sterling cost in the case of purchases). This is what happens with primitive, cash-based systems of accounting. In a normal double entry system, invoices are raised in currency, and converted into sterling at the date the invoice is issued or received. Then, when payment is received from the overseas customer (or payment is made to the overseas supplier), the actual sterling proceeds (cost) are compared with the previously computed sterling amount, and any difference treated as a cost (or gain).

Only in most exceptional circumstances (eg were the currency to be devalued between the two dates) would this cost or gain be disclosed separately; it forms part of operating profits.

SWAPS, INTEREST CAPS AND THE FOREIGN EXCHANGE FORWARD MARKET

To prevent *currency conversion losses*, many companies selling overseas at prices expressed in overseas currency sell the foreign currency forward (for sterling) on the foreign exchange market; and those buying overseas at prices expressed in overseas currency buy (for sterling) the foreign currency forward on the foreign exchange market. This is simply prudent management, and few companies refer to it in their accounts.

The use of swaps, interest rate caps and similar devices is rarely mentioned in accounts, though it may be mentioned in a Financial Review. It is an entirely proper feature of international operations and should not normally give rise to undue currency profits or losses, provided always that the other party to the swap is financially sound and permitted by its constitution and local legislation to engage in the operation. Unfortunately, as the banks learned to their cost in 1989-90, it is not always easy to be sure that the other party (a local authority in their case) is in law permitted to engage in swap deals.

Playing the currency markets

To play the currency market using swaps simply with a view to profit, and not in support of one's trade, which is what some local authorities were doing, is, to put it mildly, undesirable.

In the case of a bank, which by its very nature deals in many currencies, it is necessary to take a position as regard currencies – but even this needs to be the subject of stringent controls. Several banks (including Lloyds and, more recently, Midland, which in 1989 was reported to have suffered losses of around £250m on currency dealing) have been embarrassed by costly, sometimes unauthorised, foreign exchange dealings by staff.

For a trading company (a company not primarily involved in finance) to play the currency markets with a view to profit (or perhaps worse still, in an attempt to recoup losses), is inappropriate even where it is permitted by the company's objects and can result in heavy, unexpected, losses. Unfortunately, it is difficult for the outsider (and even, it would appear, for the board) to detect.

ALLIED-LYONS *Summary of reports in* Sunday Telegraph *24 March and 5 May 1991*

On 19 March 1991 Allied-Lyons announced currency trading losses of £147m. It seems that the first indication

that then chairman Sir Derrick Holden-Brown had that all might not be well came in June 1990 when he was asked, at a regular informal meeting with the Bank of England, whether Clifford Hatch, former finance director, knew the full extent of the company's foreign exchange dealings. The situation was discussed with the Bank by Clifford Hatch and group treasurer Timothy Dalton. In September 1990 Dalton reported that the treasury department's currency centre was considerably over the £500m ceiling which had been set on its foreign exchange exposure.

The currency centre was not originally set up as a profit generator. Hatch, it seems, who joined the group when it bought the Hiram Walker drinks group for £1.3bn, had other ideas, and recruited a number of high-flying currency dealers with American banking experience – including one who publicly extolled the virtues of using the option market aggressively. In this way, the centre had begun active currency options writing and trading.

The situation was taken in hand and by February 1991 the losses had been cut to below £10m, but Allied-Lyons was left with an aggressive bear position on the US dollar.

The Gulf war finished at the end of February 1991, and the dollar shot up and in the space of 10 days the currency centre's exposure doubled and redoubled until by 14 March it had reached £1bn.

NatWest bank was called in to sort out the mess. At that stage losses were around £100m. NatWest immediately set about closing out the remaining positions against a market which knew just what was happening. Rates moved inexorably against Allied-Lyons to leave currency trading losses of £147m.

Study of the group's accounting policies, and previous reports and accounts, including the interim statement published some weeks before, gave no clue of currency dealing or risk. But it seems that the chairman and group board were equally ill-informed until a late stage. Indeed, the board only heard of the problem on 13 March 1991.

Group Finance Director, Clifford Hatch resigned, though Allied accepted that he did not authorise the deals which led to the £147m loss – whether he should have known about them in time to call a halt is entirely another matter.

It seems that in October 1990 the group's auditors queried with Hatch the currency dealings, but that he did not report the matter to the board – there is surely a lesson in this both for auditors (who cannot rely on communicating doubts to one person be he finance director, chairman or chief executive) and for directors who should (unless there is a separate properly constituted independent audit committee) not only insist on seeing, but should themselves consider, all audit comments.

Nor, it seems, do companies always learn by past mistakes. In 1978, the then independent J. Lyons used Swiss francs to do deals in America (because interest rates were low in Switzerland) but took such a knock when the Swiss franc appreciated vis a vis the £ that a takeover by Allied Breweries seemed the only way out.

The financial review and foreign exchange

A small but growing number of companies now publish either a Review of Operations *and Finance,* or a separate Financial Review. This may be used to inform, even reassure, shareholders regarding foreign exchange dealings.

WELLCOME *Extract from Review of Operations and Finance 1992*

During 1992, Wellcome strengthened its treasury team and introduced a comprehensive range of measures to enhance the performance of its Treasury function.

The most important of these included more active foreign exchange (FX) management and selective hedging of forecast exposure to net trade and intra-Group FX transactions. During the year, Wellcome traded more than $1bn in FX in the UK, a substantial increase on any other year.

This increased activity has been accompanied by tightly controlled policies, standards and procedures for the UK's FX and money market dealing activities.

We have also introduced formal rating assessments for all deposit-taking institutions, which set strict limits of acceptable creditworthiness. ...

TATE & LYLE *Extract from Financial Review 1992*

Exchange rates & interest rates
Group policy is to translate the profit and loss account using a weighted average exchange rate and the balance sheet at year end rates. The average rate for the US$ has weakened against the £ over the past three years, although short-term fluctuations have been significant. In contrast, the year end exchange rate of US$1.72 to the £ has strengthened as compared with the prior year, increasing the sterling equivalent of our dollar-denominated debt.

The net debt exposure of the group is principally in US$, which, together with other debt in Australian and Canadian dollars which are broadly linked to the US dollar, amounted to 92% of the total Group net debt at the balance sheet date. Interest rates on the currencies fell sharply during the year and are expected to remain relatively low during 1993.

Accordingly as fixed debt matured it was decided to increase the floating debt element of net US dollar debt from 15% to 59%.

Sharp movements in exchange rates during September gave balance sheet gains on the Group's non-sterling net assets. 48% of Group net assets were in dollar currencies and 22% were in European Exchange Rate Mechanism currencies at the year end.

The weighted average exchange rate of US$1.82 (1991 – $1.78) to the £ was well above the year end rate of US$1.72 (1991 – $1.74). Compared with last year's average exchange rate there was a translation loss of $2.3m on profits before tax from operations in dollar currencies, but since all such profits were retained locally, rather than being paid as dividends to the UK, this translation loss was recovered by the balance sheet date through the rise in the sterling equivalent value of the dollar based Group reserves.

Other companies, like BOC, warned that as a result of Britain's leaving the ERM (and the consequent fall in sterling) their profit performance in 1992 was flattered, and that growth at the same rate in future was unlikely.

FOREIGN REGISTERED SUBSIDIARIES

Why groups have foreign subsidiaries

Groups use foreign-registered subsidiaries for a variety of purposes, and it is important where possible (though it often is not) to discover the purpose for which subsidiaries are employed.

The most obvious use is to provide local incorporation of manufacturing, distribution and/or trading units – rather than to operate through a branch system.
This:

1. Simplifies the making of contracts locally;

2. Simplifies the raising of on-the-spot finance and the provision (possibly a legal condition) of local participation;

3. Encourages local loyalty - since working for a local company is perceived as different from working for a foreign company, even if all or most of the shares in the local company are held overseas;

4. Facilitates the assessment of taxation.

But overseas incorporation may be used where there is no trading connection for a variety of purposes, some legitimate, some of doubtful validity and some downright illegal or dishonest:

1. As a device to avoid taxation (which may be regarded as legitimate) or to evade it (which is unlawful); or as a way of retaining funds largely free of tax (insurance funds in the Isle

of Man or the Channel Islands); or just post-poning the need to pay.

2. As a way to hide information (by using a country such as Panama with weak disclosure requirements) – or simply to make it more difficult to obtain information, since it is much more trouble to run a search in, say, Grand Cayman, than in the UK.

3. In raising finance:

   (i) In connection with a Eurobond issue;

   (ii) To enable the group to account for a transaction in one way, when, had it been made directly, its balance sheet effect would have been quite different (ie less favourable);

   (iii) To build a wall such that one class of creditor is favoured or protected against others.

4. To launder money, as is reported to have been the case with BCCI.

Types of investment in foreign companies

The UK's growth as a world power was due to the combination of manufacturing capacity, maritime strength, an empire capable of providing cheap raw materials, and trade surpluses which made possible massive overseas investment.

Many of UK's special advantages have been eroded or lost entirely, partly as a result of two world wars, but the freeing of international trade and the improvements of communication which have taken place in the last 20 years, have encouraged international trade generally, and international finance in particular. In this the UK remains a key player.

The removal of exchange controls in 1979 has made it possible for a UK group to consider investment on a world-wide basis. If returns are better in the US or Japan, Spain or Argentina, funds may be channelled there rather than into UK operations (having, in the short term at least, an adverse effect on the UK's overall balance of payments). Equally, if returns appear better in the UK than in the US, funds may be channelled there by US companies rather than into US operations.

The flow of capital funds tends, at any point in time, to be one way, though this is not necessarily the case.

We spoke earlier, somewhat vaguely, of returns being better overseas; what do we have in mind?

Investment can be divided broadly into:

1. *Portfolio investment*, where funds are invested in stocks and shares but there is no control over operations of the companies concerned; and

2. *Operational investment*, where a part is played in the management of the organisation.

In portfolio investment, the investor has regard to the overall yield, income plus capital gains. Investors have, from time to time, been prepared to invest (eg in Japan) on the basis of a negligible (even zero) dividend yield, in the expectation of substantial capital growth.

In assessing this overall yield regard needs to be paid:

1. To the relative risks involved (in the past bankers and others seem to have considerably underestimated the additional risks in investing or lending overseas); and

2. To relative exchange rate movements (the £ has tended over recent years to fall against many major currencies eg the DMark – but it is always possible that this could change).

In operational investment, a part is played in the management of the organisation. We consider here:

1. The reasons why groups operate abroad;

2. The special problems inherent in overseas operations.

Essentially, groups operate overseas:

1. To expand in a way not possible at home without fundamentally changing the nature of the business; there is, for example, a limit to the number of Marks & Spencer stores which can operate profitably in a given area;

2. To spread risk, on the basis that trade downturns tend to be regional in character;

3. To seek growth opportunities greater than those to be found in the UK – less developed economies may be expected to develop faster than those of more advanced countries – a number of UK companies have recently opened manufacturing facilities in China;

4. To raise capital, or to operate, more cheaply or effectively. For example to exploit a pool of suitably skilled labour in a non-unionised low-wage economy.

5. To benefit from favourable tariffs, eg Japanese electronics and car manufacturers fabricate within the EC to gain the advantages of EC companies.

6. To take advantage of exchange rate advantages or anomalies.

But most of these favourable factors change (probably disappear) with time. That is one important risk of overseas direct investment.

There are other risks and difficulties too:

1. Exchange controls may be introduced either in the UK or in the overseas country;

2. Local legal requirements may be introduced regarding control by foreigners (calling for

majority ownership locally, or for a substantial local management presence);

3. Nationalisation;
4. Worse still, expropriation;
5. Taxation systems may change to the disadvantage of foreign-ownership – the introduction of ACT hurt many UK groups with the major part of their earnings abroad;
6. Import / export restrictions may be introduced by the country in which the overseas investment is made, or by countries from which the local company imports or to which it exports;
7. Language differences;
8. Differences of ethics. Business behaviour abroad is not necessarily that expected in the UK, eg insider dealing is not viewed in the same light either in Germany or Japan, and not only are below-the-counter payments to facilitate business normal in many less developed countries, business may be difficult without them. Nor is it unknown for such payments to be taken fraudulently, no advantage being obtained by the payer.

SSAP 25, 'Segmental Reporting', ensures that companies provide far more information than ever before, nevertheless reports and accounts still provide only a very limited indication of:

1. Why a group has invested abroad;
2. The extent and nature of that investment; and
3. Any special risks attaching to it.

Where useful information is provided, it may appear anywhere in the report and accounts; and some types of information (eg why the investment was made in the first place) may not be repeated in later years. What the reader of accounts needs to know if he is to assess the risks involved is:

1. Precisely where the assets are (in order to estimate expropriation risk);
2. Where products are made (to estimate the risk of strikes, rising labour costs etc);
3. Where purchases of raw materials, components etc are made and in what currency

prices are expressed, and how they are transported;
4. From where sales are made, to where, priced in what currency;
5. Where the cash is – and how easy it would be to move it;
6. What, if anything, has been done in the way of forward sales of currency, swaps etc.

Segmental reporting goes part of the way, but only part and it is unlikely that accounts as at present conceived will go much further.

Methods of organising foreign operations

Foreign operations may be organised in several distinct ways:

1. Agency;
2. Branch;
3. Subsidiary;
4. Associated company;
5. Franchise.

Unfortunately, it is often impossible to tell which method has been employed. Nothing currently requires a company to disclose even the existence of agents; or of local branches (either in the UK or abroad), and present accounting requirements on franchise operations leave a great deal to be desired.

Some methods of organisation, for example agencies and branches, result in currency conversion differences which while deducted in arriving at the profit from operations are not disclosed separately in the accounts, rather than translation differences, which are.

Even where reference is made explicitly to branch operations, one cannot usually tell what proportion of operations takes which form.

Where overseas subsidiaries are separately quoted, or where they are major companies in the country concerned, they may publish information in advance of the UK parent's annual accounts or interim report. Analysts need to be aware of this possibility and to try to obtain the information rather than be left behind by their competitors.

ACCOUNTING TREATMENT OF OVERSEAS ACTIVITIES

The treatment of overseas transactions or operations in the accounts of individual companies is entirely different to that in group accounts. The reader is entitled to ask: 'Does that matter? I only look at the consolidated balance sheet'. It matters because the accounts of the individual companies are the primary books of account; it is they that record the transactions and form the basis of the audit. It is they that determine the profit or loss, assets and liabilities, of individual companies – and

the security of lenders. The consolidated accounts are simply a memorandum, academic exercise – they do not exist as books of account.

In the accounts of the individual company

Generally, all foreign currency transactions entered into by a company should be translated into its own local currency at the exchange rate ruling on the date the transaction occurs – though use of the average rate for the period is permissible if rates have not fluctuated significantly; and where a transaction is to be settled at a contracted rate, that rate should be used.

At the balance sheet date, monetary assets and liabilities denominated in foreign currencies resulting from unsettled transactions should be translated into the company's own local currency using the closing rate. Again, where a transaction is to be settled at a contracted rate, that rate is used.

Non-monetary assets (eg land and buildings, plant and machinery, stocks) are not retranslated in the accounts of an individual company but remain translated at the rate they were originally recorded.

Exchange differences arise:

1. When transactions are settled at exchange rates different from those used when the transaction was recorded;
2. On any unsettled transactions at the balance sheet date where the closing rate is different from that at which they were recorded.

Exchange differences are included as part of the profit for the period from ordinary activities unless they arise as a result of events which are themselves properly treated as extraordinary. This treatment applies equally to short- and long-term transactions and irrespective of whether the result is a gain or a loss. The amounts charged or credited to profit in respect of such exchange differences are not required to be disclosed separately in the profit and loss account – though their existence can often be detected from the cash flow statement (which should always be studied with care in this regard).

Example 15.1 Borrowing in $US

On 23 March 1993 Economise plc borrowed $10m at 7.0% from a US bank, repayable in March 1998, to finance its UK operations. On 23 March 1993 the rate of exchange was $1.82 to the £, so the transaction was recorded at £5,494,506. At 31 December 1993 the rate of exchange was $1.95 so the item was retranslated at £5,128,205, and £366,301 was credited to the profit for the period from ordinary activities. Note that the normal rules of providing immediately for a known liability but not anticipating a gain do not apply to foreign currency translations of this type.

At December 1994 the rate of exchange has become $1.65 to the £. The loan therefore appears as £6,060,606, and a loss of £932,401 is taken against the profit for the period from ordinary activities.

However, where there are doubts as to the convertibility or marketability of the foreign currency, it is necessary to consider on grounds of prudence whether any exchange gain, or the amount by which exchange gains exceeds past exchange losses recognised as profit, should be restricted.

One exception to the rule that non-monetary items are not retranslated is where foreign equity investments have been financed by foreign currency borrowings, or where the borrowings have been taken out to hedge exchange risks associated with existing investments. The standard recognises that in such situations a company may be covered in economic terms against any movement in exchange rates and states that it would be inappropriate in such cases to record an accounting profit or loss when exchange rates change.

Subject to the conditions set out below, companies in such situations may, under paragraph 51 of SSAP 20, treat the cost of investments as being denominated in the appropriate foreign currencies and retranslate them at the closing rate each year. Where this is done, the resulting exchange differences are taken not to the profit for the period from ordinary activities but direct to reserve. The exchange differences arising on the related foreign currency borrowings should also be taken to reserves and not to the profit for the period from ordinary activities.

The conditions are:

1. Exchange differences on the borrowings may be offset only to the extent of exchange differences arising on equity investments in that particular period.
2. The foreign currency borrowings must not exceed the total amount of cash that the investments are expected to generate, whether from profits or otherwise.
3. The accounting treatment must be applied consistently from period to period.

Example 15.2 Purchase of shares in a German company

Foreign Enterprises plc, a UK company, purchases equity shares in a German company for DM 9m on 1 November 1992, when the exchange rate is DM 2.80 to the £. It finances the transaction partly by borrowing DM 6m on the same date. The investment would be recorded at £3,214,286 and the loan as £2,142,857.

At Foreign Enterprises' year end of 31 December 1992, the closing rate is DM 3.00 to the £. The loan would be retranslated at £2,000,000 resulting in an exchange gain of £142,857. The investment would be translated at £3,000,000, resulting in an exchange loss of £214,286. Both the exchange gain and the exchange loss would be taken to reserve, appearing as a net loss of £71,429

If Foreign Enterprises did not adopt the procedure outlined in paragraph 51, and it is free to choose, the exchange gain of £142,857 would be taken to the profit for the period from ordinary activities, and the investment would have been retained at its original cost of £3,214,286, with no exchange loss being recognised.

In the group accounts

In their group accounts, most companies with overseas subsidiaries simply translate the entire historical cost balance sheets of such subsidiaries at the closing rate of exchange, putting (charging) any difference between the sterling amount of the opening figures (ie the corresponding figures) as translated at the rate ruling at the previous balance sheet date and that rate ruling at the current balance sheet date, direct to reserve.

It is instructive to ask just what the significance of this figure is. It is necessary to show it in order that the closing balance sheet should balance. But what does it indicate? Not a lot. Unless, that is, an overseas subsidiary is used as a means of investing at high interest rates reflecting currency risk – more about which later.

A historical balance sheet is not a valuation statement. It does not indicate either the value of individual assets (with the exception of cash) or that of the business as a whole (ie what someone would pay for it). Pedants define it as a list of the balances remaining in the books after the profit and loss account has been prepared. That there is a difference between the amount of the net assets translated at one rate of exchange and their amount translated at a different rate of exchange a year later, tells us something of the way rates of exchange have moved, and nothing more.

Example 15.3 Assessing progress of a foreign subsidiary

You are managing director of Progress (UK) plc, a company formed on 1 January 1993 with an issued capital of £10m, consisting of 20m 50p ordinary shares.

This is a summary of the accounts of the company for the years 1993 and 1994:

	1993 £m	1994 £m	Growth %
Turnover	40.000	44.800	12.000
Profit after Tax	3.300	3.729	13.000
Earnings per share (p)	16.500	18.645	13.000
Dividend per share (p)	8.250	9.140	10.784
Equity Shareholders' Funds at 31 Dec.	11.650	13.551	16.318

How would you rate your progress?

'Profit to sales ratio: 8.25% in 1993; 8.32% in 1994. Profit to opening ESF: 33.00% in 1993; 32.01% in 1994. ... A sound first year, followed by a healthy, but prudent, rate of growth overall in 1994.'

Imagine now that Progress (UK) plc is the wholly owned subsidiary of a foreign company which uses the closing rate method in its consolidated accounts.

Imagine, first, that it is the wholly owned subsidiary of DownCast Inc, a US company.

Rates of exchange were:

	1 Jan 1993	31 Dec 1993	31 Dec 1994
$ to £	$2.000	$1.950	$1.800

Your US Group managing director is assessing your progress. He has before him your sterling accounts (as above) and a summary of the accounts 1993–94 translated into $ for the purpose of consolidation:

Summary of Accounts 1993–94 translated into $:

	1993 $m	1994 $m	Growth %
Turnover	78.000	80.640	3.385
Profit after Tax	6.435	6.712	4.308
Earnings per share ($)	0.32175	0.33561	4.308
Dividend per share ($)	0.160875	0.16452	2.269
Equity Shareholders' Funds	22.718	24.392	7.371

How does he judge your progress?

He invested $20m ie 10m x $2.000 on 1 January 1993. Using that yardstick, the profit after tax ($6.435m) represents 32.175% on his investment – not quite the same as you got, because he has translated the profit after tax into $ at the closing rate of 1.95.

Using the opening ESF expressed in $ ($22.718m) as his yardstick for 1994, the profit after tax ($6.712m) represents 29.545% on his investment – rather less than you got, partly because he has translated the profit after tax into $ at the closing rate of 1.80.

He is also very confused. You report sound growth in 1994. But he is disappointed to see from the translated accounts that this not the case: 4.308% growth in earnings (when you referred to 13.00%), for instance, is far from spectacular; and a mere 2.269% growth in dividend is not at all what he was expecting.

He is even more disturbed by the translation losses charged to reserve:

	1993 $m	1994 $m
Differences on translation	(0.500)	(1.747)

(being: In 1993 $20m – (10m × 1.950) = $–0.500m

In 1994 (11.650m × 1.950 – 11.650m × 1.800) = $ – 1.747m)

– the latter representing 26.03% of the dollar profit.

Where *differences on translation* appear in the group accounts, favourable differences are often netted against unfavourable.

The effect of exchange rate changes *on the trading results* is not usually shown as such, but in segmental figures or their review of operations, the directors may draw attention to exchange rates in so far as they have caused a marked change in overall turnover or profitability.

Now let us consider instead the possibility that Progress (UK) plc was the wholly owned subsidiary of a German company.

The DM has behaved differently from the dollar:

Rates of exchange were, shall we say:

	1 Jan 1993	31 Dec 1993	31 Dec 1994
DM to £	2.650	2.750	2.950

Summary of Accounts 1993–94 translated into DM:

	1993 DMm	1994 DMm	Growth %
Turnover	110.000	132.160	20.145
Profit after Tax	9.075	11.001	21.218
Earnings per share (DM)	0.454	0.550	21.218
Dividend per share (DM)	0.227	0.270	18.943
Equity Shareholders' Funds	32.038	39.976	24.778
Translation gain (loss) transferred to reserve	1.000	2.330	

A very different, even flattering, position.

How then should the local management be judged? Almost certainly on the basis of accounts expressed in local currency.

But in judging its own investment policy the holding company needs to have regard also:

1. To the underlying reasons for the investment; and
2. To its effect on the group accounts.

A holding company with overseas subsidiaries has a choice when it comes to translation of overseas profits and losses: it can translate using (a) the closing; or (b) the average rate of exchange. Companies which produce monthly or quarterly sterling accounts for overseas companies for management purposes, or which produce half-yearly interim statements, often use the average rate method – otherwise the closing rate could be somewhat different from that used for interim purposes.

Because of volatility of exchange rates, a number of companies have recently changed over to the average rate method, and most FT–SE 100 companies now use that method.

By financing, where practicable, overseas subsidiaries by local currency borrowings or capital, and hence reducing the net investment, currency translation differences can be minimised. A growing number of (but still relatively few) companies spell out their policy in this regard.

Few companies provide sufficient information on exchange rate changes for one to judge properly their effects. A company which does is GKN.

GKN *Extract from accounting policies 1992*

... Where practicable, transactions involving foreign currencies are protected by forward contracts. Assets and liabilities in foreign currencies are translated at the appropriate forward contract rate or, if not covered, at the exchange rate ruling at the balance sheet date. ...

Where practicable, the group's overseas equity investments are covered by borrowings in the currencies in which those assets are denominated. ...

The exchange rates used for the currencies most important to group operations are ...

Example 15.4 Closing rate / net investment method

Imagine that the US parent of Progress (UK) plc (see above) borrowed £10m by way of a 3 year loan on the Eurocurrency market. Accounting standards permit the set off of this in the group accounts (what is termed the closing rate / net investment method). The group's net investment in Progress (UK) plc at 1 January 1993 then becomes £0, and the difference on translation becomes $0 in 1993 and (£11.650m – £10m) × 1.950 – (£11.650 – £10m) × 1.800 = $– 0.2475m in 1994.

Many companies borrow in overseas currencies to finance operations generally, rather than to finance operations in the country in which the money is raised. Danger lies where no trade connection exists, and there is simply an attempt to take advantage of lower interest rates abroad (possibly investing the proceeds on the higher yielding UK money market as Hanson and TI Group did recently). If this comes unstuck, as it is will do if exchange rates move adversely, the exercise can be very costly indeed – as a number of companies have found to their cost over the years.

High inflation and hyperinflation

Cases have arisen where companies have deposited money in bank accounts in overseas countries offering a high rate of interest for the simple reason that local inflation is very high and the currency is likely to depreciate. If the interest is then credited to profit and loss account among income from ordinary activities, and the adverse translation difference due to the falling value (in sterling terms) of the investment is taken against reserves, the result is unfairly flattering.

Example 15.5 When the answer is a Lemon

On 1 January 1994, a UK Group invests £140m in setting up a wholly-owned subsidiary C in a central Mediterranean country, Citrus, the currency of which is the Lemon (L). The whole £140m is placed on deposit with a bank in Citrus where it earns 45% interest in 1994. For simplicity we will ignore tax and any operating expenses.

On 1 January 1994 £1 = L100. At the end of the year, on 31 December 1994, £1 = L140.

The interest of L6,300,000,000 is translated (using the closing rate method) as £45,000,000 and included (as interest received) among operating profits of the group.

The opening investment of £140,000,000 (L14,000,000,000) is retranslated at the closing rate as £100,000,000, and the £40 million translation difference taken against reserves. This is unduly flattering. The truth is, the high rate of interest reflected the likelihood of high inflation, and it might be fairer to say that the effective interest was £45m – £40m = £5m.

That something of this sort of thing happened with Polly Peck was detectable from its accounts (substantial conversion gains were apparent from the funds flow statement and there were massive adverse translation differences).

POLLY PECK *Extracts from Sunday Telegraph 28 October 1990*

...

It is doubtful if many [banks] knew either the extent of the £300 million of investments in Northern Cyprus, a state recognised only by Turkey and Bangladesh.

The remittability of funds from Northern Cyprus has turned into a major issue. PPI claims to have had £100 million on deposit there. Why could it not get it back when it needed it? One suggestion is that PPI's cash flow effectively doubles as the central bank reserves. ...

In fact, one place to look for information on overseas activity was the funds flow statement, and is now the cash flow statement. We mentioned Tate & Lyle earlier. The extract from Note 29 (below), a note supporting the cash flow statement, puts borrowings into perpective, and certainly suggests that the group knows what it is doing.

Where a foreign enterprise operates in a country with a very high rate of inflation use of the closing rate / net investment method would cause anomalous results in other ways, as is shown by this Example 15.6.

TATE & LYLE *Note 29 to the 1992 accounts*

After taking into account the various interest rate and currency swaps entered into by the Group, the currency and interest rate exposure of the borrowings of the Group as at 26 September 1992 was:

Currency and interest rate exposure

	Total net borrowings	Fixed rate net borrowings	Fixed rate gross borrowings	Average interest rate (%) of fixed rate gross borrowings	Average years to maturity of fixed rate gross borrowings
	£m	£m	£m		
Sterling	24.7	45.4	45.4	12.8	8.3
US dollars	552.4	224.1	236.7	8.5	2.4
Canadian $	6.2	–	–	–	–
Australian $	31.3	–	–	–	–
ERM currencies	37.8	20.6	27.9	8.5	5.0
Others	(10.5)	0.1	0.1	14.3	2.1
	641.9	290.2	310.1	9.1	3.5

The analysis of average interest rates and years to maturity on fixed rate gross borrowings is after adjustments for interest rate swaps.

Example 15.6 Assets in a country with a high rate of inflation

On 31 December 1993 a UK group acquired a property in Bananaland (the currency of which is the BananaSplit) for BSplits 1 million.

	Purchase price BSplits	Exchange rate BSplits to £1	£
31 December 1993	1,000,000	0.25	4,000,000
31 December 1996	1,000,000	32.80	30,488

If the closing rate were used, the property would have virtually disappeared from the 1996 balance sheet.

SSAP 20 therefore suggests that where a very high rate of inflation exists (which it did not define) the local currency financial statements should be adjusted where possible to reflect current price levels before the translation process is undertaken; but it does not specify how current price levels should be arrived at (whether to use CPP or CCA principles).

In the US, SFAS 52 defines a highly inflationary economy as one that has cumulative inflation of approximately 100% or more over a three year period (ie about 26 per cent per annum compound). On that basis, the currencies of Argentina, Brazil, Ecuador, Ghana, Jamaica, Mexico, Nigeria, Peru, Poland, Sierra Leone, Tanzania, Turkey, Uganda, Zaire and Zambia are among those so regarded in recent years. Unfortunately, most companies do not state clearly where they draw the line.

Urgent Issues Task Force Abstract 9, 'Accounting for operations in hyper-inflationary economies', required adjustment for periods ending on or after 23 August 1993 where the cumulative inflation rate over three years is approaching or exceeds 100% ('a level widely accepted internationally as an appropriate criterion') and the operations are material

Where it is not practical to adjust the local currency financial statements to reflect current price levels an alternative is to translate them using the temporal method (explained below). This, in fact, is the required treatment in the US.

Some UK companies adopt a mixture.

RECKITT & COLMAN *Acounting policies 1992 (extract)*

The accounts of overseas subsidiary and associated undertakings are translated into sterling on the following basis:

Assets and liabilities at the rate of exchange ruling at the year-end date except for fixed assets of undertakings operating in countries where hyperinflation exists which are translated at historical rates of exchange.

Profit and loss account items at the average rate of exchange ruling during the financial year. An inflation adjustment is charged in arriving at local currency profits operating in hyperinflation countries before they are translated to reflect the impact on the undertakings' working capital requirements.

Where severe long-term restrictions substantially hinder exercise of the rights of the parent company over the assets of an undertaking FRS 2 requires subsidiaries to be excluded from consolidation.

BOOKER *Extract from accounting policies 1992*

Certain subsidiary undertakings operate in countries overseas where the amount of profit that may be remitted is restricted or where freedom of action may be limited. In the opinion of the directors it would be misleading to consolidate these subsidiaries and the group share of their results is therefore included in profit only to the extent of remittances received. The group's total investment in these subsidiaries is shown as an asset at attributable net asset value either at the date from which this accounting policy was adopted for such companies adjusted for capital subsequently invested or withdrawn, or attributable net asset value at the balance sheet date, whichever is the lower amount.

It behoves the analyst to be on the look out for any evidence of money tied up in areas from which remittance might be difficult or impossible (eg Kenya, Zimbabwe, Northern Cyprus).

The temporal method

In certain circumstances the closing rate/net investment method is inappropriate and the standard then requires the temporal method.

The temporal method is to be used where the trade of the foreign enterprise is more dependent on the economic environment of the investing company's currency than that of its own reporting currency. Under it the consolidated accounts reflect the transactions of the foreign enterprise as if they had been carried out by the investing company.

REUTERS HOLDINGS A*counting policies 1992 (extract)*

Where it is considered that the functional currency of overseas operations is sterling the financial statements are expressed in sterling on the following basis:

1. Fixed assets are translated into sterling at the rates ruling on the date of acquisition as adjusted for any profits or losses from related financial instruments.
2. Monetary assets and liabilities denominated in foreign currency are translated into sterling at the foreign exchange rates ruling at the balance sheet date.
3. Revenue and expenses in foreign currencies are recorded in sterling at the rates ruling at the dates of the transactions.
4. Any gains or losses arising on translation are reported as part of profit.

Practice

1. Obtain the latest report and accounts of Lonrho. Endeavour to establish:

    (i) What Lonrho does, where, and why;
    (ii) Where it raises its money;
    (iii) Where it holds its cash?
    (iv) How it was affected by currency factors in that year?
    (v) How it treated subsidiaries operating in areas of hyper-inflation (if any)?
    (vi) How it perceives its exposure to risk - risk of recession, currency risk, insurrection?

2. Another company with substantial overseas exposure is Grand Metropolitan, assess its international risk; its policies on hedging and on overseas funding.

3. Compare the overall risk of the two investments. Does the market support your assessment?

Chapter 16

PENSIONS AND PENSION FUNDS

The problem with pensions

SSAP 24, 'Accounting for Pension Costs', ensures that readers of accounts today know more about a company's pension plans, pension funding and pension costs than ever before. But as recent developments at Mirror Group Newspapers and Maxwell Communication Corporation have shown, weaknesses and potential problems remain.

Recent press coverage might lead one to believe that at the heart of all the difficulties with pension funds was one man, the late Robert Maxwell. But, without in any way seeking to minimise the depredations of the Mirror Group Newspapers and Maxwell Communication Corporation pensions funds, for all blame to be laid at the door of one person would not only be wrong but most unwise. One thing we can say: Robert Maxwell has put the spotlight on pensions; and that is no bad thing.

The legal system under which pension funds operate must bear part of the blame; so must the conflicts of interest to which it gives rise and the complex but ineffectual regulatory system.

It would be reassuring to believe that the raiding of a pension fund, and / or the misapplication of its investments, could not long remain undetected by audit. But that is not necessarily the case.

The auditor of a company with a pension scheme is required to verify pension costs and payments made to the pension fund trustees; but not to audit the fund itself.

The auditor of a pension fund is appointed and reports in accordance with the rules of the scheme. At the present time, with the exception of contracted out funds, there is no statutory requirement for pension fund accounts to be audited – which will undoubtedly be changed (see p. 97).

The problem with pensions is that there is not one problem but many.

The first difficulty is the variety of pension arrangements which exists, making both reporting and control difficult. Often there are several, sometimes many, distinct arrangements and funds within a single business. BAT, for instance, operates 130 separate pension plans; and most worldwide groups have quite different plans in their various areas of operation.

There are three types of arrangement of which the first two are the most common:

1. *Unfunded pension schemes:* where neither employee nor employer makes contributions over the period of the employment but the employer undertakes either:

    (i) to take care of the ex-employees in their retirement; or
    (ii) to pay a defined pension paid 'out of the till' at the time of payment (which is what happens with civil servants).

    The liability involved can be considerable. At the end of 1992, Unilever Group made provision in its accounts for £1,574m in respect of pensions, almost entirely unfunded ones.

2. *Defined contribution schemes,* under which contributions at a stated rate, sometimes only by the employer but generally by employee and employer, are set aside, frequently with an outside institution such as an insurance company. The cost to the employer can be measured with reasonable certainty, but the benefits depend upon the success with which that outside institution manages the underlying investments.

Most small schemes, and a growing number of those of larger companies, are defined contribution schemes.

3. *Defined benefit schemes*, where in return for contributions, again normally by both employee and employer, the scheme plans, on the retirement of the employee, to pay a pension, based sometimes on average salary but mostly on final salary. In addition, the scheme may provide a lump sum at the time of retirement. In this type of scheme the employer's commitment is open ended (in the case of a defined contribution scheme it is not) and the final cost to him is subject to considerable uncertainty.

Despite recent switching to defined contribution schemes, most schemes operated by large companies are defined benefit schemes.

The three types of scheme give rise to different problems:

1. In the case of a *non-contributory scheme* the employee is entirely dependent on the continued existence, goodwill and profitability of the organisation for which he works or worked. If it goes to the wall, is taken over, or rationalised, he may see nothing.

2. Members of a *defined contribution scheme* generally have greater security in that their money is usually invested with, say, an insurance company, but they depend upon its financial stability and the competence and skill with which it manages the fund. Cases continue to arise of companies which, short of money, fail to pay over not only their contributions but those of employees for some months before finally going into liquidation.

3. By far the greatest problems arise in connection with *defined benefit schemes* (which most frequently are self-administered) and it is upon these that we largely focus.

Defined benefit schemes do not have to be self-administered; and a number of companies, like Bredero, operate schemes based on pensionable salary 'near or at the date of retirement' with the assets 'held separately from Group assets and ... administered by Scottish Widows' Fund in whose managed fund they are invested' ie pass over the management role to outsiders upon whose performance Group costs largely depend. This may well increase costs to the company, but it does provide an element of security to employees.

Who calls the tune?

Historically, company pensions developed for a number of distinct reasons:

1. Altruistic reasons – as already mentioned: the owners of the business may feel some sort of responsibility for long-term employees in their retirement.

2. As a way of retaining key employees.

3. As a means of attracting staff (or possibly simply keeping up with the competition).

4. For the tax advantages they bring.

In short, though, they are in one way or another an exercise in employee relations.

Pension arrangements normally involve a trust set up by the employer; and it is the trust deed which gives the trust its legal status and lays down how it is to operate. This gives rise to the next problem: trust law is arcane, somewhat archaic, and unfamiliar to most businessmen.

Because it is usually the employing company which sets up the trust, the trust deed is normally drafted, and its content laid down, by that company and its legal advisers, rather than jointly by employer, employees and their representatives, or by existing or future pensioners.

It is also the case – whether that is seen as fair or unfair, right or wrong – that the rules of the fund (subject to Inland Revenue and Occupational Pensions Board approval) tend to be laid down, in the first instance at least, by the employer.

In the case of a defined benefits scheme, consultant actuaries are normally employed to assess the levels of contribution necessary to fund the benefits to be provided. If, for any reason, on an actuarial revaluation the fund proves insufficient (ie 'there is a deficiency') the employer is expected in the long run to meet it (though conceivably the rules could provide otherwise).

Can one really rely on the trustees?

The employer, and, perhaps to an even greater extent, employees, ex-employees and pensioners, place considerable reliance on the trustees appointed to run the fund.

Currently, unless the trust deed provides otherwise, there is:

1. Nothing to ensure that trustees are fit and proper persons or have the necessary skills and independence to enable them properly to perform their duties.

2. Nothing to prevent the chairman or managing director of the employing company also being chairman of the trustees (as Robert Maxwell was, and many other chairmen are).

3. Nothing to prevent the finance director of that company being a trustee – indeed it is quite usual.

4. In most cases, nothing to require a specific proportion of the trustees to be employees.

5. Nothing to require ex-employee or pensioner representatives to act as trustees – and this is far from universal, indeed it is relatively unusual.

6. Nothing to ensure that meetings of the trustees are called regularly, with due notice, with a proper agenda and supporting papers – in the case of the Maxwell companies they were not.

7. Nothing to protect trustees who take a stand against what they regard as improper behaviour by their employer.

Pensioners do well to be wary.

Inflation is a key problem

A key problem with all types of pension scheme is inflation:

1. Unless a defined benefits scheme is based on final salary (or some approximation to it), the benefits are likely to be inadequate.

2. Unless a defined contribution scheme is invested in such a way as to provide a hedge against inflation, it too will provide insufficient in the way of pension.

Indexed-linked securities apart, and they are a relatively new development, no form of investment gives both security and perfect protection against inflation. The choice for most of the post-war era for those involved in investing long-term to provide pensions has been between the comparative safety of gilt edged and other fixed interest stocks, the value of which in real terms has declined progressively, and, more risky, investment in property or in equities, both of which over a period have grown, frequently ahead of inflation. But there have been long periods of stagnation and a number of sharp setbacks. The overall growth has not been regular but the result of a limited number of marked upsurges in the equity market. And as investors in general are continually reminded: 'The value of investments can go down as well as up'.

SHELL TRANSPORT AND TRADING *Extracts from Notes 25 to the 1991 and 1992 accounts*

	1992 £m	1991 £m	1990 £m	1989 £m
Plan assets held in trusts, at fair value	14,857	12,862	11,509	13,573
Actual return on plan assets	1,254	1,861	(836)	2,207

The problem of variability of return and the sheer scale of the amounts involved are well illustrated by SHELL TRANSPORT AND TRADING (see bottom of previous column). Shell, in fact, provides an example well worth further study: the 1992 report and accounts devoted no less than one and a half pages to employee retirement plans, their cost and status, and to post-retirement benefits other than pensions (for which, as a result of a change in policy, there was a provision of £793m).

Who owns a surplus (and who makes good any deficit)?

Throughout the 1970s, many defined benefit schemes showed an actuarial deficit. By the end of the 1980s most schemes showed an actuarial surplus. But it was not at all clear to whom that surplus belonged. There were three potential categories of claimant:

1. The employing companies, on the grounds that they set up the scheme, were in a position to dictate the rules, had made most of the contributions for example in 1992 LONRHO reported that the company was expected to bear any deficiency and as a consequence it contributed as much as 34% in respect of some UK schemes, and BRITISH LAND that 'The resulting contribution rate is 28% of pensionable salaries, pending completion of the 1991 triennial valuation'.

2. Employees, ex-employees and pensioners, on the grounds that the pension fund simply represented deferred remuneration (that if they had not been promised a pension they would have expected a higher salary); and that any surplus should be used to provide (so far as the law permits) enhanced benefits. In this they have the support of trade unions.

3. The Inland Revenue, on the ground that contributions by the employer must have been excessive in the past, and that he has had tax relief on them, so if they are repaid, the Revenue are entitled to tax the refund.

Before going further, it should perhaps be emphasised that although it is normal for accounts to place a precise value on an actuarial surplus:

1. It represents a professional opinion;

2. At a particular point of time (commonly only once every three years);

3. On conditions which will prevail (for example inflation, salary increases, pensions and other benefits and investment yields) up to forty or more years hence; and

4. On probabilities (eg life expectancy) even further into the future.

Traditionally actuaries employ three basic methods of valuing the investments held by a pension scheme: (a) historical cost (rarely used); (b) market value; and (c) discounted value; and (d) a number of variations on these methods.

Because values both of equities and properties go up and down (are uncertain), in order to arrive at a prudent valuation, actuaries often take for this purpose not the market value of the assets at a particular date but an adjusted market value based on expected dividend and income streams (the result can be regarded as a sort of smoothing adjustment designed to reduce or eliminate temporary fluctuations).

This commonly gives a valuation below market value – but that is not always the case, as the BAA illustration shows.

BAA *Extracts from the Notes to the 1992 accounts*

... at the latest actuarial valuation, the actuarial value was sufficient to cover 128% of the benefits that have accrued to members.

... At the date of the latest actuarial valuation, the actuarial value of the assets of the Scheme was £462.7m with a market value of £442.6m.

Any smoothing effect would almost certainly be insufficient to protect against a major stock market collapse (such as occurred in the 1920s or 1973–74).

Pressure to reduce surpluses

Nevertheless, there has been pressure upon companies in recent years to reduce pension scheme surpluses. The Pension Scheme Surpluses (Administration) Regulations 1987 set out the assumptions which have to be used to establish the extent of any surplus and procedures for disposing of a surplus. Memorandum No 66 'Pension Scheme Surpluses', published by the Inland Revenue, clarifies practical points.

If the assets of a scheme exceed its liabilities by more than 5% (on the basis of a valuation made in accordance with the Regulations), the trustees must (whether they think it prudent or not) make arrangements to reduce the surplus to 5% or below.

The trustees have four options (any one or combination of which they may choose):

1. Contributions may be reduced or suspended by the employer and / or the employees for up to five years – this is known as taking a contribution holiday.
2. Pension benefits may be improved within Inland Revenue limits. For example: widows' benefits could be provided, pensions in payment could be increased to maintain their purchasing power and / or members' pensions

could be increased up to two-thirds of final remuneration.
3. Dependants' pensions could be introduced.
4. The surplus could be returned to the employer (subject to a flat tax charge of 40%).

This was by no means a prudent change. It entirely disregards the fact that:

1. Investment, both in equities and in property, is by its very nature risky.
2. Property values can fall (in some areas prices fell 25% or more between 1989 and 1992) and remain depressed for long periods.
3. Equity prices rise and fall sharply over quite short time spans (the FT–SE 100 index fell 13.8% over the 8 weeks following from its immediate post-election peak on 11 May 1992) and its not unknown for prices to fall 70% and more between peak and trough (as they did in 1974).

The normal way of handling overfunding if the company does not want to improve benefits is either to take a reduction in contributions or a contribution holiday. Some see this as imprudent. But it may, in fact, be the more prudent choice: once benefits are improved it is difficult, if not impossible, to reduce them again, and the liability has a very long tail.

Few companies seem to seek simply a return of contributions. One which did recently is AITKEN HUME INTERNATIONAL.

AITKEN HUME INTERNATIONAL *Extract from Note 22 to the 1991 accounts*

The actuarial valuation of the UK scheme disclosed a surplus in excess of the maximum permitted by the Surplus Regulations of the Finance Act 1986. In order to reduce the surplus pension benefits have been enhanced and, with the approval of the Superannuation Funds Office, £510,000 was refunded to the principal company, Aitken Hume International plc, on 15 August 1991. The remainder of the surplus will be absorbed by a pension holiday in respect of the participating companies' contributions for the period from 1 October 1990 to 30 November 1991.

The problems are complex as MOLINS explained in a full and frank note in its 1992 accounts.

MOLINS *Extract from Chairman's statement 1992*

Shareholders will recall that a review of the assets and liabilities of the Company's UK pension schemes at 1 January 1992, using the assumptions prescribed by the legislation relevant to the proposed repayment to the Company, indicated combined surpluses of approximately £38m.

We have now agreed proposals with the independent trustees to the schemes which provide for the surpluses to be shared between a gross repayment to the Company (subject to tax at 40%) and the enhancement of members' benefits. After making provision in the schemes for a continuing contribution holiday, the proposals envisage the company receiving a net repayment which, at current market values, would be about £10m after tax. As to members' benefits, the proposals provide, for most people, a 10% increase in pension or pensionable service.

The proposals are being submitted to the members of the schemes for their approval, and are conditional upon 80% acceptance. Subject to members' approval, and then to the necessary formalities for tax clearance, the trustees will be in a position to effect the repayment to the Company. The schemes will continue to enjoy very substantial actuarial surpluses even after implementation of the proposals. Indeed, on the basis of the less restrictive assumptions recommended for funding purposes by the independent actuaries to the schemes, the review of the assets and liabilities at 1 January 1992 showed surpluses of £90m, less than half of which is earmarked for the current proposals.

At the AGM the Chairman added:
The proposal for providing for part of the surpluses in the UK pension schemes to be shared ... has been taken a step further. In particular, the condition requiring acceptance by a substantial majority of the members of the pension schemes has now been satisfied. Members' acceptances are still coming in ...

Things to look out for

The Molins illustration highlights the need to study the usual note on pensions with care and suggests many of the things to be on the look out:

1. Subnormal (or abnormally high) charges in the profit and loss account;
2. Pensions holidays;
3. Prepayments, refunds, deficiencies and surpluses;
4. Changes to benefits; and
5. Changes to assumptions (or unrealistic assumptions).

Downright fraud, especially if there is collusion among top management, is difficult for an auditor to detect, and virtually impossible for the outsider to spot from the accounts alone. The existence of a dominant chairman / chief executive, an absence of independence on the part of trustees (eg if they are chaired by that same chairman / chief executive), and any use of family controlled investment companies, should be sufficient to give rise to suspicion. But it will not be easy to detect, except perhaps on a company visit, when it is perfectly legitimate to ask about pensions.

Dishonesty apart, companies employ a number of devices in relation to pensions some of which are undoubtedly questionable. The relative independence of trustees (and often their lack of

commercial/investment experience), the fact that in many cases the need to make pension payments from the fund is somewhat distant, means that despite the vast sums involved (around £400 billion), control is weak.

The assessment of pension fund contributions and the valuation of the fund are a matter for the professional expertise of the actuary. EUROPEAN LEISURE explains very clearly what is involved.

EUROPEAN LEISURE *Note 4 to 1992 accounts (Extract)*

Contributions to the Company's major defined benefit pension scheme are determined by a qualified actuary on the basis of triennial valuations using the defined accrued benefit method. Under this method a stable contribution percentage is set based upon calculating a series of contribution rates over a period of not less than forty years following the valuation date. These rates are obtained by dividing the sum of the following items by the present value at the beginning of the year of members' earnings in that year:

(a) the present value at the beginning of each year following the valuation date of the benefits which will accrue in the year in question by reference to service in that year and projected salaries at the end of that year; and

(b) the present value at the beginning of the same year of the increase in that year, if any, in the accrued liability (as defined below) by reference to service prior to the year in question and salaries at the end of that year.

The calculations allow for the anticipated demographic projection of the membership including, in the case of the Company, the addition of new entrants. Withdrawals are allowed for in the calculation of the contribution rate but not in the calculation of accrued liability. The accrued liability at any time is calculated as the present value of the wind-up benefits as defined in the trust deed and rules and, in the case of the Company, allowance is made for 5% per annum increases on accrued benefits in excess of guaranteed minimum pensions up to the date of normal retirement.

Even if there is no surplus, then maybe the actuary will (or can be persuaded by the company to) change his assumptions. If not, it could always find another actuary who was prepared to take a more rosy view of future investment returns (or to assume lower pay, or existing pension, growth).

BM GROUP *Comparison of 1988 and 1992 accounts*

1988 Accounts: assumed that investment return would exceed wage and salary increases by 1%. 1992: assumed investment return 10% and pay growth 7%.

Changes in assumption of this magnitude have a substantial effect on any apparent pensions deficit (possibly converting a deficit into a surplus) and on pension costs.

Some companies, like ROYAL BANK OF SCOTLAND report the actuaries' assumptions in real terms (ie after making due allowance for the Retail Price Index).

ROYAL BANK OF SCOTLAND *Extract from Note 3 to the 1992 accounts*

The principal assumptions were that the annual rate of return on investments would be 2.5 per cent higher than the annual increase in salaries, 4.5 per cent higher than the annual increase in present and future pensions and 4.0 per cent higher than the annual increase in equity dividends.

On the basis that wages and salaries typically rise 1 per cent or so more than the going rate of inflation, this implies a return of about 3.5 per cent more than inflation. Recognising how difficult it is to match, let alone beat, inflation over the long term, the bank's assumptions could, to some, appear ambitious. Nevertheless, 'The actuarial valuation [at 30 June 1991] ... disclosed that the actuarial value of the assets was sufficient to cover 115 per cent of the benefits that had accrued to members after allowing for expected future increases in earnings ... The surplus is being corrected by a suspension of the cash contributions made by the Bank ...'

At one time it was easy to create a surplus (and in 1979–81 many companies did) by making people redundant, creating so-called 'early-leavers' whose pension was frozen (or grew minimally) until 65. The state pension scheme now provides employees with some protection in this regard, but a company can still use the method to gain at the ex-employees' expense.

BURNFIELD *Extract from Note 27 to the 1990 accounts*

Following the reorganisation of the group's activities in the UK the actuary has assessed that a surplus of £187,000 has arisen as a result of redundancies in the eleven months ended 31 December 1990. This surplus has been dealt with as a reduction of the extraordinary cost [of restructuring] (note 8) and as part of the increase in the pension prepayment (note 18).

Pension schemes and the acquirer

The acquisition of a company with an over-funded scheme offers useful opportunities. Many companies, in an inflationary period, provide a greater element of protection than they are required to under the terms of the fund (eg out of loyalty to former employees, they increase pensions, where possible, in line with inflation even though the scheme's provisions do not require this). An acquirer who feels he owes no such loyalty to the staff of an acquired company won't do this, and may even close the fund, take any surplus into account in his acquisition calculations, and use it elsewhere in the business eg to prop up an existing fund. Merging funds neatly spreads any acquired surplus around. There was, however, an outcry over HANSON's treatment of the Imperial Pension Scheme when that group was acquired and, more recently, over Government plans possibly not to transfer all the BR pension fund on privatisation.

Self-investment

In the past pension funds were free to invest either in shares of the company or in land and buildings which were then rented by it, or to lend money to it. Thus, not only were the fortunes of employees tied to those of their company, so sometimes, and to an unpredictable extent, were their future pension benefits. Occasionally, loans to the parent were on such favourable terms that they bordered on the dishonest. Nevertheless, the directors of the parent were reasonably assured that on any contested vote the pension fund trustees (whom they had appointed) would loyally follow the party line.

Pension funds are now, generally, prohibited from tying up more than 5% of their assets in their parent company. But until trustees are truly independent, there is nothing to prevent their investing in other companies at the request of their parent.

Sex equality and other recent developments

The ruling of the European Court of Justice *Barber & Guardian Royal Exchange* raised the question of the need to pay pensions to men and women at the same age. To avoid any contingent liability, a number of companies (including ECC GROUP) have over the past couple of years changed the rules of their pension schemes so that men and women retire at the same age (65 in the case of ECC), which can substantially affect costs.

Another area which is causing concern is the need for companies to follow from 1994 UITF 6, 'Accounting for Post Retirement Benefits'. This involves changing from a system of recognising the cost of retiree health benefits when the money is paid out, to a system recognising the expense when the obligation is incurred. Retiree health benefits are largely an American phenomenon, so UITF 6 is unlikely to have a major impact on most UK companies. But this is potentially a major problem for companies like SHELL, BP and ICI. To put things into perspective: in the US, GENERAL MOTORS grasped the nettle in February 1993 with a $20.8 billion charge after tax, representing $33.38 a share (and estimated the annual ongoing charge would be $1.4bn, or, in 1992 terms, $2.05 a share.)

Several UK companies have replaced defined benefit schemes with non-contributory defined contribution schemes because recent changes in pensions legislation would, under the existing scheme, impose an open-ended liability which could not be countenanced.

The recent recession caused a number of companies to question the automatic increase of pensions in payment for inflation. Most schemes provide for a stated (maximum) level of automatic protection (eg 3 per cent) but in the buoyant 1980s many in fact provided much better protection than that.

Pension costs and the concept of prudence

The prudence concept, under which:

1. Revenue and profits are not anticipated but are recognised by inclusion in the profit and loss account only when realised in the form of cash or of other assets the ultimate realisation of which can be assessed with reasonable certainty; on the other hand,
2. Provision is made for all known liabilities whether the amount of these is known with certainty or is a best estimate in the light of the information

does not apply to pension costs. Variations from regular cost, such as:

1. Experience surpluses or deficiencies;
2. The effects on the actuarial value of accrued benefits of changes in actuarial assumptions or methods;
3. Retroactive changes in benefits or in conditions of membership;
4. Increases in pensions in payment or to deferred pensions for which provision has not previously been made

are, instead, spread forward over the remaining service lives of current employees. This can result in future cost levels considerably greater than perhaps they ought to be, ie it is a form of rear-end

loading of costs, which is ordinarily viewed by accountants as unacceptable, and imprudent.

The recession of the early 1990s caused a number of companies to rationalise, and to create large scale redundancies. Since this involved transferring or repaying substantial sums in respect of past pension contributions of former employees, it had spectacular effects both on degree of funding and on the size of funds (see in particular the effect on BT in the year to 31 March 1994. It plans (1) to resume contributions from April 1993; and (2) make a special contribution in 1994 of £800m; after a period of pensions holiday).

Pension law reform

The report of the Pension Law Review Committee chaired by Professor Roy Goode has recommended wide-ranging changes. They include the appointment of a Pensions Regulator; no contribution holidays if the funding level would fall below the 100% minimum solvency level; funded schemes would have to meet a minimum solvency standard; the actuarial profession should tighten its methodology and range of assumptions; trustees should be automatically disqualified on grounds similar to those under the Company Directors Disqualification Act 1986; active members should be entitled to appoint one third of trustees in earnings related schemes and two-thirds for money-purchase schemes; auditors of occupational pension schemes must report serious irregularities to the Regulator; flexible guidelines for investment; establishment of a compensation scheme; the report and accounts should be available to members and lodged with the Pensions Registrar.

Practice

Obtain the latest report and accounts of the Shell Transport and Trading Company. Consider:

1. The way in which Shell provides for pensions and accounts for pension costs;
2. The significance of the total amount of Shell's pension fund investments;
3. The adequacy or otherwise of information on the actuarial assumptions employed.

Chapter 17

EFFECTS OF INFLATION

Traditionally, accounts are prepared on a historical cost basis. That is to say, assets and liabilities, income and expenditure, are all stated on the basis that a £ is a £, and a $ is a $, whether paid (or received) in 1991, 1981, 1971, ... or 1901, and will be the same in 2001 or 2101. In terms of purchasing power, that is manifestly untrue.

As inflation has, from time to time risen, accountants and others have expressed dissatisfaction with the historical cost convention, and have sought alternatives. But no obvious alternative acceptable to all (preparers and users of accounts, companies and investors, taxpayers and taxgatherers, academics and laymen) has emerged, and before agreement on a satisfactory compromise has ever been reached, the rate of inflation has always fallen back to a level at which the pain of change appears to exceed that brought by the unsatisfactory nature of accounts in an inflationary period (to less, say, than 10%).

Evidence suggests a degree of satisfaction, not to say self-satisfaction, on the part of preparers, not matched by the users of historical cost accounts.

Why the present position is unsatisfactory

Lack of agreement on a solution must not be allowed to hide the fact that:

1. Inflation is undesirable.
2. It is particularly painful:

    (i) To certain types of individual (eg those holding fixed interest securities and others on fixed incomes); and

    (ii) To those sectors of the economy, eg trade, industry and finance, hit by the higher interest rates which it brings.

3. In an inflationary situation, accounts provide an unsatisfactory view either of the profitability or the state of affairs of a business;

4. The 'cult of the equity' depends upon the concept that equity shares provide a hedge against inflation. Without inflation there would be no need to provide a hedge; no cult of the equity, and no reverse yield gap. That is to say, the traditional order would return under which gilts and bonds provided security of capital and income, preference shares a higher yield with somewhat greater risk, and equities a higher yield still with more risk.

Inflation is difficult to measure

Economists and laymen differ in the way they define inflation. But both recognise it when they see it. We will use the term to indicate a situation where the £ ($, or any other local currency) in one's pocket gradually buys less and less of things generally (apparently, the £ seems to become worth less and less).

It is necessary to distinguish this *general inflation* from changes in price of specific products (eg because of shortage or glut, locally or worldwide, changes which are possibly temporary or seasonal in nature, but which may be permanent).

Even prices of goods and services which do not suffer from seasonal effects, shortage or glut, do not change uniformly; and the existence of seasonal and other specific price changes makes it difficult to estimate the rate of general inflation.

To estimate general inflation, therefore, it is necessary to arrive at some agreed basket of goods and services. There are in the UK several measures of general inflation which, because they adopt different baskets of goods and services, produce somewhat different indices of inflation.

The most general measure of inflation, and that preferred by economists, is the *gross domestic product deflator*, which is a measure of inflation for the economy as a whole. Gross domestic product is a measure of the total annual output of a country, excluding income from abroad. It can be calculated in three ways: based on income, output or expenditure. In theory each method should give the same answer; but because of errors in measurement and estimation, they rarely do.

The gross domestic product deflator is found by dividing the current value of consumers' expenditure by the volume estimate measured at constant prices. This adds another imponderable: how does one measure, accurately, the volume of activity of an entire economy? To add to the difficulties, while the GDP is estimated quarter by quarter, those estimates are revised from time to time over a period of several years. Since the GDP deflator does not become finally known for perhaps two years, it is useless for the purpose of annual accounts.

Another possible measure of general inflation is the *index of factory gate prices* but this reflects published price lists, and overstates prices in time of recession since it takes no account of discounts offered by companies desperate to sell.

This virtually compels accountants to base their figures on the *Retail Prices Index* (and those indices which derive from it). But it is ease and speed of availability, rather than the suitability of the RPI, that has led to its being adopted as a measure of general inflation in almost all the various methods of inflation accounting put forward by the accountancy profession.

The RPI is a measure of the change in a basket of goods and services which sets out to be typical of all but the top 4% of the population in income terms. But there almost certainly is no such person. By aiming to make the index typical of a wide range of individuals whose ages, incomes and tastes differ greatly, statisticians ensure that the RPI is probably representative of no one.

The UK RPI is a measure of the changes in the average price of a basket of those goods and services on which most households spend their income. The actual goods and services included in the basket and the weights given to each item are determined by the Family Expenditure Survey, in which approximately 7,000 households (a figure which has grown over the years from 2,000 in 1914) a year provide a record of their spending over a fortnightly period. Furthermore, they are changed from time to time.

The main goods and services represented are food, alcoholic drink, tobacco, housing (though there is argument over whether mortgage payments should be included), fuel and light, household goods (which cover everything from furniture and furnishings to pet care), household services (postage, telephones, domestic services, fees and subscriptions), clothing and footwear, motoring expenditure, fares and other travel costs, leisure goods (eg audio equipment, records and tapes, toys, photographic equipment, books and newspapers, and gardening), and leisure services (television licences and rentals, entertainment and recreation).

The RPI is untypical of any one family, or type of consumer. And it does not even pretend to be a measure of business (manufacturing, trade or service industry) prices.

Nevertheless, general price inflation clearly exists; and makes figures for one year or period difficult to compare with those for another.

We consider the problem of changing prices under seven heads:

1. Depreciation is insufficient;
2. Is revaluation the solution?
3. Rents in an inflationary period;
4. Stocks and stock profits;
5. Other components of working capital in an inflationary period;
6. Gains on borrowed money;
7. Adjusting figures in historical summaries.

Finally, we look at what, if anything, accounts tell us about the effects of inflation.

Depreciation is insufficient

In accounting terms, depreciation is simply the writing off of an asset over its effective life. Provided that the method chosen is appropriate, the historical cost convention accepts that, unless its value has been permanently impaired, an asset may be stated at cost less provision for depreciation to date; it is not necessary to revalue it, or to have regard to any possible difference between its saleable value and book value.

But the writing off of depreciation does more than this: in the case of a business the profits of which equal or exceed the charge for depreciation, it prevents the distribution by way of dividend (which *might* otherwise take place) of profits equal to that depreciation charge.

It is sometimes suggested that depreciation *provides funds* for the replacement of the asset at the end of its effective life. This is an oversimplification. It neither produces the money in the first place, nor does it prevent its being spent on anything else – dividends apart. Subject to the qualification already made about the business being profitable:

1. Depreciation ensures that the capital (ie the business is maintained, not that cash is available for the replacement of assets.
2. Depreciation does nothing to determine the form of those net assets. Indeed, most businessmen expect most of the time to find a better (more profitable) use for funds than retaining them in the bank. That is the last place the money will be.
3. So long as a business generates each year, or is in a position to raise by way of loan or share capital, sufficient to replace fixed assets at the end of their effective life, all is well, and the retention of cash balances specifically for this purpose is unnecessary, even undesirable.
4. Historic cost is a relatively poor indicator of the cost of replacing an asset at the end of its effective life, because:

    (i)   Asset cost reflects a complex economic, possibly monopoly, situation in which suppliers come and go, integrate vertically and horizontally, and change both pricing and product policies.
    (ii) Assets are rarely replaced by an identical unit: improvements and other modifications are made. Consider, for instance, the way in which the medium-priced saloon car has evolved over the last 20 years – disc brakes, anti-lock brakes, power steering, electrically adjustable wing and door mirrors, central locking, sun-roofs, manufacturer-supplied stereo equipment, have all become common-place over that period. One car is thus not a direct replacement for its predecessor, except in the broad sense of being a means of transport.
    (iii) Methods of manufacture, and the product range, change over time, so the plant used to make them necessarily changes.

5. Depreciation is also seen as a cost, as a measure of fixed asset consumption, in arriving at stock values and in fixing selling prices. Here, again, inflation brings problems.

    Imagine a manufacturer with two identical lathes; one cost £10,000 in 1986; the other £20,000 in 1993. Estimated useful life is 10 years at the end of which the saleable value will equal the cost of removal. The manufacturer expects each lathe to be used for 1,000 hours per annum. Each lathe makes the same product, which takes 5 hours to produce. On a historical cost basis, the cost of items produced on the first lathe will include £5 in respect of depreciation, and those on the second £10. But is it appropriate to use (these) differ-

ent figures: (a) in placing a value on stock for balance sheet purposes; or (b) in setting selling prices? Or should regard be had to replacement cost? Almost without exception, industry adopts the historical cost basis in valuing stock (probably using average depreciation for a group of similar machines of different ages), though prices charged will often reflect replacement cost.

To summarise: critics of historical cost accounting maintain that in a period of inflation (and the effects live on long after one):

1. The value of fixed assets tends to be understated.
2. The depreciation charge is an inadequate measure of asset consumption.
3. Insufficient funds may be available to enable fixed assets to be replaced at the end of their effective life.
4. The problem is made worse by the present UK tax system:

    (i) Relief in respect of capital allowances is restricted to the historic cost of an asset.
    (ii) There is no relief from corporation tax on any profits ploughed back in order to provide for the *increased* cost of replacement.

Is revaluation the solution?

UK generally accepted accounting practice permits the revaluation of fixed assets, but does not require it. Few UK companies revalue plant and machinery or fixed assets other than freehold and leasehold land and buildings. One notable exception is BRITISH AIRWAYS, which at 31 March 1992 showed its fleet, as valued in 1988, at £3,873 million.

There is a growing tendency for companies, more especially small and medium sized companies which formerly revalued land and buildings to cease doing so – cynically one might add, now that values are no longer going up.

Where revaluation for balance sheet purposes of fixed assets is adopted, the reserves normally increase, and the charge for depreciation rises. While this may provide a better measure of consumption (or would if the principle was applied to all fixed assets), it has a doubly adverse effect on return on capital employed: (1) the return goes down; and (2). the capital employed goes up, as is shown by Example 17.1 on page 101.

There is, in historic cost accounting, no rationale for revaluation of fixed assets, and many countries do not permit it. There is certainly none for revaluation on a piecemeal (even asset-by-asset) and irregular basis.

Example 17.1 The effect of revaluation

Extra plc revalues its leasehold property at the beginning of an accounting year as follows:

Balance Sheets (extracts):

	Before Revaluation £	Effect £	After Revaluation £
Fixed Assets:			
Leasehold Land & Buildings (25 year life assumed)	400,000	600,000	1,000,000
Capital	500,000		500,000
P & L A/C	100,000		100,000
Revaluation Reserve	–	600,000	600,000
Capital employed	600,000	600,000	1,200,000

Imagine that the profit and loss account for the year is:

	Before Revaluation £	Effect £	After Revaluation £
Profit before Depreciation	100,000		100,000
Depreciation	16,000	24,000	40,000
Net Profit	84,000	24,000	60,000

Return on opening capital employed:

After:

$$\frac{84,000}{600,000} = 14\%$$

Before:

$$\frac{60,000}{1,200,000} = 5\%$$

The Alternative Accounting Rules in Part C of Schedule 4, Companies Act 1985 recognise in addition to historic cost the following bases of valuation:

1. Tangible fixed assets may be included at market value or current cost.
2. Intangibles, except goodwill, may be included at current cost.
3. Investments may be included at market value or at directors' valuation.

This is not entirely satisfactory, and to make matters worse, neither market value nor current cost is clearly defined for this purpose.

Companies which revalue fixed assets use a variety of bases, often employing one basis for some assets, and another for others.

ED51, *Accounting for Fixed Assets and Revaluations* (published in May 1990) attempts to bring some order into a diversity of practice by restricting piecemeal valuations and proposing that valuations

be kept up to date (not allowing those over five years old to be used) but it has not yet become a Financial Reporting Standard.

ED51 makes it clear that:

1. Mere revaluation of fixed assets is an inadequate response to the problem of reflecting the effects of changing prices on an undertaking; and
2. Under neither the historic cost, nor the current cost, convention, is the balance sheet intended to be a statement of the value of an enterprise as a going concern.

And it might have added: Nor under historic cost is the profit and loss account framed to provide an indication of the current cost of the fixed assets consumed during the period.

The ASB Discussion Paper, 'The Role of Valuation in Financial Reporting', published on 25 March 1993, suggests a move towards regular revaluation is afoot. US GAAP do not permit revaluation of fixed assets at all.

Rents in an inflationary period

One factor neglected by either of the methods of inflation accounting explored by the accountancy profession (CPP and CCA) is that of rents.

The tradition has grown up of regular, often upward-only, rent reviews of shop, office and factory premises. Rents thus rise in discrete steps, sometimes very sharply. Inflation accounting ignores this threat altogether; yet the effects of rent rises can be sufficient to turn an organisation, eg a high street store, from profit into loss.

What is more, the effect can be delayed. If, for instance, a lease with 5 year rent reviews was negotiated in 1986 at £100,000, and rental values rose sharply in 1987–88, to, say, £350,000, after which rents flattened, an increase of £250,000 could surprise in a market seen as flat, but that is what would be likely to happen. Big organisations may be in a position to resist such an increase by threatening to move; most small ones, it seems, cannot. Though that could change.

Gains on borrowed money

Arguably, a company which borrows money and later repays gains, if the value of the currency unit in which the debt was expressed fell over the period, at the expense of the creditor. Reference to this gain rarely appears either in published accounts or reviews of operations.

Stock and stock profits

The effect of all generally accepted methods of stock valuation is the same: the charge to the profit and loss account represents earlier purchases and the stock in the balance sheet, the cost of those items received latest.

In the case of the first-in first-out basis:

1. In, and shortly after, a period of inflation, or more strictly, one in which unit stock values have risen (fallen), there will be stock gains (losses). Accounts rarely disclose stockholding gains or losses separately, so gross profit margins are inflated when prices are rising, and this flattering disappears, and margins appear to fall, once inflation is under control.

2. The RPI gives a relatively poor indication of changes in unit stock values, which are heavily industry (or even manufacturer / supplier specific).

3. After a period of inflation, a company which continues to hold the same physical stock as it did will tie up more working capital in stock. If it does not retain, or raise, money to cover this, its capital base (measured in real terms) will be eroded, and there is likely to be pressure on liquid funds.

4. No stock relief currently exists for corporation tax purposes: stockholding gains are profits for tax purposes.

5. Where, as is the case with GUINNESS, financing costs are added to stock values of maturing stocks, the higher levels of interest due to inflation become part of stock values (rather than fall against profits for the period).

GUINNESS *Extract from Note 15 of 1992 Accounts*

Stocks of maturing whisky and other spirits include financing costs amounting to £528m (1991 – £504m). A net adjustment to stocks of £17m (1991 – £13m) has been credited to the profit and loss account within net operating costs comprising £125m (1991 – £116m) of interest incurred during the year less £108m (1991 – £103m) in respect of sales during the year.

Stockholding gains (losses) are rarely disclosed separately. In some industries, like the oil industry, their effect differs spectacularly from year to year.

Consider, for instance, BP , a summary of whose accounts for 1991 and 1992 is shown alongside. In 1990 there had been a gain of £477m. So the effect on the historical cost profit of stock gains and losses swung between 1990 and 1991 by £1,106m (a swing which was roughly 1½ times the entire HC profit for 1992!).

Other components of working capital

Even though no account is taken of the fact in historic cost accounts, in a period of rising prices debtors and creditors tend to increase as result of price

---

BP *Extract from Group Income Statements 1992*

	1992 £m	1991 £m
Gross profit	5,938	6,431
Distribution and administration expenses	4,307	4,145
Exploration expenditure written off	316	425
	1,315	1,861
Other income	569	510
Replacement cost operating profit	1,884	2,371
Profit on sale of operations	70	242
Restructuring costs	(1,064)	(58)
Replacement cost profit before interest and tax	890	2,555
Stockholding gains (losses)	(106)	(629)
Historical cost operating profit before interest and tax	784	1,926
...		

---

changes (the same volume of goods being sold (purchased) at a higher price than in the previous period, and it is necessary to plough back profits (or raise capital) in order to meet this, otherwise liquidity comes under strain.

Some companies actually benefit from inflation, eg food shops and stores groups have stocks wholly or largely financed by suppliers, customers pay cash and they gain from rising property values, financed by debt.

Adjusting figures in historical summaries

In studying historical summaries it is necessary to have regard to changes in the underlying value of the reporting currency (normally the £). Most companies do not publish this information, and hope that the analyst will not bother, since it tends to be unflattering. One which does is BP (see page 103). Without using either the index of retail prices or the adjusted figures, ask yourself:

1. In which year(s) did turnover fall in real terms?

2. In which year was (a) the replacement cost operating profit greatest; (b) the historic cost profit greatest?

3. Have (a) earnings per share; (b) dividends per share kept up with inflation?

4. Which measure of profit: replacement cost or historic cost best indicates BP's success?

BP *Information on price changes 1992 accounts*					£ million
As reported:	1988	1989	1990	1991	1992
Turnover	24,706	29,056	33,039	32,613	33,250
Replacement cost operating profit	2,314	2,423	2,725	2,371	1,884
Replacement cost profit before exceptional items and discontinued operations	937	890	1,039	928	536
Historical cost profit (loss)	1,210	2,134	1,688	415	(458)
Earnings (loss) per ordinary share					
On profit (loss) for the year	20.0p	39.0p	31.5p	7.7p	(8.5)p
On replacement cost profit before exceptional items and discontinued operations	15.5p	16.3p	19.4p	17.2p	9.9p
Dividends per ordinary share	13.50p	14.90p	16.05p	16.80p	10.5p
Ordinary share price: High	295p	341p	376p	357p	296p
Daily average	257p	293p	335p	329p	240p
Low	233p	249p	304p	276p	184p
Adjusted for average UK Retail Price Index of	106.9	115.2	126.1	133.5	138.5
Turnover	32,009	34,933	36,288	33,834	33,250
Replacement cost operating profit	2,998	2,913	2,993	2,460	1,884
Replacement cost profit before exceptional items and discontinued operations	1,214	1,070	1,141	963	536
Historical cost profit (loss)	1,568	2,566	1,854	431	(458)
Earnings (loss) per ordinary share:					
On profit (loss) for the year	25.9p	46.9p	34.6p	8.0p	(8.5)p
On replacement cost profit before exceptional items and discontinued operations	20.1p	19.6p	21.3p	17.8p	9.9p
Dividends per ordinary share	17.49p	17.91p	17.63p	17.43p	10.5p
Ordinary share price: High	382p	410p	413p	370p	296p
Daily average	333p	352p	368p	341p	240p
Low	3021p	299p	334p	286p	184p

Accounting for Inflation

Very few companies now produce either CCA or CPP accounts. One which still prepares a group current cost profit and loss account and balance sheet as its primary accounts is BRITISH GAS.

Others in the privatised sectors, including water companies (eg ANGLIAN WATER SERVICES which produces four pages of regulatory information of which two are devoted to current cost data),produce CCA information. Note the spectacularly different HC and CCA balance sheets of ANGLIAN WATER.

SOUTHERN ELECTRIC includes no less that eight pages in its 1992 accounts devoted to CCA, including a CCA cash flow statement.

A number of manufacturing companies make reference to inflation in their directors' report, but few mention it in the accounts themselves.

Practice

Obtain a copy of the accounts of BAT Industries. Consider the significance of inflation to the group. Why is it more difficult to account for or explain the effects of inflation in the case of a group like BAT than is the case for a UK-based company?

ANGLIAN WATER SERVICES *Extract from Historic Cost and Current Cost Balance Sheets at 31 March 1992*

	£m	£m
Historic cost balance sheet		
Assets employed		
Fixed assets	1,814.3	1,596.4
Working capital	(505.6)	(383.8)
Net assets employed	1,308.7	1,212.6
Financed by		
Called up share capital	294.9	294.7
Profit and loss account	1,013.3	917.9
Share premium account	0.5	–
	1,308.7	1,212.6
Current cost balance sheet		
Assets employed (extracts)		
Fixed assets	11,409.0	10,714.6
Working capital	(96.7)	(116.5)
Net assets employed	10,777.4	10,288.2
Financed by		
Called up share capital	860.0	860.0
Profit and loss account	163.0	87.1
Current cost reserves	9,754.4	9,341.1
	10,777.4	10,288.2

Chapter 18

INTERIM REPORTS

Uses and shortcomings

Unless a listed company makes a share or debt issue, or an acquisition, or is involved in a takeover bid, its interim statement provides the major, if not the only, source of financial information available to investors on its fortunes and activities from the publication of one year's accounts to the next.

Nevertheless, interim reports do have numerous shortcomings:

1. There is currently no legal requirement to produce other than annual accounts.
2. No accounting standard calls for half yearly figures.
3. The Stock Exchange requirement, first introduced twenty years ago, has shown little or no development since. Changes are being considered, but not before time. Currently, it does not reflect the many improvements which have taken place either in the Companies Acts or in accounting standards regarding annual accounts. For example, it does not insist on the interest charge being shown.
4. In the past they have normally been unaudited. Indeed, the auditor has often not been involved with them in any way, so the treatment of items at the interim stage was not that which he insisted upon at the year-end. The Yellow Book, the Stock Exchange's *The Listing Rules*, requires it to be stated if the half-yearly report has not been audited, and for the auditor's report to be included if it has.
5. They are not required to include a balance sheet.
6. Financial Reporting Standard 1 on 'Cash Flow Statements' does not apply to interim statements. It should.

7. Exceptional items need not be disclosed separately. FRS 3 does not mention them.
8. No requirement exists for them to disclose either the effect on turnover or profits of acquisitions or disposals; their planned accounting treatment; or balance sheet effect.
9. Interim statements are not required to present a true and fair view.
10. The chairman's comments on progress (and even on aqcuisitions and disposals) in the first half are often sketchy.

A shame there is no balance sheet

Although interim statements currently do not have to include a balance sheet, over a quarter of FT-100 companies do so, and the position is improving all the time. One cannot help wondering whether the failure of the other three-quarters to do so:

1. Reflects the fact that they did not actually produce one internally. (It is *possible* to estimate profits without reference to a balance sheet, and some companies do.)
2. Stems from reservations on the part of management about the accuracy of the balance sheet at the interim stage (and thus presumably about the profit and loss account which gives rise to it); or
3. Suggests a failure to see the significance of a balance sheet to shareholders; or
4. Is a deliberate decision: a balance sheet might reveal too much (eg financial strain); or
5. Reflects unwillingness to bear the additional expense; or
6. Simply represents slavish following of the Stock Exchange requirement.

Most, though not all, listed companies prepare an interim balance sheet for internal use, and we suspect where a balance sheet is lacking, that is due to a combination of factors 2 to 6.

Ironically, in presentations to analysts and fund managers, after the interim results companies often in the past disclosed at least summary balance sheets, but did not publish them.

Audit and the true and fair view

Although there is no requirement for interim statements to give a true and fair view, they are clearly intended and expected to do so. But, in their present form (ie lacking a balance sheet) it is unlikely that any self-respecting auditor would accept that they do.

The very idea that a once a year check on the accuracy and fairness of figures is sufficient is surely outdated – recent events in MIRROR GROUP NEWSPAPERS (where the auditors apparently sought to conduct an interim audit of the pension fund but were not allowed to do so) have shown just how quickly matters can change. Six-monthly audit would narrow the window of opportunity for fraud or error.

Unless specifically asked to review the half-year's figures, auditors have tended to pay scant regard to interim statements; possibly none at the time they were produced. Most auditors do examine them later but largely as a means of detecting:

1. Trends which might affect their view at the end of the year, for example, a sharp downturn in sales in the half-year which might suggest that stocks were overvalued.
2. Inconsistencies and anomalies (lest they cause them embarrassing questions).

Auditors also use management information (eg monthly reports) to support the annual figures, but they are not called upon to audit it as such. Perhaps if they were (and what we are talking about is checking the basis and accuracy of the information which management is using to steer the business from day to day), not only would the idea that interim statements should be audited present less of a problem, but analysts (and management) would have more confidence in the information on which decisions were being made.

The present shortcomings of unaudited interim statements are well-illustrated by the 1989 interim figures of JAMES WILKES (alongside).

The chairman's statement which accompanied these interim results made no mention of any profits on the sale of property.

FRS 3 should ensure that in future companies do not take material property profits as part of the profit for the year without disclosing the fact.

JAMES WILKES *Extract from Half-year's results – unaudited*

	Six months ended 30 Jun 1989 (Unaudited) £	Six months ended 30 Jun 1988 (Unaudited) £	Year ended 31 Dec 1988 (Audited) £
Turnover	10,706,900	2,900,727	9,164,243
Profit before Tax	2,015,700	424,507	1,318,863

The following November Wilkes wanted to make a large acquisition, financed by a 1 for 1 rights issue. To do so it needed to make a forecast for the full year, and was forced to admit that the interim results had included a £1.1m profit on the sale of a property where completion wasn't due to take place until June the following year.

JAMES WILKES *Extract from circular to shareholders and report and accounts for 1990*

... your Directors forecast that the profit on ordinary activities before taxation of the James Wilkes Group for the year ending 31 December 1989 will be not less than £2.3 million.

In its interim results for the six months ended 30 June 1989, the Group recognised a profit amounting to some £1.1 million on the sale of a property ... the terms of sale were that completion will take place in June 1990.

Your directors now consider that in the context of the profit forecast for the current financial year, it is prudent not to recognise a profit on the sale of the property until completion in 1990 and accordingly it is excluded from the forecast ... above.

Extract from annual report and accounts for year ended 31 December 1990:

	1990 £000	1989 £000
Profit on ordinary activities before taxation	5,613	2,502
Earnings per share (p)	22.4	20.3

There were no Exceptional or Extraordinary items, and no mention of whether the property sale that was due to complete in June 1990 had gone through or not. If it in fact went through, the profit of £1.1m made it possible for the company to report a rise, rather than a fall, in eps.

The James Wilkes example enables us to make another point: the need to follow through from one annual report to the next, and from interim results to annual report, being on the look out for inconsistencies and subtle changes of emphasis.

Do interim reports give warning of impending disaster?

Interim statements sometimes provide clear warning of trouble ahead; though, because of the lack of a balance sheet, not always. A classic case is PARKFIELD.

PARKFIELD *Extract from Interim Report – October 1989*

Half year ended	31.10.89	31.10.88
Group results (unaudited)	£000	£000
Turnover	168,640	132,390
Profit before taxation	17,346	8,087
Earnings per share (p)	17.7	9.9

Chairman's Review of the half year

For the first six months of the year I am pleased to report another set of record results with pre-tax profits up 103% to £17.3m and earnings per share up 79% to 17.7p. Your board has declared an interim dividend of 5p (net) compared with 3p (net) at last year's interim stage.

... the Group [is] in a strong position to maintain over the coming years our exceptional record of growth in earnings per share.

This review was dated 9 January 1990. On 21 June 1990 the company announced that profits for the year ended 30 April 1990 were going to be disappointing as they were unlikely to exceed those of the previous year.

The shares were suspended on 18 July 1990, and on 24 October the company announced the appointment of Michael Gercke and Colin Bird of Price Waterhouse as Administrative Receivers to the company.

Prior to the suspension of listing, there were rumours in the City that the auditors had refused to sign off Parkfield's annual accounts to 30 April 1990, which were due out towards the end of June 1990. We wonder whether the interim results to 31 October 1989 would have got past an auditor.

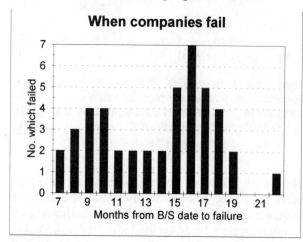

When companies fail

Example 18.1 Company failures: Time of death

Example 18.1 shows the number of months which elapsed between the last published balance sheet and the date of failure of companies in the 'Company Pathology' research referred to in Chapter 9. Had interim results been audited, we think the two peaks would have been about the same.

The seasonal business

Most businesses are to some extent seasonal:

1. *Turnover* varies, sometimes quite widely, between one month and another.
2. *Debtors* will tend to be high, where sales are made on credit, immediately after the seasonal peak, and then to fall.
3. *Stocks* are likely to be built up before the seasonal peak and run down after it.
4. *Creditors* for goods will typically be highest immediately before the seasonal peak.
5. *Employment costs* are likely to vary from one month to another (eg staff will be taken on by a store around Christmas).
6. *Liquidity* is likely to be most under pressure at or around the seasonal peak, but is sharply affected by tax and dividend payments (which have a seasonal pattern).

Accounting ratios of a seasonal business at the year end are not typical of those at other times (that is one reason why it would be useful to have a balance sheet and cash flow statement in an interim statement, and perhaps even better to have quarterly figures). Sudden collapse through liquidity failure might then come as less of a surprise to investors analysts and financial journalists alike.

Using the interim statement

Most companies which produce an interim statement show alongside the figures for the current half-year those for the corresponding half-year the previous year and those for the full year. It is often useful to deduce figures for the previous year's second half – many analysts use spread sheets and computer programs such as Lotus 123 or Quattro Pro. On page 107, we use this technique to discover what we can about BUCKINGHAM INTERNATIONAL, a small hotel group with international connections, the directors of which later ran into trouble with the Panel on Takeovers and Mergers; but that is not relevant to our exercise.

The Cadbury report

The Cadbury Committee's final report on Financial Aspects of Corporate Governance (December 1992) with its Code of Best Practice has important implications for listed companies whether or not legislation is eventually imposed.

BUCKINGHAM INTERNATIONAL Extract from interim statement 1992, with deduced figures for second-half 1991

	--------------Published--------------			Deduced
	Six months ended		Year to	Second
	3 May 92	30 April 91	3 Nov 91	Half 1991
	£000	£000	£000	£000
Turnover	21,915	15,602	49,129	33,527
Operating profit	1,275	440	6,170	5,730
Net interest	(4,008)	(1,728)	(4,919)	(3,191)
(Loss)/Profit before exceptional items	(2,733)	(1,288)	1,251	2,539
Exceptional items	520	(866)	(9,465)	(8,599)
Loss on ordinary activities before taxation	(2,213)	(2,154)	(8,214)	(6,060)
Taxation	–	–	(230)	(230)
Loss on ordinary activities after taxation	(2,213)	(2,154)	(8,444)	(6,290)
Extraordinary item	–	(68)	(609)	(541)
Loss for period	(2,213)	(2,222)	(9,053)	(6,831)
(Losses)/Earnings per share	(1.84)p	(1.78)p	(7.01)p	(5.23)p

Extracts from Notes:

2. Interest is stated net of capitalisation of £0.6m (1991: £1.8m).

3. Exceptional items include the surplus on an asset disposal and insurance claim proceeds for a Jersey hotel that burned down in 1989. For 1991 the exceptional items principally represent the cost of arranging a new bank financing facility.

4. The extraordinary charge relates to expenses and provisions in respect of former business activities.

5. The calculation of losses per share is based on a loss of £2,213,000 (1991: loss of £2,154,000) ...

Commentary:

1. *Turnover*: Grew year-on-year by 40.46%, substantially ahead of inflation

2. *Seasonal effect:*

	Turnover	Operating Profit
	£000	£000
First half 1991	15,602	440
Second half 1991	33,527	5,730
First half 1992	21,915	1,275

ie (i) 68.24% of turnover in 1991 was in the second half;
and (ii) the second half produced 92.87% of the operating profit.

3. *Operating margin:*

	%
First half 1991	2.82
Second half 1991	17.09
First half 1992	5.82

Note the marked improvement in 1992; and the substantial difference in margins between seasons. This is a hotel group and low room occupancy off season has a substantial effect.

4. *Net Interest:*

	£000
First half 1991	(1,728)
Second half 1991	(3,191)
First half 1992	(4,008)

Note the marked, and continuing, deterioration. Interest rates were falling in early 1992, so it seems at first sight that liquidity may have suffered – this is where a balance sheet and cash flow statement would be helpful. But the chairman does tell us: Net borrowings at 3 May 1992 were £82.1m, an increase of £0.9m since 3 November 1991. So that is not the explanation. Note 4 explains that a substantial amount of interest was capitalised (apparently in the first half of 1991 if the statement is consistent in its usage of '1991'): £1.8m; and much less (£0.6m) in the first half of 1992. The difference, of course, falls into the net interest charge; and explains part of the growth.

Capitalisation of interest is not uncommon among hotel groups.

5. *Exceptional items:*
The exceptional item in first half 1992 represents in part the proceeds of an insurance claim in respect of a fire in 1989.

The cost of arranging bank finance reflects, in part at least, the ease or difficulty of raising money.

6. *Divisional analysis:*
The divisional analysis, which we do not reproduce, showed, inter alia, that hotels in Texas accounted for £2,844,000 of the turnover growth, swinging from loss-making (£90,000) to profit (£786,000); that those in Holland had swung from a loss (£299,000) to a very small profit (£5,000); and that tour operations (turnover £2,382,000) continued to be loss-making (£796,000).

Among the recommendations of Cadbury are that:

1. Interim reports be extended to include balance sheet information;

2. They be reviewed (not audited) by the auditors, and that their findings be discussed with audit committee.

Companies are beginning to do this; and more: WHITBREAD, for example, adds a group cash flow statement and segmental analysis. And ELLIS & EVERARD includes graphs of turnover, profit and earnings over 10 half-years – both of which we commend. Another useful example of what an interim statement can provide is that of GRAND METROPOLITAN: a two page chairman's statement, group profit and loss account, balance sheet, cash flow statement, segmental analysis, and report by KPMG Peat Marwick on a limited review made by them. In time there will undoubtedly be a Stock Exchange requirement and / or legislation.

Would quarterly statements be better?

US companies are required to prepare quarterly statements and a number of British, generally those with a US listing, do so. Advantages are:

1. They provide a better indication of annual sales/profit pattern of a seasonal business.
2. They provide the investor more quickly with information (and put him more nearly on a par with management, the banks and lenders who insist on at least quarterly figures).
3. They compel companies to improve internal reporting.
4. Although there is no requirement for either audit or review of quarterly reports, many US companies do ask their auditors to review their interim statements. (Review, while short of a full audit, offers directors a degree of assurance that the published figures were properly prepared and are thus likely to prove true and fair).

Analysts who prefer the existing UK system of half-year figures suggest that 'Quarterly figures take the patient's pulse too frequently – what we need are interims to include a Balance Sheet and Cash Flow Statement, and to be audited'; and in saying this are at least half-right.

In a consultative document on the way listed companies handle price sensitive information, a working party formed by the London Stock Ex-change recommends a policy of announcing regular updates on the trading position and immediate prospects. These statements could either be an unaudited, quarterly financial trading statement or an update with no financial figures at the close of the year and half year.

THORN EMI announced early in 1994 that it would publish quarterly trading results in future. Apparently the leisure and electronics group has installed new financial reporting systems for internal management accounting. This will enable the group to produce quarterly reports without incurring additional costs. THORN EMI may sell its system to other companies.

Certainly the pressure from the London Stock Exchange is leading to the issue of far more trading statements from listed companies, as witnessed by those of TESCO, SAINSBURY, MARKS & SPENCER, and others early in 1994.

Practice

SmithKline Beecham publish quarterly statements. Obtain those for all three quarters of their last financial year and deduce the fourth quarter.

Answer the following questions:

1. To what extent, if any, are SKB's activities seasonal?
2. Does the usefulness of:

    (a)   the balance sheet;
    (b)   cash flows;
    (c)   segmental information;
    (d)   quarterly figures;

    justify their publication generally?
3. Consider how, if at all, the publication of the quarterly reports affected the share price.

Chapter 19

SECTORS AND SEGMENTS

Sectors and segmental analysis share one feature: they are both ways of expressing what a company or group does. To identify a company as forming part of a particular sector is a convenient way of focusing on its similarity to other companies long familiar to analysts.

Segmental analysis, which answers similar questions: 'What does it do?' and 'Where does it do it?' is a more recent development. For convenience we treat them in a single chapter.

GETTING TO GRIPS WITH A SECTOR

How sectors differ

Investors, financial journalists and stock exchange professionals have long seen the equity market as comprising a number of distinct sectors. They have not always agreed among themselves either: (a) just what those sectors are, or (b) which sector a particular company or group falls into.

It is, however, both helpful and convenient to treat market segments separately for several reasons:

1. *Asset structure differs widely*; compare, for instance, property companies, almost all the assets of which consist of land and buildings, oil companies with vast sums tied up in plant, and heavy sunk costs (which may not appear in the balance sheet at all) in respect of exploration to produce reserves for the future, and package tour travel, where the main 'assets' tend to be reputation, the latest tour brochure, and advance bookings (both by customers and of suitable aircraft and hotels.)

2. *Commercial risk tends to be very different.* Compare, for instance, a regional electricity utility, supplying millions of customers, industrial, commercial and domestic, with a drug company a major part of whose profits come from a single spectacular drug, which could, in matter of months be superseded by a more efficacious one produced by a competitor – or which could be shown to have unfortunate, previously undiscovered, side-effects.

3. *Market sentiment tends to be sector oriented.* A sector which is growing in favour (as property did in much of the 1980s) tends to outperform relative to the FT-SE Actuaries Index and those which are out of favour (like building and construction, and property were in the early 1990s), to under perform.

4. *Some sectors (like food) are little affected by a downturn in the economy* whereas others (like construction) feel the full effect. In a recovery, the same is likely to be true (food, both manufacturing and retailing, may show little expansion compared with construction).

5. *Some sectors lead and others lag the general pattern* in a downturn / recovery. Thus personal car purchases tend to fall away (and recover) fast, whereas commercial vehicle sales are slower to respond (if a company has a budget it may be spent even though times are hard, but if a year or two later there is as a result of hard times no budget, replacement may well have to wait).

6. *P/e ratios tend to differ widely from sector to sector.* For example on 7 February 1994:

	Average p/e ratio	Average dividend yield gross
Building & Construction	43.2	2.32%
Media	30.1	1.87%
Water	16.7	4.43%
FT–SE Actuaries Non-Financial Share Index	22.4	3.37%

The *FT–SE Actuaries Non-Financial Share Index* breaks down into five equity groups:

> Mineral extraction
> General manufacturers
> Consumer goods
> Services
> Utilities

each of which contains a number of sectors. If one adds on to this:

> Financials (including Banks, Insurance, Life Assurance, Merchant Banks, Property, Investment Trusts etc)

one arrives at the components of the *All-Share Index.*

7. *Investors seek to build a diversified portfolio.* Few private investors, and even fewer professional investment managers, are prepared to put all (or even a high proportion) of their eggs in one basket; and one simple way of building a diversified portfolio is to spread one's investment over several distinct sectors.

Companies come in all shapes and sizes

The trouble is, companies cannot neatly be categorised and fitted into boxes. Like people, they come in all shapes and sizes. Their origins differ, they develop differently, in ways shaped in many cases by particular individuals, each with their own skills and personalities. So that even companies in the same broad area, like MARKS AND SPENCER and STOREHOUSE (BHS) often have a very different product range and ambience.

Nor do most companies specialise on one activity to the exclusion of others. Many are to a greater or lesser extent conglomerates or investment holding companies. Others just grew like Topsy, perhaps under an opportunist chief executive. Both types are difficult to categorise.

The division of companies into sectors is a convenience but it is easy to jump to the wrong conclusions. All companies in a particular sector will not be affected equally by particular events.

In this book, we look at some, but not all, the 38 sectors into which the FT–SE Actuaries Index is broken down.

We do so for two reasons:

1. The risks, the accounting problems, and even to some extent the ratios used differ from sector to sector;
2. In good times, the sector specialist is among the most highly rewarded occupations in the City.

Of these, the first is pre-eminent in importance. We cannot hope to make the reader a sector specialist overnight. If he is prepared to devote the time, and do the work, he may well get there in the end. But it takes time. Most of those who today head sector research teams have lived their specialisation for a number of years. But we can provide a start.

Where to start

Whatever the sector, one first needs a sense of perspective:

1. How important is the sector as a whole in market terms ie vis à vis other sectors?
2. Who are the key players?
3. Is it dominated by one group, or do two or more groups rival one another for pride of place? What is the relative importance of:

    (a) overseas owned; and
    (b) private groups?

4. How big are the major players compared with the rest of the sector eg at time of writing (February 1994), nine egineering, vehicles companies had a market capitalisation in excess of £100m (the top three – GKN, LUCAS and T & N – between £1.1bn and £1.6bn) and there were five companies from around £100m to £100m. Whereas UNILEVER dominated the food manufacturing sector (nearly £23bn in total, or £9.89bn for Unilever plc) against CADBURY-SCHWEPPES nearly £4,200m. Hemmington Scott's *Performance Ranking Guide*, published twice a year, provides useful comparative tables of key ratios for companies generally and the leaders and laggards in individual sectors, which we find invaluable in gaining a perspective.
5. Is the sector highly regarded by the market (expensive?) or out of favour (cheap)? How has the pattern changed historically?
6. Where does the sector stand currently in the trade cycle?
7. Is it due for re-rating? If so, why?
8. What are the sector's particular strengths and opportunities?
9. What are the special risks and threats?
10. Where are the sector leaders going in share price terms? Up, down or sideways?

11. What have those companies got that others lack (or do they now lack that they once had)?

12. Who made the market leader what it is? Dominant chief executives who will brook no challenge are a danger sign. Nevertheless, one rarely finds a committee-dominated organisation at the forefront. There is a happy medium; and most successful businesses depend heavily upon the leadership and general ability of someone at the top, hopefully that of their chief executive. Because of the special factors involved, and the opportunities and risks, the accounting problems and difficulties of interpretation they bring, we have chosen 15 sectors, which we group into 10 chapters:

1. Building and materials, building and construction;
2. Leisure and hotels;
3. Retailers, food and retailers, general;
4. Health care and household goods;
5. Business services;
6. Utilities;
7. Oil, integrated, and oil exploration and production;
8. Banks and Merchant banks;
9. Insurance and life assurance;
10. Property.

SEGMENTAL ANALYSIS

Using segmental information

Segmental information aims to provide information which will assist the users of financial statements:

1. To appreciate more thoroughly the results and financial position of the entity by permitting a better understanding of its past performance and thus enabling them to make a better assessment of its future prospects; and
2. To be aware of the impact that changes in significant components of a business may have on the business as a whole.

SSAP 25, 'Segmental Reporting', develops somewhat the requirements of Paragraph 55 (1) of Schedule 4 of the Companies Act 1985 regarding businesses which carry on several classes of business or operate in several geographical areas, with different rates of profitability, different opportunities for growth and degrees of risk.

Segmental information is certainly improving as a result of SSAP 25, but it is very doubtful whether it yet fulfils that standard's objectives. But those objectives do set out clearly what the reader should be endeavouring to glean from the accounts.

Like the Companies Acts, the standard leaves a great deal, some would say too much, to directors.

What the user of the financial statements is looking for is more information than provided for by consolidated accounts where an entity carries on operations either: (1) in different classes of business or (2) in different geographical areas that:

(i) Earn a rate of return on investment that is out of line with the remainder of the business;
(ii) Are subject to different degrees of risk;
(iii) Have experienced different rates of growth;
(iv) Have different potentials for development.

And that is what directors should have in mind in identifying separately reportable segments.

Each class of business or geographical area that is significant to the entity as a whole forms a reportable segment. For this purpose, a class or geographical area is *significant* if:

1. Its third party turnover is 10% or more of the total third party turnover.
2. Its segment result, whether profit or loss, is 10% or more of the combined result of all segments in profit or all segments in loss, whichever combined result is the greater.
3. Its net assets are 10% or more of the total net assets of the entity.

The *geographical analysis* is designed to help the reader decide which activities are subject to:

1. Expansionist or restrictive economic climates;
2. Stable or unstable political regimes;
3. Exchange control regulations;
4. Exchange rate fluctuations.

According to the Standard, the entity should define in its financial statements each reported class of business and geographical segment. Many are far from explicit.

The result of the reportable segment shown should be before tax, minority interests and extraordinary items – and, *normally*, before interest (para 22), but there are exceptions.

The net assets of each reportable segment are disclosed, *in most cases*, as being the non-interest bearing operating assets less non-interest bearing operating liabilities. But if interest is allocated to segments so, of course, should be the associated liability.

If associated undertakings account for 20% or more of the total result, or 20% or more of total assets, segmental information will be provided as regards associates. One company which does this very well is GENERAL ELECTRIC and the figures are striking: in 1992 £3,285m, almost 40% of turnover and £227m, 25% of profit, came from associates.

The total of the amounts disclosed by segment may be expected to agree with the related total in the financial statements. If it does not, the reporting entity is supposed to provide a reconciliation between the two amounts, properly identifying the reconciling items and explain them.

The media

Press comment on segmental information varies from knowledgeable, highly sophisticated, and useful to worse than useless, even dangerously misleading. So consider it with care.

We often see dismissive comments such as this: 'It is disturbing to find that three-quarters of the turnover produces only one-quarter of the profit.' There is no reason to suppose that the margin in one segment should be the same as that in another, and if that is the implication it is clearly wrong.

Let us consider some imaginary figures.

Example 19.1 What is disturbing about this?

	Segment A	Segment B	Total
	£m	£m	£m
Turnover	30.000	10.000	40.000
Operating profit	1.500	4.500	6.000
Operating profit/Turnover	5.0%	45.0%	15.0%

What *is* disturbing here is not so much the *low* proportion of operating profit that comes from Segment A as the *high* proportion of the operating profit which comes from a small, high profit margin segment, Segment B, and the effect this has on overall risk.

What one needs to know is:

1. Is 5% a reasonable margin for Segment A? It may well be. Everything depends upon what Segment A does. How does this level of profitability compare with other companies in the same industry?
2. What is it that causes the spectacular margins in Segment B? It could be a patent (with a finite life), or some other form of monopoly eg the high cost of entry into an industry like oil.
3. Will those advantages last (or can they be made to last)? Is there danger from incoming competition, or is the company in some way protected – for example by tariffs or other restrictions.
4. What will happen if competition comes?

Case study: Courts

COURTS is well-known in the UK as a High Street household furniture store. Study the profit and loss account for 1992 shown alongside.

CONSOLIDATED PROFIT AND LOSS ACCOUNT

for the year ended 31 March 1992

	Notes	1992 £000	1991 £000
Turnover	1	183,973	175,048
Cost of sales		(148,408)	(139,989)
Gross profit		35,565	35,059
Distribution costs		(3,388)	(3,171)
Administrative expenses		(20,910)	(19,358)
		(24,298)	(22,529)
Other operating income		6,779	5,948
Net operating expenses		(17,519)	(16,581)
Operating profit excluding associated undertaking	2	18,046	18,478
Net interest payable and similar charges	4	(5,369)	(5,515)
		12,677	12,963
Income from interest in associated company		1,280	–
Profit before transfer to deferred profit	1	13,957	12,963
Transfer to deferred profit –			
subsidiaries		(3,986)	(5,551)
associate undertaking		(1,326)	–
Profit after transfer to deferred profit and before property disposals		8,645	7,412
Profit / (loss) on property disposals		(560)	1,637
Profit after transfer to deferred profit before taxation		8,085	9,049

It is immediately obvious that:

1. Turnover increased in 1992 by £8.925m (5.1%), and the cost of sales by £8.419m (6.0%), reducing the operating margin from 20.0% to 19.3%.
2. Distribution costs as a percentage of turnover rose slightly from 1.81% to 1.84%, as did administrative expenses, from 11.06% in 1991 to 11.37% in 1992.

One could be forgiven for thinking that this was a UK furniture store weathering the 1990–1992 recession relatively well. But one would be wrong: read on.

EXTRACT FROM DIRECTORS' REPORT 1992

Principal activities

The group has continued to trade successfully as a retailer of household furniture, carpets and bedding in the United Kingdom, Guernsey and Jersey, and in these goods, together with gas, electrical and electronic equipment and other household and household related products and bicycles in Antigua, Barbados, Fiji, Grenada, Jamaica, Malaysia, Mauritius, Papua New Guinea, St Lucia, Singapore and Trinidad. The company does no direct exporting, specific orders from Courts stores as well as active encouragement, advice and support in the exporting of their products generally are given to manufacturers in countries where the group trades. The company owns an insurance subsidiary, based in Bermuda, which transacts, inter alia, motor, property and credit insurance for the group. An investment company also operates in Bermuda. Further opportunities are being sought for expansion within the group's prime merchandising areas both in the United Kingdom and overseas.

NOTE 1 TO THE FINANCIAL STATEMENTS:

Turnover and profit before taxation

Turnover consists of the invoiced price of goods and charges for deferred terms but excludes sales taxes. Turnover including VAT was £201,116,000 (1991 £188,660,000). Intragroup sales are excluded. The turnover of our associate undertaking in Trinidad was £10,600,000, of which the group share was 50%.

£000	1992	1991
Goods sold	166,740	158,503
Charges for deferred terms	17,233	16,545
Turnover	183,973	175,048

The group's geographical analysis of profit / (loss) on ordinary activities after deferred profit and before taxation is as follows – in the accounts this is stated in continuous text, which we have turned into a table:

	1992 £000	1991 £000
United Kingdom	(46)	1,175
Caribbean	3,841	4,756
Far East	1,490	707
Pacific/Indian Ocean	2,800	2,411
	8,085	9,049

The group's net assets are split geographically as follows (again to make it easier to understand we have turned text into a table):

	1992 £000	1991 £000
United Kingdom	38,453	39,239
Caribbean	24,728	28,373
Far East	16,965	11,500
Pacific/Indian Ocean	17,870	15,340
	98,016	94,452
The net assets of the insurance activity are	5,477	4,950
	103,493	99,402

These totals cannot be identified in or built up from the balance sheet.

	1992 Turnover £000	1992 Profit before deferred profit £000	Profit before taxation £000	1991 Turnover £000	1991 Profit before deferred profit £000	Profit before taxation £000
Analysis by activity:						
Furniture retailing	183,973	12,614	7,371	175,048	11,689	6,262
Insurance	-	1,343	1,274	-	1,274	1,150
Property disposal (losses)/profits	-	-	(560)	-	-	1,637
	183,973	13,957	8,085	175,048	12,963	9,049

Page 10 (which lies between the chairman's statement and directors' report) provides further details.

Meanwhile, let us explain why we chose Courts as a case study. We did so to make a number of points:

1. Segmental information frequently provides a perspective not immediately obvious from a study of the accounts themselves.

2. It may raise questions which it does not answer; but those questions are to some extent an indication of the risks.

3. SSAP 25 does not call for a standard presentation, but it does require some of the information to be in the accounts or notes.

4. All the available segmental information is not, however, presented in the accounts and notes.

5. Wherever it is given, information does not always take the form of a table. It may help to tabulate it.

6. The total of the amounts disclosed by segment *should,* according to the Standard, agree with the related total in the financial statements. If it does not, the reporting entity *should* provide a reconciliation between the two amounts, but it does not always do so.

7. The statement of activities to be found in the directors' report should be studied but often it is vague to the point of being useless. Here it is not.

GEOGRAPHICAL ANALYSIS OF TURNOVER AND PROFITS

	Turnover	Operating profit	Profit before deferred profit	1992 Profit after DP before property disposals	Turnover	Operating profit	Profit before deferred profit	1991 Profit after DP before property disposals
	£000	£000 [A]	£000 [B]	£000	£000	£000 [C]	£000 [D]	£000
United Kingdom, Guernsey & Jersey	102,516	2,025	568	514	95,486	1,564	(853)	(452)
Caribbean Antigua, Barbados, Grenada, Jamaica, St Lucia & share of profit from Trinidad	23,164	6,312	5,258	3,841	30,138	6,627	5,662	4,746
Far East Malaysia & Singapore	32,832	5,904	4,433	1,490	25,249	4,897	3,713	707
Pacific/Indian Ocean Fiji, Mauritius & Papua New Guinea	25,461	5,085	3,698	2,800	24,175	5,390	4,441	2,411
	183,973	19,326	13,957	8,645	175,048	18,478	12,963	7,412

To sum up: In 1992:

1. 55.7% of the turnover came from the UK; 39.2% of the assets excluding insurance activity were there; but only 4.1% of the profit came from the UK; and the UK operations showed a loss of £46,000 before tax.

2. The operating profit came almost entirely from the three overseas areas: rather more from the Caribbean and the Far East and less from the Pacific / Indian Ocean.

3. The net effect of deferred interest (ie the overall change in the provision) was unfavourable in every area (and in all apart from the UK in 1991) – (compare columns A and B, and C and D.) But the effect is most marked in each year in Malaysia. In 1992, for instance, a profit of £4.433m was reduced by (additional) profits carried forward as unearned of £2.943m.

    It is instructive to ask why? Were more people taking advantage of deferred terms (which would involve the need for more working capital)? Were margins higher, entailing more profit being deferred per £ of sales? Or were the interest rates charged getting higher? Or was the credit period offered/taken increasing (leading to greater risk and the need for more working capital.

4. Operating margins were much higher overseas than in the UK (1992: eg UK 2.00%; Caribbean 27.25%).

The reader is entitled to ask, indeed should ask, how much of this difference in profitability is due to:

1. Differences in the state of the economies, home and overseas;
2. Entirely different market demands overseas;
3. The somewhat different product mix overseas (eg bicycles and electrical goods);
4. Lack of competition overseas;
5. Exchange rates;
6. Borrowing overseas;
7. Favourable overseas taxation

and how all this affects the overall risk of the investment?

This is not so much a criticism of Courts, as an admission of the inevitable fact: the analyst with much information can always see the need for more.

Practice

From time to time, the FT–SE Actuaries Classification Subcommittee reclassifies shares. Indeed it has just completed a major overhaul. But there is a tendency, it seems, for it to be the smaller less well-known company which is moved.

Neverthless a number of larger companies appear to have ended in unexpected sectors. Find three examples.

Solution

As required, we give three examples, but there are countless others:

1. BASS, classified as breweries, but a substantial part of its profits comes from Holiday Inns.
2. POWELL DUFFRYN treated as diversified industrials though a large part of its profits are from fuel distribution and engineering.
3. HARRISON AND CROSFIELD, which comes under diversified industrials, although a large part of the business is now in builders merchants.

Chapter 20

BUILDING MATERIALS AND MERCHANTS, BUILDING AND CONSTRUCTION

General overview

In this chapter we consider special features of companies in the building materials and merchants, building and construction sectors which form part of the general manufacturers sub-section of the FT-SE Actuaries Non-Financials Share Index and are thus included in the All–Share Index.

There under 30 companies in the FT–A Index in the building materials and merchants sector of which seven stand out in terms of market capitalisation:

    REDLAND
    BLUE CIRCLE
    CARADON
    WOLSELEY
    RMC
    TARMAC
    PILKINGTON

– each with a market capitalisation in excess of £1,500m.

The building and construction sector, although more numerous overall, again has about 30 companies in the FT-A Index, is headed by companies which though many of them are well-known even to the man in the street, are somewhat smaller in terms of market capitalisation:

    GEORGE WIMPEY
    TAYLOR WOODROW
    WILSON BOWDEN
    BARRETT DEVELOPMENTS
    WILSON (CONNOLLY)
    BRYANT

– each with a market capitalisation in excess of £475m.

The fortunes of the two sectors are obviously interconnected and closely related to those of the Property Sector (see Chapter 28). So much so that it is sometimes difficult to say whether their estate development activities are best described as property or construction ie just how much building work a group itself does.

The building materials and construction sectors themselves overlap: companies placed in the building materials sector (like TARMAC) have considerable interests in contracting and both commercial and residential property; and a number of those placed in the construction sector have interests in building materials.

They are part of a single macro-economic unit, the profitability of which is largely determined by the volume of new orders for construction in four main areas (on which there are useful government statistics):

1.   Housing;

2.   Public works;

3.   Industrial construction;

4.   Commercial construction.

Nevertheless, the problems and special features of the building materials and construction sectors are sufficiently different for us to consider them separately.

BUILDING MATERIALS AND MERCHANTS

The building and construction industry uses a wide variety of materials, like: aggregates, bricks, clay and concrete tiles, cement (dry and ready mixed), stone, glass (including double-glazing), timber, fabricated timber and metal work, pipes, bathroom, kitchen and central heating equipment, roofing materials and insulation. There is a good deal of specialisation, with companies like Pilkington focusing largely on one material (glass), though other groups like Redland are involved in a range of related areas world-wide.

This means that: (1) there are wide differences in the asset and cost structure of companies in the sector; and (2) it is often unfair directly to compare ratios of one company with another.

Activities in building materials can be broadly divided into:

1. Manufacture (eg brickmaking, glass manufacture, timber fabrication);
2. Extractive activities (eg quarrying, the extraction of sand and gravel);
3. Merchants;

each of which we will consider separately.

1. Manufacture

The financial and accounting problems of building materials companies involved in manufacture differ little from those of other manufacturing businesses, apart from the fact that traditionally they sell largely to a cyclical industry (construction) upon whose fortunes they depend, and often to a number of large construction companies, the failure of any one of which would be very damaging. That tradition has broken down slightly with sales to a considerable do-it-yourself market; though that too is cyclical, but follows more closely that of retail sales.

Five key ratios are:

1. *Gearing*: any cyclical business with excessive gearing is in trouble when sales fall away sharply – and all parts of the construction sectors are highly cyclical.
2. *Stock / Sales*: watch, in particular, finished goods / sales. If sales fall away, this ratio will inevitably rise unless stocks are reduced. But the danger lies in stocks increasing (because while sales have fallen, production has continued at the old rate). Excessive stocks produce financial strain and increase the risks of deterioration and obsolescence. Sometimes, as with bricks in 1991–92, the overhang is industry-wide.
3. *Collection period*: construction companies whose finances are under strain endeavour to stretch the credit period taken from suppliers of materials.
4. *Fixed assets per employee*: traditionally most parts of the sector used to have a relatively low capital investment per employee, but fixed capital investment was so great during the 1987–90 boom that some companies face the need to reduce capacity if they are to survive.

BPB INDUSTRIES *Extracts from 1988–92 accounts*

	Turnover	Fixed assets at year end	No. of Employees	Fixed assets per employee
	£m	£m	000s	£000
1992	1,021.0	860.2	12.6	68.27
1991	1,139.0	845.7	14.1	59.98
1990	1,033.2	616.9	12.4	49.75
1989	960.8	455.9	11.9	38.31
1988	869.7	365.2	11.8	30.95

---

5. *Operational gearing*. Fixed costs increase and operational gearing tends to rise as processes become more automated. It is sometimes possible to assess the effects of fixed costs by estimating the operational gearing:

$$\text{Operational gearing} = \frac{\text{Change in Operating Profit}}{\text{Change in Turnover}}$$

(expressed as a percentage).

PILKINGTON *Extracts from Note 1 to the 1991 accounts – with additional data from the 1992 accounts*

	1991 Turnover	1991 Operating Profit	1990 Turnover	1990 Operating Profit
	£m	£m	£m	£m
Flat & Safety Glass	2,061.6	197.6	2,260.7	292.8
Insulation	100.9	(4.6)	136.5	6.4
Visioncare	295.3	9.6	311.8	24.6

Estimated operational gearing:

Flat & Safety Glass*	47.9%
Insulation	30.9%
Visioncare	90.9%

* ie $((197.6 - 292.8) / (2061.6 - 2260.7)) \times 100 = 47.9\%$

which suggested that if fixed costs were not cut in the flat and safety glass operation, a further fall in turnover of:

£197.6m / 0.478 = £413m

would put it on break even, so that segment is quite sensitive to volume.

It is possible with the benefit of hindsight to assess the (un)reliability of the technique. Turnover did not fall in the flat and safety glass operation in 1992, but the operating profit did. On the other hand, turnover in insulation continued to fall, but the operation was brought back into (limited) profit:

	1992 Turnover	Operating Profit	1991 Turnover	Operating Profit
	£m	£m	£m	£m
Flat & Safety Glass	2,080.4	138.6	2,061.6	197.6
Insulation	79.8	1.1	100.9	(4.6)
Visioncare	306.1	21.5	295.3	9.6

The extremely high operational gearing in Visioncare suggested distorting factors eg Contact lenses. In the USA in 1991 that company instituted further substantial cost cutting and rationalisation measures, reducing its employee numbers at all levels and in total by 30%. The costs of these actions resulted in a loss in the second half of 1990–91 but Visioncare began 1991–92 with a cost base substantially lower than the previous year.

In an ideal world with no inflation, no acquisitions or disposals, no major changes in policy, production, production methods ... this way of estimating operational gearing might work. But it is management's job to manage; to change its policies, to improve products and methods of production. To assume it won't is generally wrong. If a business hits problems, its managers know (or should know) long before the annual accounts are prepared – and they should already be doing something about them. And this technique assumes that they don't. So it rarely works very well.

2. Extractive activities

Extractive companies purchase freehold or leasehold interests in land with mineral rights, or simply acquire the mineral rights over land, with a view to extracting sand, aggregates, stone and the like.

Three points to look for:

1. Do they have adequate reserves of mineral-bearing land and planning permission to extract?
2. How do they amortise the cost of land and / or mineral rights?
3. What provision is made / necessary in respect of land restoration (or subsidence)?

Although it is very difficult to win new planning permissions for mineral extraction in the UK, and even in Europe and the US, most extractive companies do not separate the value of mineral rights in their balance sheet (an exception is TARMAC, another is BARDON), and it is generally necessary to look for hints as to any mineral bank (the value of which can be significant) in the review of operations.

In common with most companies, extractive companies do not normally depreciate either freeholds or long leaseholds (over 50 years) but write off short leaseholds over the life of the lease.

Policy with regard to mineral rights varies:

GEORGE WIMPEY *Accounting Policies 1992*

'Quarries are depreciated over the last 15 years of the operating life'.

BARDON *Accounting policies 1992*

'Freehold land is not depreciated and mineral resources are amortised over their estimated commercial lives where this is less than ten years'.

REDLAND *Accounting policies 1992*

'Depreciation is provided on mineral bearing land to reflect the diminution in economic values as a result of mineral extraction. As a result, no provision is made where the remaining life is judged to be in excess of 20 years since the amount is not material'.

This means that the depreciation charge of similar companies can be very different; and the amounts can be significant.

Mining companies, like the NATIONAL COAL BOARD, make significant provisions for restoration and subsidence, though these are admittedly very long term liabilities and difficult to assess. No mention of potential liability is normally found either in the accounting policies, provisions or contingent liabilities of building materials companies, though it is possible that such costs, were they to arise, would be considerable (BEAZER had in 1990 'Environmental provisions £175.3m)', mostly as regards the US.

3. Merchants

The problems of companies involved in merchanting eg the stocking and sale (wholesale or retail) of central heating equipment, pipes, bathroom and kitchen equipment, are not dissimilar to those of retail and wholesale businesses in general. Though they tend to follow somewhat the construction cycle, they are considerably affected by the existence of repair, maintenance and improvement work (both industrial and DIY).

CONTRACTING AND CONSTRUCTION

Contracting and Construction covers:

1. House building;
2. Repair, maintenance and improvement work (RMI);
3. Commercial building eg shops, shopping malls, offices, hotels, leisure centres;
4. Civil engineering eg roads, bridges, dams, airports, docks

and more specialist activities like:

5. Second home / retirement home building;
6. Scaffolding and access services;
7. Plant hire;
8. Ground engineering (ie advising external clients on difficult sites);
9. Oil and gas pipelines;
10. Contract management.

Some companies specialise in one area eg scaffolding (WESTMINSTER SCAFFOLDING) or the construction of retirement homes, nursing homes and second homes abroad (McCARTHY & STONE). Most operate rather more generally.

It is important in studying the accounts of a construction company to ascertain just what it builds and where it earns its profits. Who are its main customers: government, local authorities, supermarkets or their superstores? SSAP 25, 'Segmental Reporting', makes this somewhat easier than it used to be. Traditionally, many construction companies were remarkably silent on the breakdown of turnover and profit and, as the J. Smart illustration alongside shows, despite SSAP 25 some still are.

One needs to know just what a construction company builds and where it earns its profits, for:

1. Although construction generally tends to be cyclical, the cycle is not necessarily the same in various types of activity. For example:

    (i) *Housebuilding* is affected by interest rates, the residential property market (if the would be purchaser cannot sell his existing property, he cannot buy a new one), the ease or difficulty of obtaining a mortgage, tax relief (eg on mortgage interest or on endowment policies), prices, and by the general economy, eg income growth, unemployment and confidence).

    (ii) *RMI* tends to hold up somewhat better in a recession than most construction work.

    (iii) *Shop and office building*: there is at present an oversupply which, even when

business fully recovers, will take some years to absorb.

    (iv) *Roadbuilding* depends on national budget considerations, and varies from year-to-year, and more especially over the slightly longer term.

    (v) *School and hospital building* is affected by similar considerations.

    (vi) *Overseas contracting* eg dam building, major road schemes and pipe-lines, are affected by the world economy, national budget considerations, lending by the more developed countries and so on.

J. SMART & CO (CONTRACTORS) *Extract from report and accounts for the year to 31 July 1992*

REPORT OF THE DIRECTORS:
The principal activities of the company and its subsidiaries are building and public works contracting of all types, building for sale of private houses, carrying out of industrial and commercial developments for sale or lease, and the manufacture for sale of concrete building products.

Turnover during the year decreased by £1,043,133 and rental income from investment properties increased from £2,088,413 to £2,787,417, resulting in an operating profit of £3,349,061.

PROFIT AND LOSS ACCOUNT

	Notes	1992 £	1991 £
TURNOVER	2	12,528,667	14,783,689
Change in stocks of finished goods and work in progress		1,464,634	252,745
Own work capitalised		3,045,861	2,885,265
		17,039,162	17,921,699
Other operating income		2,787,417	2,088,413
		19,826,579	20,010,112
Raw materials and consumables		5,927,915	5,480,206
Other external charges		3,498,544	4,315,423
Staff costs		6,072,798	5,879,316
Depreciation		394,828	474,240
Other operating charges		583,433	390,783
OPERATING PROFIT		3,349,061	3,470,144

...

NOTE 2:

...

	1992 £	1991 £
The net profit on ordinary activities before taxation may be attributed to:		
Construction activities	803,222	1,608,506
Investment activities	2,487,120	2,830,791
	3,290,342	4,439,297

Construction - A cyclical industry

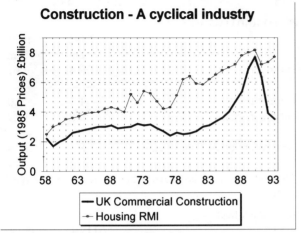

Example 20.1 Note the long cycle, the slow build up to a 1990, and the diffferent patterns of the two segments

2. Margins differ considerably in the various areas.

3. The risks involved differ from one area of activity to another eg operating abroad in inclement conditions, a long way from base, with long lines of communication, often with local semi-skilled labour, is very different from operating in the UK. There is much greater risk of not being paid, of adverse currency movements, local unrest or disturbance.

4. The consequences of a fall in volume are different:

    (i) *House building*: A lot depends on the cost of the land. Traditionally a large part of housebuilders' profits has come from the effect of inflation on the value of their land bank.

    Much house building is speculative; that is to say, houses are not sold until partly or fully completed. If prices fall after a property is complete, prices may have to be cut. If the bottom falls out of the market, it may be difficult to sell even at a loss; and the builder will suffer from liquidity problems. Building can be halted, and staff laid off, but nothing deteriorates quite as fast as an empty house, except perhaps a partly completed one. Materials on site disappear, and children play on the part built units, so that all too soon they are worthless.

    (ii) *Office building*: empty offices are perhaps not quite as hazardous to the builder as empty homes, though they are likely to remain empty longer, and involve payment of rates. It is not unknown for new offices to remain unoccupied for up to 5 years.

    (iii) *Shopping complexes and other major developments*: where the contractor takes on the role of developer of a major project, he is likely to have borrowed heavily against the project, and be highly dependent for survival upon sales (which may be non-existent) to maintain his liquidity, and upon property values (which will fall heavily) to convince bankers.

    (iv) *Contracting*: payment for work on building contracts tends to be spread over the life of the contract (which may take several years). Despite a downturn in new work, work on existing contracts continues to generate turnover and profit and, provided that the customer is sound, payments continue to be received month by month. Lay-offs can thus be phased and so long as overheads and interest charges are not too great, there is not too much strain on liquidity. Nevertheless, in the longer term, lack of work means lack of turnover and much reduced profits or even losses.

    This leads to highly competitive tendering, companies being willing to take work at prices which are *too* keen. This is difficult for someone outside the industry to spot until the consequences work through into profit (or loss).

What to look for in construction company accounts

Construction company accounts have a number of special features:

1. *The treatment of long-term contracts.* SSAP 9 requires that companies disclose their accounting policies in respect of long-term contracts, in particular the method of ascertaining both turnover and attributable profit. This is important.

    The policies of some companies are noticeably more prudent than others, but some rear-end load profits to such an extent that in a down-turn profits appear to be being earned when the volume of new work, and that of work being done, has fallen sharply.

WILSON CONNOLLY *Extract from Accounting Policies 1992*

Contracts:

Turnover comprises the cost of work executed in the year together with profit attributable to contracts, where applicable. Profit is taken on short-term contracts on practical completion. Profit is taken on long-term contracts at the rate of 75% of anticipated profits once the contracts have reached 75% completion. Full profit is taken on practical completion.

Unfortunately, little or no information is provided in accounts on:

(i)   The volume and value of *new* work;

(ii) The total value of *contracts in progress*;

(iii) Long-term *contract completions*;

any information there is being buried deep in the notes or given in the chairman's statement or the review of operations.

2.   *Financial gearing.* As with any cyclical business it is important to have regard to financial gearing and interest cover.

3.   *Geographical risk.* Many construction groups are involved in public works contracting worldwide. The economic climate is at times more favourable than that in the UK. It is often entirely different. But so are the risks and margins. Segmental analyses should be studied with care.

4.   *Unusual contingent liabilities.* Such as those found in the example below. These became more common in the difficult trading conditions of the early 1990s.

5.   *Stocks.* Signs of weakness are:

(i)   Falling turnover coupled with increasing stocks of completed properties and, possibly, work-in-progress

(ii) Excessive stocks in relation to sales especially where found in conjunction with high borrowings and high interest rates.

McCARTHY & STONE specialises in the private retirement housing market at home and overseas. Until the surge in interest rates and the depression of the housing market it did so very successfully – but its results (shown alongside) well illustrate the problem of excessive stocks.

It will be seen that while turnover fell in 1989, and more dramatically in 1990, and continued to fall in 1991 and 1992, stocks remained high. At the end of the 1992 accounting year they equalled 1.64. years' turnover – most of it being finished stock.

McCARTHY & STONE *Extracts from 1992 report and accounts*

FIVE YEAR RECORD:

Year	Turnover	Profit after tax	Share-holders' funds	Earnings per share	Net assets per share
	£m	£m	£m	p	p
1992	71.4	(18.8)	76.9 (29.3)	81	
1991	73.1	(10.4)	98.3 (21.9)	112	
1990	87.7	(9.0)	98.7 (18.9)	152	
1989	131.4	4.9	107.8	5.9	168
1988	149.7	22.5	104.4	43.9	163

PROFIT AND LOSS ACCOUNT:

	1992 £m	1991 £m
Turnover	71.4	73.1
Trading profit	1.1	2.0
Interest expense	9.8	13.9
Loss before exceptional items	8.7	11.9

(Note the lack of brackets, where some would expect them.)

BALANCE SHEET:

Stocks	117.1	132.1
Net cash and cash equivalents	(60.6)	(58.1)
Creditors due after more than 1 year		
Loan stock, lease and hire purchase contracts	(26.0)	(25.2)
Shareholders' Funds (including minorities)	(77.0)	(98.4)
Gearing:	112%	85%

(1992: (£60.6m + £26.0m / £77.0m)

EXTRACT FROM NOTE 19

In 1993 the group may be called upon to repurchase a development sold in 1990. The net cash consideration would not be less than £2m. In the directors' opinion, no material loss would arise on repurchase.

The group operates a scheme under which it will pay interest on bridging finance taken out by a purchaser of a unit for a maximum period of two years if it is not sold within the two year period. Under the scheme the group will be required to purchase the bridged property if it is not sold within the two year period. The group could be required to pay a maximum of £5.4m to purchase all properties falling under the scheme at the balance sheet date. ...

Disturbingly:

1.   Land for development (1992: £22.6m; 1991 £30.2m) fell more than finished stock (1992: £72.9m; 1991: £75.1m); and

2.   Interest represented 891% of trading profit.

The illustration demonstrates once again that it is not losses which kill companies, but the inability to raise sufficient funds to meet commitments as they fall due.

Companies which batten down the hatches and have banks / shareholders with faith in their future can, while loss-making, survive for a surprisingly long time. Indeed McCarthy & Stone continues at the time of writing to survive, although no dividend was paid in 1993.

Practice

Obtain the latest accounts of:

Pilkington;
Redland;
Meyer International;
Wilson Connolly;
John Laing.

1. Ascertain, so far as possible:

    (i) what the group does;
    (ii) where it does it;
    (iii) where the profits are made; in which:

    (a) sectors;
    (b) activities; and
    (c) countries).

2. From the historical summary (if any) assess the degree to which profitability was affected by the downturn in 1990–93.

3. Assume that you are advising a private client with a substantial, well-diversified, portfolio: estimate the relative risk involved in investing in each company for the long term.

Chapter 21

LEISURE AND HOTELS

Overview of the sector

In this chapter we consider the problems and special features of companies in the leisure and hotels sector (which forms part of Services Group in the FT-SE Actuaries Non-Financials share index).

The sector is dominated by five companies:

THORN EMI
LADBROKE
FORTE
RANK ORGANISATION
GRANADA

but includes a wide variety of companies from ZETTERS and SAVOY HOTEL to TOTTENHAM HOTSPUR.

Hotels, caterers and leisure industries such as gaming, package-tour travel, and the operation of golf clubs and fitness clubs, share a common feature: they are heavily dependent for their success upon the personal spending power of individuals.

They are adversely affected by such things as high interest rates, high levels of unemployment, general insecurity causing people to save more (and hence to spend less), recession, or any failure of wages and salaries to keep pace with inflation (whether as a result of wage restraint or general weakness of the economy).

The success of hotel, catering and leisure companies also depends heavily on the level of business activity. Companies which are under pressure typically cut back on travel (restricting it generally and, in particular, first class travel).

Hotels and catering

Apart from general economic factors, and special factors in the case of overseas hotels (such as fuel costs and the threat of war which greatly reduce

international tourism and business travel) the success of hotels and catering establishments depends heavily on:

1. The location, and site value, of their outlets. Many hotel companies therefore combine an interest in property with that in leisure activities.
2. Ambience.
3. Room occupancy in the case of hotels, and the number of covers (people served) in the case of restaurants.

Although the annual report will often list details of hotels and restaurants owned by the group, and where they are situated, none of the factors listed above figure directly in the accounts; it is their effects which are apparent.

To be successful a hotel must meet the needs of customers; generally focusing on those of a particular type of customer: businessmen, conferences, package tours, those of individuals or families touring alone – and those needs do not necessarily coincide. Businessmen and individuals travelling alone do not like restaurants, bars or reception facilities, overwhelmed by groups of package tour travellers.

The regular business traveller, possibly spending many weeks each year in hotels, seeks assurance that the ambience, quality, and general feel of a new hotel will meet his expectations. This has been achieved by the development by hotel chains of a brand image, like Hilton or InterContinental, with international standards of decor and service, which make it difficult for the world traveller to know without looking out of the window whether he is in London, Munich or Auckland.

A similar trend developed in roadside restaurants. Chains like Happy Eater and Little Chef became recognised as providing a good standard of food with clean, comfortable speedy service.

Major hotel groups such as Forte have developed or acquired a number of distinct hotel and restaurant 'brands' (Forte own both Happy Eater and Little Chef, as well as Harvester, Wheelers, Kentucky Fried Chicken (GB) and Travelodge) which retain their individual stamp and place in the market and are treated almost as separate divisions.

The hotel industry has a good deal in common with the property industry. Indeed:

1. Hotel values tend to reflect site value – those occupying a key location may be difficult to operate so as to yield an attractive return on capital employed.
2. Because hotels represent easily mortgageable fixed assets, hotel groups sometimes overgear.
3. Interest may be capitalised while a hotel is in course of construction (or even refurbishment).
4. In a recession such as the early 1990s, these factors combine to make hotel valuations both difficult and suspect.

Accounting features of hotels and catering

In accounting terms, the different categories of leisure business have little in common. One thing they do share is high operational gearing. If any leisure business is to be financially successful it must operate substantially above break even point – though the way in which break even is expressed will differ from one type of activity to another.

A hotel needs to meet room (or bed) occupancy targets. Typically, if a 5-star hotel cannot achieve 80% bed occupancy throughout the year, it will not be profitable. Management thus focuses on three factors, ensuring that

1. The break-even bed occupancy does not rise, through inefficiency;
2. The hotel is filled; and
3. Restaurants, bars and function rooms attract custom.

Published accounts rarely reveal much about these factors, but the chairman may.

In the same way, a restaurant must serve a certain number of meals (or 'covers') if it is to break even. Again, published accounts rarely reveal this sort of information.

Typically, hotel operation tends to be a high profit margin (perhaps 20%), high investment, labour intensive, activity. But if due allowance is made for the cost of capital, it is likely to appear less adequate – that was the reason GRAND METROPOLITAN gave when it sold the InterContinental

Hotel chain in 1988 (another way of looking at things might have been that it could find better ways of investing its money). In a period of inflation the property value of hotels, especially those on prestige town centre sites, tends to increase, making the total long-term return *to disposal* attractive, while the return to a hotelier may seem inadequate.

Restaurant operation is again a high margin activity, labour intensive operation. The sales value of a meal needs, for successful operation, to be somewhere between 3 and 5 times its food content, in order to cover wages (which are a major component of costs) and accommodation. Wines apart, stocks tend to be low, and little credit is given, so net current assets may well be negative.

Accounts are complicated by the fact that many hotel groups operate hotels under contract (and receive fees for doing so), or allow others to operate their hotels for them (paying them a fee).

In the US it is quite normal for the ownership and management of a hotel to be in different hands; and this seems to be spreading to the UK.

A group which combines catering and healthcare is COMPASS GROUP, whose accounts (extracts overleaf) provide an interesting illustration of segmental analysis.

What is worth noticing are:

1. The very different margins:

	1992	1991
Catering & Facilities –		
	%	%
United Kingdom	9.66	10.11
North America	insignificant	
Healthcare United Kingdom	21.50	20.54

2. The very different return on net assets:

	%	%
Catering & Facilities –		
United Kingdom	infinite	infinite*
North America	insignificant	
Healthcare United Kingdom	12.60	13.51

* capital employed being negative.

It is important to know exactly what a company does, and Compass is not a typical restaurateur – a management buyout from Grand Met in 1987, it specialises in catering in the workplace, in educational establishments, hospitals, in executive dining, in sporting and events catering – most of which involve it in little investment in property assets. Hence the negative capital employed. It operates under the names of Bateman Catering and, most recently, Travellers' Fare.

It operates private hospitals and nursing homes, and is keen to take advantage of recent NHS reforms, seeing 'worthwhile opportunities.'

COMPASS GROUP *Extracts from annual report for 1992*

CONSOLIDATED PROFIT AND LOSS ACCOUNT

	Note	Period ended 27 Sept 1992 £m	Period ended 29 Sept 1991 £m
Turnover	2	345.1	320.9
Operating costs	3	(305.1)	(282.8)
Operating profit		40.0	38.1
Interest receivable and similar income		0.3	0.8
Interest payable and similar charges		(5.4)	(6.9)
Profit on ordinary activities before taxation		34.9	32.0

NOTE 2

Turnover, operating profit and net assets

	Period ended 27 Sept 1992 £m	Period ended 29 Sept 1991 £m
Turnover		
Catering & Facilities –		
United Kingdom	285.8	261.0
North America	2.1	3.9
Healthcare United Kingdom	57.2	56.0
	345.1	320.9
Operating profit		
Catering & Facilities –		
United Kingdom	27.6	26.4
North America	0.1	0.2
Healthcare United Kingdom	12.3	11.5
	40.0	38.1
Net assets		
Operating profit		
Catering & Facilities –		
United Kingdom	(15.4)	(13.4)
North America	0.2	0.4
Healthcare United Kingdom	97.6	85.1
Total	82.4	72.1
Interest bearing liabilities (being loans less cash in hand)	(38.0)	(41.1)
Net assets	44.4	31.0

The total for net assets agrees with the total per the consolidated balance sheet; and the interest bearing liabilities represent the closing net borrowings as shown by the notes to the cash flow statement.

Gaming

Racing and gaming are again labour intensive, but, because a substantial part of the take is returned as winnings or paid over in betting duties and levy, the profit margin is much lower (5% or rather less). There are few stocks or debtors, and very few creditors.

Papers often write of the heavy losses sustained by bookmakers when a favoured horse wins. This is nonsense. Bookmakers seek to operate a balanced book (and rarely fail in doing so) so that they win whatever the result of, say, a race.

The real risks lie in:

1. *Fraud*. Racing and gaming attract people who believe that they can get rich quickly at the bookmaker's expense. Fraud and collusion within the bookmaker's own operation are constantly guarded against but the possibility of successful fraud cannot be ruled out.

    Casinos take the risk so seriously that they sometimes operate three separate internal chains of command which run from the *gaming* room right up to the board (responsible for croupiers, cashiers, and general gaming room staff respectively).

2. *Loss of the entire operation*, eg withdrawal of a casino's gaming licence (as happened relatively recently in the case of several well-known London casinos) or the imposition of a ban on off-course betting (which is unlikely, but not beyond the bounds of possibility). As GRAND METROPOLITAN found recently, off course betting does not always have the relative respectability overseas that it today enjoys in the UK).

3. *Possible competition from a National Lottery.*

Package tours and holidays

The accounts of package tour companies have a number of special features:

1. Cash is received in advance, in the form of deposits and prepayment of holidays (most ask for the balance around 28 days before travelling), and 'Revenue received in advance' forms the main element of creditors.

2. The tour operator places deposits with, and makes prepayments to, hotel and airline operators in order to ensure firm bookings. These make up the major part of debtors and represent in a sense the goodwill of the business.

3. Cash balances tend to be high for most of the season.

4. This permits operation with a low capital base; but therein lies danger: a number of tour

companies which used deposits to finance equipment, brochure and other selling costs, have been forced into liquidation. An inadequate capital base is a danger signal.

5. It is quite normal for tour companies to carry forward brochure and promotional costs and charge them to the season to which they relate. This is reasonable provided that the business has adequate capital, and does not need to use deposits for this purpose.

6. Tour companies depend heavily on effective planning, booking, cash collection and investment, systems.

7. Cost of sales, ie travel, hotel accommodation etc, tends to be relatively high, leaving a gross profit margin to cover (substantial) selling and administration costs.

Tour companies differ in the way they arrange travel. Some have their own air fleet; others depend on charter arrangements. In either case, profitability depends heavily upon the operator's ability to fill flights to capacity with full-paying passengers, and to match demand against pre-booked accommodation. This is no easy task. Demand for overseas holidays is affected by:

1. Changes in the UK economy. For instance, interest rates and unemployment, directly affect demand. The relative strength of the £ affects oil prices, hotel prices and the spending money in the traveller's pocket, and quickly hits demand.

2. Changes in the economies of countries to which the tour operator provides holiday packages. Quite apart from the tour price which will change relative demand, countries known to be 'dear' tend to be unpopular.

3. Climate and changes in taste. A bad season in the UK, or in an overseas centre, may well change demand for that area for a year or more afterwards. Bad publicity (a resort becoming known as a centre for 'yobbos') may rule out a resort for the majority.

4. Political instability or threat (or perceived threat) of terrorism. Consider recent events in Yugoslavia, Israel, and the Lebanon (which little more than a decade or so ago was a country attractive to tourists). Note, too, how the UK's attractiveness to tourists from the US fell in the months following the Lockerbie bomb.

5. The balance in supply and demand for charter aircraft and for holiday accommodation. Heavy discounting even by one or two carriers affects the entire market. Note, in particular, the aggressive attitude of market leader, THOMSON.

6. Attempts to dominate the market. Note the recent failed bid by AIRTOURS for OWNERS ABROAD, which, had it succeeded would have meant a UK travel industry dominated 70% or so by Thomson and Airtours. Thos Cook (now German-owned) has taken a stake in Owners Abroad. We seem likely to see a period of change, with companies becoming more integrated – with their own retail outlets, own airline and own packaged holidays etc.

Practice

1. Study the latest report and accounts of:
   THORN EMI
   LADBROKE
   QUEENS MOAT HOUSES
   EUROCAMP
   FAIRLINE BOATS.

2. Ascertain:
   (i) what each does;
   (ii) what kind of markets it serves; and
   (iii) what its special risks and features are.

3. A client with a substantial and well-diversified equity portfolio is considering putting £50,000 into leisure companies in the hope of superior growth once the recession is over. Having studied their reports and accounts, recent history and relative price performance, which company(ies) would you prefer, and why?

Chapter 22

RETAILERS, FOOD AND RETAILERS, GENERAL

Overview of the sectors

This chapter considers the special problems and factors of two sectors which appear in the FT-SE Actuaries Share Index in the Services section under the headings Retailers, Food and Retailers, General.

There are about 17 listed and USM companies in the retailers, food sector, three of which stand out:

SAINSBURY
TESCO
ARGYLL

with market capitalisations in excess of £2,900m. They are followed by:

KWIK SAVE
WILLIAM MORRISON
ASDA GROUP
ICELAND FROZEN FOODS

which, while big, do not compare with Sainsbury, Tesco or Argyll in size or market dominance.

In the same way, while six retailers, general groups may be said to dominate that sector, MARKS AND SPENCER stands out:

MARKS AND SPENCER
BOOTS
GREAT UNIVERSAL STORES
KINGFISHER
SEARS
W H SMITH

– all with a market capitalisation in excess of £1,500m.

Grasping the essentials

Stores, supermarkets and other retailers have obvious similarities in that they all buy, stock and display, goods for resale, but do not normally manufacture the goods themselves.

In retailing of any type, location is a key factor, though customers more readily use distant retailers or inconveniently located ones where:

1. Specialist items are required, for example outsize clothes; or
2. The quantity purchased and / or the savings justify; for example a family may well use an out-of-town supermarket for weekly shopping to save money and provide additional choice, but use a local store for smaller items during the week.

It is important, therefore, in trying to understand a retail group, to know:

1. What type of business it operates (general or specialist);
2. What sort of locations it favours;
3. Its policy as regards store expansion (how many stores, and of what size?).

If this emphasis on location echoes the rules of sound property investment, that is no coincidence. Many stores and supermarket groups dabble in property development (though some, having burned their fingers, retired from that scene in the early 1990s).

Stores

Department stores are retail organisations departmentally organised to cover a range of specialisms, eg fashion, general clothing and shoe departments, fashion jewellery and cosmetics, hairdressing, household equipment and linens, radio and television, lighting, toys, cameras, records, garden equipment, travel, food and a restaurant.

The very variety of specialist departments which may be included makes it somewhat difficult to compare the results of one department store group with another. The stock turnover in a food department will be far greater than that in fashion goods or jewellery; but the gross margin, far less.

Although most retail groups take pains to produce for internal purposes sales analyses of many types, eg departmental and sectional figures, and week by week comparisons, store by store, few make much of this information public. Indeed much of the focus in the past has been on turnover (with the production of statistics on sales per employee, sales per £ of employment costs and sales per square foot of selling area) rather than on gross profit (which was not readily available).

This drive to maximise sales is found especially in modern high-rental shopping complexes and may produce a deterioration in customer service – goods with a low demand (eg very small sizes of ladies shoe) simply not being stocked. But there is a neat balance: one of the advantages of the large store is that it sells everything under one roof. Once that claim fails to be met, it loses its attraction.

The broad range of activities of departmental stores means that, in an economic downturn, individual departments are affected differently, and the least affected, like food, tend to cushion the worst affected.

This has been recognised by a number of stores groups, such as KINGFISHER, which has added B&Q, COMET and SUPERDRUG – and more recently the French specialist electrical retailer Financière Darty, to its original Woolworth base; but a general downturn is difficult to avoid.

The term *specialist stores* is used to cover those which concentrate their activities in one area. Examples include LLOYDS CHEMISTS, the specialist multiple chemist retailer and drugstore operator.

The division between department stores and specialist stores tends to become blurred as groups develop. For example, W H SMITH, long one of the UK's foremost stationers and distributors and retailers of newspapers and magazines, has in recent years moved into books, recorded music and videos, and (with BOOTS) into out-of-town do-it-yourself stores. And BURTON, long thought of as a multiple men's tailor, owns Debenhams (department stores) and various ladies fashion chains.

There is also a tendency for groups which are at first sight retailers, through a process of vertical integration, to add or develop manufacturing activities, which increase the difficulty of interpreting their accounts. For example, AUSTIN REED, at first sight a retailer of fashionable top-quality men's (and women's) clothing, owns general clothing, shirt and knitwear manufacturing companies.

Retail groups also frequently add an industrial service element to their range of activities. For example, SKETCHLEY, at first sight a high street retail dry cleaners, but now classified as Support Services, in 1990 took more from vending services than from its retail cleaning activities; and 71.4% of its turnover came from vending, office cleaning and similar services, and the supply of corporate clothing and workwear.

Points to look for in the accounts of stores companies

In looking at the accounts of a stores company expect:

1. *A relatively high gross profit margin.* Not all stores companies disclose their gross margin, but you should look for something between 20% and 40% – higher in the case of specialist stores like the BODY SHOP and WORLD OF LEATHER, but much less where the group verges on the supermarket (in 1991–92 half the total sales area of STOREHOUSE was BHS, the remainder HABITAT, MOTHERCARE, and RICHARDS AND BLAZER).

	Accounts to:	Gross Profit £m	Sales ex VAT £m	Gross Margin %
Austin Reed	Jan 1993	22.526	58.677	38.39
GUS	Mar 1992	957.9	2,597.1	36.88
Kingfisher	Jan 1993	1,123.2	3,547.9	31.66
Liberty	Feb 1993	31,925	82,388	38.75
Marks and Spencer	Mar 1993	2,071.2	5,950.8	34.81
WH Smith	May 1992	668.5	2,127.5	31.42
Storehouse	Mar 1993	92.3	1,139.3	8.1
The Body Shop	Feb 1993	90,280	168,272	53.65
World of Leather	Dec 1992	11.457	25.563	44.82

2. *A relatively low stock-turnover ratio* (certainly compared with a supermarket), though this will depend very much on the type of goods sold – the more specialist, the lower the stock-turn, and the more like a supermarket the group is, the higher it will be:

	Accounts to:	Stocks £m	Cost of Sales £m	Stock-turn
Austin Reed	Jan 1993	16.597	36.151	2.18
GUS	Mar 1992	233.5	1,639.2	7.02
Kingfisher	Jan 1993	571.7	2,424.7	4.24
Liberty	Feb 1993	18,597	50,463	2.71
Marks and Spencer	Mar 1993	344.2	3,879.6	11.27
W H Smith	Jun 1992	249.8	1,459.0	5.84
Storehouse	Mar 1993	122.2	1,047	8.57
The Body Shop	Feb 1993	35,255	77,992	2.21
World of Leather	Dec 1992	3.205	14,106	4.40

3. *Debtors dependent upon trading policy* – high where a major part of sales are on credit and the company finances these itself, as is the case with GUS, or where sales are made on credit to franchisees etc (THE BODY SHOP), and low where most sales are for cash (KINGFISHER):

	Accounts to:	Trade Debtors £m	Sales £m	Months Sales
Austin Reed	Jan 1993	10,801	58.677	2.21
GUS	Mar 1992	1,310.5	2,597.1	6.06
Kingfisher	Jan 1993	48.2	3,547.9	0.16
Liberty	Feb 1993	9,067	82,388	1.32
Marks and Spencer	Mar 1993	535.7	5,950.8	1.08
Storehouse	Mar 1992	11.4	1,139.3	0.12
W H Smith	June 1992	55.5	2127.5	0.31
The Body Shop	Feb 1993	22,609	168,272	1.61
World of Leather	Dec 1992	0.834	25.563	0.39

4. *Dependence on sales at high margins to cover high fixed costs*, particularly rents (which may be hidden in administration expenses) or interest. In a downturn, fixed costs must be cut sharply. If they are not, problems will quickly arise.

WORLD OF LEATHER *Profit and Loss Accounts for the years to 31 December 1989, 1990 and 1991*

	1991 £000	1990 £000	1989 £000
Turnover	24,550	24,496	23,164
Cost of Sales	13,226	13,646	12,658
Gross profit	11,324	10,850	10,506
Distribution costs	(1,099)	(1,170)	(1,244)
Administrative expenses	(10,261)	(10,426)	(9,342)
Other operating income	721	559	150
Operating profit / (loss)	685	(187)	70
Interest receivable	1	5	116
Interest payable	(571)	(641)	(274)
Profit/(loss) on ordinary activities before taxation	115	(823)	(88)
Tax on profit/(loss) on ordinary activities	(47)	(15)	22
Profit/(loss) on ordinay activities after taxation	68	(838)	(66)

Note the small operating profit (£70,000 in 1989), which turned to a loss in 1990, and the insignificant margin at the operating profit level (0.3%) in 1989, despite a gross margin of 45.4%, because distribution costs took 5.4% of sales and administration costs 40.3%, the difference representing (unexplained) other operating income, 0.6%.

In 1990 the gross margin fell slightly to 44.7%; distribution costs were reduced to 4.8% but administration costs grew (by 11.6% on sales which increased only 5.8%), absorbing a massive 42.6% of sales, so that despite £559,000 of other operating income, there was an operating loss of £187,000, ie 0.8% of sales.

Interest rates rose, liquid funds fell (as they had done in 1989), as a result of which interest payable increased from £274,000 to £641,000, by 133.9%.

What had been a small loss before tax in 1989 (£88,000) became one of £823,000.

The group returned to profit in 1991 despite static turnover, by improving gross margin (to 46.13%); cutting distribution costs to 4.5% of sales, and administration costs to 41.8% of sales; thanks to falling interest costs and 'Other operating income' (representing a disturbing 627% of profit on ordinary activities). Note 2 to the 1991 accounts explained:

	1991 £000	1990 £000
Other operating income includes:		
Profit on disposal of stores	375	126

In 1992, the profit on ordinary activities before tax was £44,000; tax on ordinary activities was £40,000 (after adjustments), to leave £4,000, representing earnings per share of 0.1p. It seems the group has some way to go.

Points to look for in the accounts of food retailers and supermarkets

The accounts of food retailers, and most especially those of supermarkets, exhibit a number of factors which distinguish them from the stores sector.

1. *Low, but growing gross profit margins.* Not all supermarket groups disclose gross profit margin (eg Asda does not) and many supermarket operators also do other things, making it difficult if not impossible to compare their figures with the rest of the industry. Smaller retailers, like M&W which operates a number of local convenience stores, may exhibit higher margins.

	Accounts to:	Gross Profit £m	Sales ex VAT £m	Gross Margin %
Kwik Save	Aug 1993	372.5	2,651.2	14.05
M&W	Sep 1993	17.024	71.495	23.81
Sainsbury	Mar 1993	996.6	9,685.5	10.29
Tesco	Feb 1993	732.5	7,581.5	9.66

Tesco's margins have risen remarkably over the past 9 years (and with just one hiccup, every year since 1980) :

Accounts to:	Gross Profit £m	Sales ex VAT £m	Gross Margin %
Tesco February 1985	133.4	3000.4	4.45
1987	226.0	3593.0	6.29
1989	377.1	4717.7	7.99
1991	558.6	6346.3	8.80
1992	661.5	7,097.4	9.32
1993	732.5	7,581.5	9.66

But while Tesco provides an impressive illustration of margin improvement:

(i)   Sainsbury, Kwik Save and M&W all produce higher margins;

(ii) Margins have improved year by year elsewhere (eg in Marks and Spencer).

And, beware: there is no standard definition either of gross profit or of cost of sales. Most retail companies treat cost of sales as the cost of the goods sold (pure and simple, with no addition for store or staff costs) – as do both M&W and Marks and Spencer. Tesco say: 'Cost of sales includes warehouse and transportation costs and all store operating costs'. Sainsbury adopts a similar definition

2.   *A relatively high, and growing, stock-turnover ratio*; though supermarkets tend to have a higher ratio than High Street grocers.

Accounts to:	Stocks £m	Cost of Sales £m	Stock-turn
Kwik Save Aug 1992	154.6	2,278.7	14.74
M&W Sep 1993	5,259	54,471	10.36
Sainsbury Mar 1993	414.9	8,688.9	20.94
Tesco Feb 1993	240.0	6,849.0	28.54

Tesco's stock turnover ratio has improved in 8 of the last 9 years but it now seems to be struggling a little:

Tesco			
1985	178.3	2867.0	16.08
1987	182.5	3367.0	18.45
1989	192.2	4340.6	22.58
1991	231.5	5767.7	25.00
1992	221.7	6,435.9	29.03
1993	240.0	6,849.0	28.54

3.   *Very low debtors*, because few sales are on credit:

Accounts to:	Trade Debtors £m	Sales £m	Months Sales
Kwik Save Aug 1993	1.5	2,651.7	0.0070
M&W Sep 1993	0.588	71,495	0.0001
Sainsbury March 1993	21.8	9,685.5	0.0270
Tesco Feb 1993	31.9	7,581.5	0.0505

4.   *Negative net current assets* (the use of what is sometimes termed 'other people's capital'), in other words a current ratio less than 1.

Accounts to:	Current Assets (unadjusted) £m	Creditors due within a year Current £m	Ratio
Kwik Save Aug 1993	202.3	318.5	0.64
M&W Sep 1993	10.414	9.082	1.15
Sainsbury Mar 1993	804.0	1,524.6	0.53
Tesco Feb 1993	525.4	1,055.7	0.50

5.   *Massive investment in property assets* (where possible, freeholds), representing a high proportion of capital employed:

Accounts to:	Properties net £m	Capital and Reserves £m	%
Kwik Save Aug 1992	344.5	347.8	99.05
M&W Sep 1993	4.12	9.99	41.24
Sainsbury Mar 1993	3,540.7	3,028.7	116.9
Tesco Feb 1993	*3,513.8	2,752.9	127.64

* including £191.6m in course of construction

Sale and leaseback is frequently used (in 1990 Tesco quoted its policy as being to finance 30% of new store development by leaseback, maintaining freehold asset backing at around 70% in the longer term).

5.   *Very low gearing.*

TESCO *Gearing*	1993 £m	1992 £m
Net Other Borrowings and Finance Lease Obligations (per Note 26)	531.5	480.4
Shareholders' funds	2,752.9	2,447.0
Borrowings/Shareholders' funds	19.3%	19.6%

6.   *Openness about strategy.* Supermarkets, tend to be very open about store development and profit improvement strategies.

7.   *Response to public and investor concern* (a) that saturation may soon be reached; (b) that discounters and new warehouse chains may make inroads; that the enormous buying power of chains like Sainsbury enables them to keep prices (unduly) high.

Practice

In April 1990 shares in ARGOS PLC were distributed to the shareholders of BAT INDUSTRIES PLC, Argos ceased to be a subsidiary of BAT and became an independent quoted company ie it was demerged. Consider the reports and accounts from 1990 to date. How successful do you regard the demerger as being? Why do you feel this?

Chapter 23

UTILITIES

General Overview

In this chapter we look at utilities: companies which fall for FT-SE Actuaries Index purposes under the headings:

1. Electricity;
2. Water;
3. Telecommunications.

Worldwide, utilities share a number of features. Because they provide a domestic service to a large number of customers:

1. A monopoly position of one sort or another;
2. Operation under the watchful eye of the state, local government or other watchdog;
3. A high profile;
4. Customer resistance to price increases, which is easily organised;
5. State interference in pricing, and possibly development, policy.

Most UK utilities are former nationalised industries which have recently been 'privatised', ie sold off by the state.

Privatised utilities

A number of organisations have, within the last ten years, been privatised, and allowed, encouraged, to operate in the private sector. They include:

1. Freight;
2. Gas

which fall outside the scope of this chapter, and

3. Electricity;
4. Water;
5. Telecommunications

which form its main subject.

Privatised organisations share a number of key features:

1. Accounts at, and to, the point of privatisation, adjusted for the purpose of sale, ie accounts which probably do not represent the published accounts of the former business, because the privatised company has been:

    (i) Trimmed of loss-making, subsidiary, and other activities to make the product attractive both to seller (the state) and to potential investors;

    (ii) Given a new capital structure.

2. A capital structure which includes one special rights redeemable preference share of £1 (the 'Special Share') issued to HM Government (carrying no right to dividend and redeemable at the holder's option). Written consent of the holder is required before certain changes in the articles are made.

3. Possibly, government finance by debenture repayable over a period (say 5 years).

4. Usually, payment by instalments for shares issued.

5. Often, discounts either against invoices for supplies from the utility or against a subsequent instalment for individuals continuing to hold the shares.

6. Some form of regulator, possibly price control structure.

7. A licence or franchise defining its areas of operation.

8. Provision for payment of property clawbacks to HM Government on the disposal of tangible fixed assets.

9. A large number of investors with small holdings (eg at 31 March 1992, Scottish Power

had 754,936 shareholders with 200 shares or less).

10. Although the denationalisation issues attracted many new small investors to the market, they are not without risk. It is always possible that:

   (i) A future socialist government might renationalise them;

   (ii) The compensation provided might be limited; – but this does not seem an election-winning policy, since many shareholders in the denationalised utilities might as a result be persuaded to vote tory when they otherwise might not have done so.

   (iii) The regulator may favour consumers at the expense of shareholders.

11. A major significance in terms of the FT–SE 100 Index. There are currently six electricity companies, four water companies and BT in the FOOTSIE index, as well as BRITISH GAS.

12. An urge to build up the proportion of their activities not subject to regulation eg water companies: by operating overseas, and in waste management.

Electricity

The companies listed in the sector all represent privatised former nationalised industries, either primarily generators or regional suppliers of power.

There are four generators:

NATIONAL POWER
POWERGEN
SCOTTISH POWER
SCOTTISH HYDRO

of which NATIONAL POWER is much the largest; though the two Scottish generators together do not fall far short of its market capitalisation. SCOTTISH POWER is a composite utility, part generator and part distributor; as is SCOTTISH HYDRO – which supplies the North of Scotland. Indeed all the generators seem to sell direct to large consumers of electricity.

There are 13 regional electricity (distribution) companies (RECs), several of which have market capitalisations in excess of £1,550m:

EASTERN
LONDON
MIDLANDS
SOUTHERN

The industry operates under the Electricity Act 1989 and its regulators are the Director General of Electricity Supply (DGES) and the Office of Electricity Regulation (OFFER). But the industry cannot escape a more hands-on approach on the part of government.

Crucial to the future success of the industry as a whole are the contracts between the generators – the original contracts expired on 31 March 1993:

1. The national interest is clearly involved:

   (i) It would be undesirable for Britain to be unduly dependent on foreign sources of supply (although it does use a link with France);

   (ii) Some potential fuels are currently provided by nationalised industries (coal), others by privatised organisations subject to regulation (gas), and others by private industry (oil and gas) – the state surely has an interest in Britain's energy balance in the medium and long term.

2. Electricity generators are in a monopoly situation.

The industry is, nevertheless, able to act with a fair amount of freedom in setting up commercial deals. For example:

1. POWERGEN:

   (i) have worldwide consultancy experience, and are looking to buy, build and operate power stations abroad and to acquire interests in overseas power generation businesses;

   (ii) have an interest in oil and gas fields in the UK and overseas;

   (iii) aim to be Britain's premier wind power generator.

2. SCOTTISH POWER acquired 17 shops from Rumbelows and now run these together with eight Atlantis superstores to give it a considerable retail presence.

3. EASTERN ELECTRICITY, SOUTHERN ELECTRIC and, more recently, MIDLAND have transferred their retailing and appliance servicing businesses to a jointly owned associated undertaking E&S Retail Ltd.

4. SOUTHERN ELECTRIC are participating in three independent generation schemes to be owned by Barking Power, Medway Power and Isle of Grain and Derwent Cogeneration. They are also involved in pipe and cable laying, the industrial gas market and environmental control systems.

5. SEEBOARD have taken advantage of the increasing deregulation of gas supply to enter into a joint venture to market and supply natural gas to commercial and industrial companies throughout the South of England.

So it unwise to ignore the complexity of the electricity companies.

Points to look for in the accounts of electricity companies:

1. Most companies do more than one thing eg distribute, supply and generate. These are often not equally profitable, so segmental information is valuable.
2. The Public Electricity Supply Licence requires accounting statements of the distribution, supply and generation businesses to be published with the annual accounts of the licensee – normally they are free of charge on application.
3. Current cost accounts are often published either as the primary accounts or supplementary to them. Typically the CCA profit is about half the HC profit.

Water

There are about 13 listed water utilities in the sector, several of which have market capitalisations in excess of £1,200m:

THAMES
SEVERN TRENT
NORTH WEST
ANGLIAN
YORKSHIRE.

The industry operates under the Water Act 1989 and companies hold appointments as water and sewerage undertakers to provide services in defined areas. That part of the water company's business is regulated by the Secretary of State for the Environment, the Director General of Water Services and the National Rivers Authority.

A feature of the accounts is the heavy investment in infrastructure assets (North West Water: 1992 £1.052 billion), operational structures and the like (which typically far exceed a year's turnover), and the substantial amount of assets in course of construction. In 1992, for example, the ratio of turnover / capital employed of North West Water was 46.48%. Typically, infrastructure assets are not depreciated but treated on a renewals basis.

NORTH WEST WATER *Extract from Accounting Policies 1992*

Tangible fixed assets
Tangible fixed assets comprise infrastructure assets (mains, sewers, impounding and pumped raw water storage reservoirs, dams, sludge pipelines and sea outfalls, and other assets (including properties, overground plant and equipment).

(i) **Infrastructure assets**
Infrastructure assets comprise a network of systems. Expenditure on infrastructure assets relating to increases in capacity or enhancement of the network is treated as additions, which are included

at cost, after deducting related grants and contributions).

Expenditure on maintaining the operating capacity of the network in accordance with defined standards of service is charged as an operating cost. No depreciation is charged on infrastructure assets because the network of systems is required to be maintained in perpetuity and therefore has no finite economic life. ...

Supplementary current cost accounts are often published. Typically the CCA profit is about 20% less than the HC profit., but the replacement cost of fixed assets is perhaps 10 times their HC carrying value (as with North West Water).

Many of the water systems inherited by the Water Authority in 1974 were dilapidated and inadequate: networks of aqueducts, mains, sewers and waste water systems were aged. Investment programmes tend to be ambitious.

In part this reflects demands, not least from the EC, for higher standards of water quality, and tighter environmental controls. As a result the cost of water has risen sharply in recent years.

Like the electricity companies, water utilities (like NORTH WEST WATER and SEVERN TRENT) have branched out into areas such as:

(i) Desalination treatment;
(ii) Waste water treatment;
(iii) Disinfection and the handling of epidemics;
(iv) Filters;
(v) Fish farming;
(vi) Sludge and solids handling.

Telecommunications

BT stands out among companies in this sector as, currently, Britain's largest company in terms of market capitalisation (in excess of £28,000m).

Other substantial listed companies include:

CABLE & WIRELESS
VODAPHONE

both over £6,000m.

BT is a denationalised utility which, until 1993 was part-owned by HM Government. It is big: with over 200,000 employees and assets in excess of £16,000m.

The accounts of BT are notable for:

1. The very heavy investment in fixed assets: in particular plant and equipment (at cost, £23,134m in March 1993);
2. Long term borrowing (much, more than 5 years);
3. Substantial use of overseas borrowing (mainly US $);
4. The use of interest rate swaps;

5. Substantial potential liability in respect deferred taxation (mostly excess capital allowances);
6. A quarterly analysis of turnover and profit;
7. Three pages of excellent financial and operational statistics; showing, amongst other things:
   (i) financial ratios (such as gearing, interest cover, growth in eps and dividends per share);
   (ii) the breakdown of expenditure on fixed assets;
   (iii) quality of service criteria.
8. Substantial reorganisation and early release costs.

Look out for comment on:

9. Competition (possibly severe) not only from MERCURY but from the US telecommunications giant AT&T.
10. Developments. There is enormous potential for telecommunications in the office, in working from home, and in security and similar systems. Telecommunications is an international business; note any new overseas links or potential competition.

The statistics reproduced alongside provide a feel for the overall report, but it is important to consider the whole document. Note how it highlights:

(i) The pressure on growth (caused by the recession);
(ii) The marked effect of prices of regulation (agreements with HM Government and OFTEL).

Practice

The trustees of a medium sized pension fund (£1m-5m) are considering investing 20% of the fund in utilities.

1. Obtain and study the accounts of:

   POWERGEN
   SOUTHERN ELECTRIC
   NORTH WEST WATER
   BT.
2. Compare these companies in terms of:
   (i) Profit performance (ie growth);
   (ii) Price performance (including volatility), past and potential;
   (iii) Risk.

3. Consider the statistical information provided by BT and develop a case for the provision of statistical data to be made more general.

BT *Extracts from operational statistics 1993*

			Year ended 31 March		
	1989	1990	1991	1992	1993
Call growth					
% growth in telephone call volumes over the previous year:					
Inland	11	10	4	1	–
International	13	13	6	4	6
Exchange line connections					
Business (000)	5,037	5,551	5,795	5,866	5,970
% growth over previous year	10.5	10.2	4.4	1.2	1.8
Residential (000)	18,703	19,246	19,573	19,729	20,114
% growth over previous year	3.3	2.9	1.7	0.8	2.0
Network modernisation					
% of customer lines serviced by type					
Digital	23.1	37.7	46.9	54.6	64.0
Semi-electronic (analogue)	40.3	38.6	37.1	35.0	31.9
Electro-mechanical (analogue)	36.6	23.7	16.0	10.4	4.1
Optical fibre					
Fibre – kilometres (000)	610	938	1,441	2,045	2,337
Cellnet					
Cellular telephones in the UK (000)	258	429	509	547	658
Price control					
% RPI movement ...	4.61	8.26	9.79	5.84	3.88
RPI formula in effect	(3.00)	(4.50)	(4.50)	(6.25)	(6.25)
% permitted increase (required reduction) in prices	2.80	3.76	5.52	(0.23)	(0.95)
% actual increase (reduction) in prices	–	3.53	5.34	(0.73)	(0.10)

Chapter 24

PHARMACEUTICALS AND HEALTH CARE

General overview

In this chapter we consider two sectors: Pharmaceuticals and Heath Care. The Pharmaceuticals sector includes one of Britain's two largest companies (in terms of market capitalisation):

GLAXO

followed by:

SMITHKLINE BEECHAM
ZENECA
WELLCOME.

A poor fourth in size (but still having a market capitalisation in excess of £900m) is FISONS, which is followed by a host of smaller pharmaceutical companies like:

MEDEVA
SCOTIA
CELLTECH
BRITISH BIOTECHNOLOGY.

The Health Care sector includes companies like LONDON INTERNATIONAL GROUP – which makes and sells consumer goods, such as contraceptives, health and beauty products; household, industrial and surgeons' gloves – which is almost 'manufacturing'.

SCHOLL specialises in manufacturing and distributing personal care products, but are best known for foot and leg care.

In between lie various other specialisms. UNICHEM, for instance, provides pharmaceutical distribution and support facilities to retail and hospital pharmacies, as well as operating a chain of its own pharmacies. SMITH & NEPHEW focuses especially on wound management, and things like orthopaedic, eye and ear implants.

A number of companies in the sector, like ASSOCIATED NURSING SERVICES, COMMUNITY HOSPITALS GROUP, GREENACRE GROUP, QUALITY CARE HOMES, and TAKARE develop and operate private hospitals, nursing homes and homes for the elderly.

As will be seen, this a complex sector, involving a wide range of activities from drugs to food, from chemicals to property; the risks involved in which vary widely. It is also a sector (particularly pharmaceuticals) in which market sentiment, and fears of government interference in pricing or licensing produce high volatility. Consider the share price of Glaxo in 1992–93; or that of Wellcome in 1987 (high 514p; low 178p).

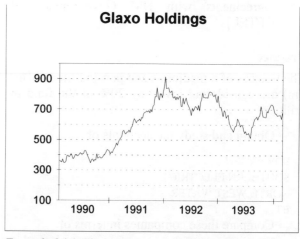

Example 24.1 Glaxo share price fell 41% between January 1992 and April 1993

What to look for in the reports and accounts of pharmaceutical companies

Pharmaceutical companies:

1. *Tend to exhibit a high rate of growth in earnings per share.*

134

	Year to	Earnings per share growth (%)
Medeva	Dec 91	147.1
	Dec 92	53.57
Wellcome	Aug 91	29.07
	Aug 92	36.0
Glaxo	Jun 92	12.1
	Jun 93	16.3

2. *Tend to have a high rate of return on capital employed.* We take ROCE to be Profit before interest and tax / Closing capital employed.

	Year to	ROCE (%)
Medeva	Dec 92	49.0
Wellcome	Aug 92	42.9
Glaxo	Jun 93	37.3
SmithKline Beecham	Dec 92	35.8

3. *Look for high profit margins.*

	Year to	Margin (%)
Medeva	Dec 92	55.6
Glaxo	Jun 93	30.9
Wellcome	Aug 92	27.7
SmithKline Beecham	Dec 92	21.9

4 *Can be divided* into those which have patented drugs already on the market and those (like PROTEUS and BRITISH BIOTECHNOLOGY) which are trying to develop drugs. The former are often heavily dependent on a single product (drug):

Glaxo	Zantac	Anti-ulcerant
Wellcome	Zovirax	Anti-viral
SmithKline Beecham	Augmentin	Antibiotic
	Tagamet	Peptic ulcer treatment

5. *Depend heavily upon* their ability:

    (i) to develop market-leading drugs;
    (ii) to obtain patent protection worldwide;
    (iii) to gain necessary approvals to enable them to be marketed worldwide;
    (iv) to avoid adverse publicity / negligence claims.

6. *Spend heavily on research and development.*

	Year to	R & D £m	Sales £m	% of turnover
Glaxo	Jun 93	739	4,930	15.0
Wellcome	Aug 92	254.6	1,762	14.4
SmithKline Beecham	Dec 92	478	5,219	9.2

This spending tends to be international (eg Glaxo in 1992 had research facilities not only in the UK but in the US, Italy, Japan, Spain and elsewhere.

International involvement may win the confidence of the regulatory boards, and make it easier to obtain international licensing.

It is not, of course, research *spending* which is important so much as *successful* research and development, and marketing. That can only be measured with hindsight.

7. *Often sell worldwide.* That is not surprising as all countries are interested in improving the health of their populations. In 1992, Glaxo estimated that the world market for pharmaceuticals was £93,400m of which the US, Japan, Germany, Italy and France (in that order) accounted for £64,700m. The UK came a poor sixth at £3,100m.

8. *Often overlap into consumer products*, eg SmithKline Beecham produce Horlicks, Lucozade and Ribena; and are into animal health.

9. *Also sometimes spread into the area of garden and horticultural products* (eg Fisons, although they are trying to sell these interests).

What to look for in the report and accounts of health care companies

Because of their diverse nature, the companies in the sector are difficult to compare. The first thing to do is to find out what the company does, and where it does it. Upon whom does it depend for its success (eg the NHS). This dependence may be direct (eg the purchasing of bandages or surgical equipment) or indirect (the worse NHS facilities are perceived to be, the more successful is private health care likely to be).

Included in the sector are companies like ASSOCIATED NURSING SERVICES and QUALITY CARE HOMES which have some of the characteristics of property and construction companies; and were hit in a similar way by the 1990 recession; and in many ways are more like hotels. This means that site costs, the costs of development and occupancy all play an important part in success (or failure).

In the case of such companies, readers are advised to examine carefully how prudent their accounting policies are, for example: on capitalisation of interest, operating costs prior to opening, marketing and training costs (see Westminster Health Care Holdings).

Practice: Medeva Case Study

The principal activities of the Medeva Group are the development, manufacture and sales of pharmaceutical products. Given the information provided on pages 136–138, prepare a report outlining the activities and financial success of the group.

Start by skimming the profit and loss account and consolidated balance sheet. See what strikes you. In our commentary we show some of the in formation which we dug out to answer our queries. If you can, obtain a copy of the full report and study it.

Commentary

1. Turnover: Substantial increase (74.9% year on year). Part due to acquisition within the year. Find out how it was financed.? Was the increase also perhaps due to acquisition in 1991?

2. Gross profit margin high (55.5%) and improving (1991: 45.8%) – although the new acquisition seems marginally less profitable.

3. Research and development: only 3.96% of turnover, but growing (1991: 3.04%).

4. Selling and marketing costs show a sharp increase (13.8% of turnover; 1991: 9.4%). Why?

5. Gain on refocussing of UK generics operations: Jargon? The Managing Director explains in his report: 'After a year of further severe price reductions in the UK unbranded generics market, the Group withdrew from a marketing presence in this non-strategic business in October 1992 [so the effect on turnover / operating profit will be felt fully in 1993] . In October 1992 stocks of unbranded generics were sold to Norton Healthcare .... At the same time Evans-Kerfoot contracted to supply products to Norton for a two year period ...'. It is nice to see a profitable disposal.

6. Interest: a sharp swing from £835,000 net received to £1,319,000 payable.

7. Taxation: a markedly higher tax charge. Note 6 (page 137) goes some way to explain.

MEDEVA *Extracts from report and accounts for 1992*

CONSOLIDATED PROFIT AND LOSS ACCOUNT
for the year ended 31 December 1992

	1992 Acquisition	1992 Continuing Operations	1992 Total	1991 Total
	£000	£000	£000	£000
Turnover (2)	14,233	129,961	144,194	82,434
Cost of sales	(8,453)	(55,648)	(64,101)	(44,678)
Gross Profit	5,780	74,313	80,093	37,756
Research and Development Expenses	(394)	(5,321)	(5,715)	(2,509)
Distribution costs	(523)	(2,531)	(3,054)	(2,538)
Selling and marketing costs	(2,221)	(17,647)	(19,868)	(7,764)
Administrative expenses	(1,760)	(13,615)	(15,375)	(9,055)
Operating profit	882	35,199	36,081	15,890
Net gain on refocusing of UK generic operations (3)			1,220	–
			37,301	15,890
Interest receivable and similar income			125	1,053
Interest payable and similar charges			(1,444)	(218)
Profit on ordinary activities before tax			35,982	16,725
Tax on profit on ordinary activities			(10,915)	(3,033)
Profit on ordinary activities after tax			25,067	13,692
Minority interests			469	(72)
Profit for the year attributable to the Members of Medeva plc			25,536	13,620
Dividends			(4,753)	(2,877)
Retained profit for the year			20,783	10,743
Earnings per ordinary share				
Basic			12.9p	8.4p
Fully diluted			12.2p	8.3p
Dividend per ordinary share				
Interim			0.75p	0.5p
Final			1.5p	1.0p
			2.25p	1.5p

CONSOLIDATED BALANCE SHEET
as at 31 December 1992

	1992 £000	1991 £000
Fixed Assets		
Intangible assets	45,339	24,753
Tangible assets	49,380	31,759
	94,719	56,512
Current assets		
Stock	27,737	26,067
Debtors	46,809	23,307
Cash at bank and in hand	4,716	40,757
	79,262	90,131
Creditors – Amounts due within one year	(84,806)	(64,438)
Net current liabilities	(5,544)	25,693
Total assets less current liabilities	89,175	82,205
Creditors due after more than one year	(15,338)	(6,298)
Provisions for liabilities and charges	(436)	(862)
	73,401	75,045
Capital and Reserves		
Called up Share Capital	19,835	19,806
Deferred Share Capital	1,087	1,087
Share Premium Account	26,326	25,842
Goodwill Reserve	(25,262)	(2,682)
Profit and Loss Account	50,784	29,856
	72,769	73,909
Minority Interests	632	1,136
	73,401	75,045

NOTE 6 TAXATION	1992 £000	1991 £000
UK – Corporation tax at 33.00% (1991: 33.25%)	1,295	1,205
– prior year	–	(102)
Overseas – Income taxes	8,249	1,260
Deferred tax	1,371	670
	10,915	3,033

The charge for taxation has been significantly affected by reliefs on the amortisation of intangibles in certain United States undertakings. Because no charge to taxation arises on the exceptional gain ... the tax effect of ... the refocussing of the generics operations is a tax credit of £1.2m.

NOTE 2 ANALYSIS OF TURNOVER, PROFIT AND NET ASSETS

(a) Turnover by destination

	1992 £000	1991 £000
United Kingdom	67,398	59,247
United States of America	65,664	14,708
Rest of Europe	8,383	5,594
Rest of World	2,749	2,885

(b) Geographical analysis by country of origin

	Turnover 1992 £000	1991 £000	Profit on ordinary activities 1992 £000	1991 £000
United Kingdom	75,919	67,400	11,690	8,374
United States of America	64,757	12,248	24,776	8,093
Rest of Europe	3,518	2,786	(484)	260

	Net assets 1992 £000	1991 £000
United Kingdom	32,769	60,993
United States of America	25,590	12,319
Rest of Europe	15,042	1,733

EXTRACTS FROM OPERATING AND FINANCIAL REVIEW

Sales growth.

Sales in the year increased ... This growth results from a combination of factors including:

- The impact of owning MD and Adams for the full 12 months in 1992 rather than the seven month period for MD and two month period for Adams in 1991.
- The impact of acquiring IMS on 1 July 1992 with the resultant sales contribution of £14.2m for the six months to the end of December
- Organic growth within the constituent businesses (including MD, Adams and IMS) and the continued expansion of branded and speciality product lines.

The overall sales for the year were some 31% greater than those achieved by the divisions in 1991 (looking at the sales for the year whether or not the division was part of the Medeva Group for any or all of the period). This is useful information all too rarely provided.

The withdrawal from the direct sale of commodity generics in the UK had little impact on 1992 sales as compared to 1991 but this will impact upon sales in 1993 and beyond. This should not have a significant effect on operating profits.

Influence of US operations

A large proportion of the group's sales and profits in 1992 arose in the US with £64.7m or 45% of turnover and £24.8m or 69% of pre-tax profits being generated by MD, Adams and IMS. The impact of owning IMS for a full year and the consolidation of the operations of Armstrong from January 1993 is likely to increase the proportion arising in the US until Medeva expands its European operations. Accordingly the reported results of the Medeva Group are very dependent on the sterling/dollar exchange rate.

Operating margins

The gross profit margin increased from 46% in 1991 to 56% in 1992. This increase represents a combination of improved operating efficiencies and a policy of concentrating upon the development, acquisition and sale of higher margin branded or speciality products.

The operating profit margin increased from 19% in 1991 to 25% in 1992, largely as a result of the factors noted above. The increased size of the group (from around 1,300 employees at the end of 1991 to almost 2,000 by the year end) has led to an increase in general and administrative costs. These expenses should abate as a percentage of turnover as the group becomes more mature and capitalises on savings which will result from combining elements of its operations.

Selling costs increased significantly in 1992, largely as a result of the impact of Adams which is primarily a sales and marketing company. The concentration on branded and speciality products will also lead to higher sales costs in the future.

Research and development

The group focuses its activities almost entirely on late-stage development of products rather than pure research.

The purchase of products in the late-stages of development and the subsequent registration of these products is considered by the Directors to be a cost-effective way of securing new products and the future of the group. Accordingly the group will purchase more products and the expenditure on development (which includes registration and compliance work) is likely to increase, albeit not to the extent demonstrated by major, research-based pharmaceutical companies.

Taxation

The overall tax rate in 1992 was 30%, up from 18% in 1991 when advantage was taken of losses brought forward.

Cash flow

The operations of the group are profitable and are cash-generative. (The review goes on spell out the background to the major cash flows – which we found helpful).

Shareholders' return

The group's policy of acquiring companies with earnings potential rather than a strong asset-base and of writing off the goodwill on acquisition of those companies means that the net assets of the group are relatively low (£73m) as are the assets per share at £0.37p (1991: 0.38p). Were goodwill to be carried on the balance sheet at the acquisition cost these figures would increase to £259m and £1.30 per share. Moreover the group has never revalued the carrying value of products purchased nor does it include brand names, trademarks or other such items within the assets other than where these have been purchased from third parties.

Research and development costs are also expensed rather than capitalised. In addition, the value of such items as customer lists, sales forces and other such intangible assets are not valued in the accounts. Accordingly the group has significant assets other than those included within these accounts.

Financial needs and resources

The major current capital expenditure programmes of the group are now virtually complete. Capital expenditure in 1993 should be significantly lower than in 1992 but there will be a continuing investment programme to ensure that the Group is in compliance with the requirements of the various regulatory authorities throughout the world and also in seeking production efficiencies. The acquisition of new products can also entail significant capital expenditure in order to achieve on-going cost savings in manufacturing.

The cash flow generated from operations will allow an underlying reduction in the bank borrowings in 1993.

Major unscheduled items of expenditure arise upon the acquisition of companies and products. The financing method is reviewed with each acquisition and therefore the cash position of the group can vary significantly from year to year. Several previous acquisitions have been financed through equity fund raisings and this is likely to continue in the future as stock market conditions and acquisition opportunities arise.

The gearing of the group at the year-end (net bank borrowings [£38.926m in 1992] to shareholders' funds) was 47% (1991: 0%). More relevant to Medeva, the operating profits covered interest by a factor of 27 in 1992.

Earnings per share and dividends

The earnings per share of the companies have increased as follows:

1990	1991	1992
3.4p	8.4p	12.9p

The key measure of the success of Medeva is the achievement of a significant long-term growth in earnings per share. The growth achieved to date is notable since it reflects the selection and pricing of acquisitions, the financing methods used and organic growth achieved after acquisitions.

Medeva is following a progressive dividend policy but will maintain a conservative approach to dividend cover for the time being.

Note 6 suggests a need to examine where sales and profits are being made. It is clear from Note 2 that there has been a sea-change (a move into the US (where turnover increased 346%). Profits are now earned 68.9% in the US (1991: 48.4%).

The Operating and Financial Review is a model, worthy of study. It is frank, prepared to look into the future. It provides a finance director's eye view of those matters which clearly engaged his attention; and as such it focuses on several of the areas already highlighted:

We sum up

Everything suggests a group which is prudent and well-managed, makes the right sort of acquisitions and knows where it is going. But we cannot resist throwing a pebble into the water. The group has ADRs in the US and thus produces a reconciliation between UK and US accounting principles. Those for 1991 and 1992 can be summarised:

	Notes	1992 £000	1991 £000
Profit after taxation and extraordinary items under UK GAAP		25,536	13,620
US GAAP adjustments:			
Goodwill and intangibles	(a)	(20,328)	(11,708)
Acquisition accounting	(b)	(2,160)	(5,502)
Pensions	(c)	(318)	(448)
Compensation expense	(d)	(2,713)	(4,625)
		--------	--------
Approximate net profit under US GAAP		17	(8,663)
		--------	--------

Rather a difference!

The notes explain:

1. Goodwill on consolidation is written off directly to reserves under UK GAAP but the goodwill is capitalised and amortised over its useful life under US GAAP - usually over 10 years but the non-complete agreement within MD is written off over 5 years. Additionally, intangible assets which are amortised over 20 years under UK GAAP are written off over 10 years for US GAAP purposes.
2. The treatment of certain aspects of the acquisition of companies is different under US GAAP than under UK GAAP. Typical differences include the treatment of provisions for re-organisation costs, imputed interest on delayed funding of an acquisition and recognition of income from the contract date rather than the closing date. Moreover US GAAP treats the value of tax loss carryforwards and the deferred tax on reorganisation provisions as a reduction of goodwill at the time the benefit is realised.
3. The methods of accounting for pension costs differ between UK and US GAAP.
4. This represents the difference between the market value of share options held by management under the Senior Executive Share Option scheme at the year end and the share option exercise price together with the difference between the market value of the shares at the date the options were granted and the price at which the share options are exercisable. Whilst this gain is both unrealised and has no impact on the profitability of the company, US GAAP requires that the imputed gain to the individual employees be treated as an expense.
5. Under UK GAAP, final ordinary dividends are provided for in the accounts in the year in respect of which they are recommended by the board for approval by shareholders. Under US GAAP such dividends are not provided until declared by the directors.
6. Under US GAAP the deferred consideration payable to former shareholders of Adams Laboratories is treated as a liability rather than deferred equity.

Ask yourself: how can the world's two leading accounting nations come to such differwent conclusions. Which results do you believe?

Further practice

Obtain and study carefully the latest report and accounts of ML LABORATORIES.

1. Contrast the treatment of research and development costs by MEDEVA and ML.
2. Obtain: (i) the share price graph for 1989 to date; and (ii) figures for turnover, profit and eps for the same period. Try to explain the price behaviour of the shares.
3. Your maiden aunt (74) has a small investment portfolio. A neighbour, who has seen an investment of £2,000 in 1988 grow to £24,000 in 1993, recommends her to buy ML. Advise.

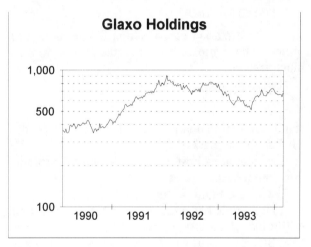

Glaxo Holdings

4. Compare this Glaxo share price graph with that on page 134. Note that it is plotted on semi-logarithmic paper, ie its vertical scale represents the logarithms of share prices. Why do analysts sometimes use this device?

Chapter 25

OIL, INTEGRATED, EXPLORATION AND PRODUCTION; GAS DISTRIBUTION

General overview

The oil sector is now divided into Oil, Integrated, with just three companies and Oil, Exploration and Production with 11. BRITISH GAS now appears in the separate Gas Distribution sector.

The three companies in Oil, Integrated are:

SHELL T & T
BP
BURMAH CASTROL

each with a market capitalisation in excess of £20 billion. The companies in the other oil sector are much smaller:

ENTERPRISE OIL
LASMO

stand out with a market capitalisation around the £1–2.5 billion mark.

But there are a host of smaller listed oil exploration companies.

In Gas Distibution, BRITISH GAS could equally well be regarded as a utility – a recently privatised utility like electricity or water. Many oil producers like BP have substantial interests in byproducts which could be said to be chemicals. They also have minimarkets selling food. But there is also close connection with shipping, since tankers may be owned or chartered. SHELL has mining interests.

The oil and gas industry is characterised by:

1. The high risk involved in exploration;
2. The high capital expenditure required to bring discoveries into production; and
3. The long lead time between initial exploration, subsequent appraisal and development and the first commercial production.

Downstream activities ie selling petrol, oil etc to the final consumer, depend heavily on the state of the economy, on fuel tax, as well as the volatility of oil and gas prices (whether as a result of OPEC or otherwise).

Interpretation of the published accounts of oil and gas company accounts is made difficult by the great variety of practices found most especially among small and medium sized companies.

Key areas are:

1. Costs of exploration and development.
2. Abandonment costs.
3. Accounting for Petroleum Revenue Tax (PRT).

Exploration and development expenditure

Policies for dealing with the costs of exploration and development fall into two broad categories:

1. Successful efforts accounting;
2. Full cost accounting.

Under successful efforts accounting, *unsuccessful* exploration is written off immediately, which seems the prudent course.

Full cost accounting is based on the view that unsuccessful efforts are an inevitable part of the search for hydrocarbons, and the costs should therefore be expensed to match income derived from all ventures within the same geographical area. Under this method, the costs of both successful and unsuccessful efforts are depreciated against income arising from the former. Net income tends to be recognised earlier; and the trend of profits tends to be more regular from year to year.

In December 1987, the Oil Industry Accounting Committee issued a SORP on *Accounting for Oil and Gas Exploration and Development Activities* which recognises that both successful efforts accounting and full cost accounting have valid conceptual justification and neither should be favoured in preference to the other.

But the method applied should be applied consistently by all companies within a group.

There is a tendency for large integrated companies to use the successful efforts method (BP, British Gas, Shell UK, Esso UK and Enterprise Oil all do), whereas, Petrofina(UK) and Premier Consolidated Oilfields are among those using full cost. Both Clyde Petroleum and Lasmo changed recently from full cost to successful efforts.

Successful efforts

The SORP on *Accounting for Oil & Gas Exploration and Development Activities* recommends that under a successful efforts policy:

1. All exploration and development costs should initially be capitalised pending determination of success.

2. Expenditure incurred prior to acquisition, and costs of exploration which are not specifically directed to an identified structure, should be written off in the period in which they are incurred.

3. Expenditure incurred in exploration and development should be written off unless commercial reserves have been established or the determination process has not been completed.

4. The costs of exploration and appraisal wells should be accumulated on a well-by-well basis, and written off on completion of the well unless the results of drilling indicate hydrocarbon reserves exist and there is a reasonable prospect that the reserves are commercial.

5. After appraisal, the net carried costs relating to a discovery of commercial reserves are to be transferred to a single cost centre. Subsequent development costs, including, if desired, the cost of dry development wells, should be included in this cost centre. But only such general and administrative expenditure as is directly related to activities the costs of which are retained may be capitalised.

6. The maximum period for retention of capitalised exploration and appraisal expenditure is three years following the drilling in offshore or frontier environments and two years in other areas. *But* if further appraisal of the prospect is under way, capital expenditure may nevertheless remain capitalised. Expenditure incurred subsequent to appraisal should be carried forward only as long as there exists a clear intention to develop the field.

Another SORP, *Disclosures about Oil and Gas Exploration and Production Activities* (sometimes referred to as the Disclosures SORP), recommends that the method adopted in respect of pre-production costs should be described in sufficient detail to make clear the precise nature of costs, including exchange gains and losses and interest capitalised or written off.

Full cost accounting

Full cost accounting involves cost pools in which expenditure is accumulated. Since cost pools form the basis both of depreciation charges and tests of impairment, the choice of their geographical boundaries has a significant effect on results.

Although the SORP makes certain recommendations, subject to these it leaves the choice of cost pool largely to the company. It makes no specific recommendations, for instance, on their size, though they should not normally be smaller in size than a country; there is no maximum limit. Only where significant interests are subject to widely differing economic or fiscal factors (eg onshore and offshore interests) should more than one pool be established for one country.

Pre-licence, licence acquisition, exploration, appraisal and development activities should, the SORP suggests, be capitalised. Other costs, like those of general and administrative work, exchange differences on third party borrowings and financing costs, *may* be capitalised. Other costs should be expensed as incurred.

Certain costs, like pre-licence, licence acquisition, exploration and appraisal costs of individual licence interests may be held outside a cost pool – and hence remain undepreciated – until the existence or otherwise of commercial reserves is established, subject to there being no evidence of impairment.

Changes in the number and size of cost pools should only be made if warranted by business developments or changes in economic factors.

Some groups use a single global cost pool, most have 3, 4 or 5 pools worldwide.

Expenditure carried within each cost pool should be depreciated on a unit-of-production basis.

Points to look for in the accounts

Look particularly at:

1. The treatment of geological and geophysical costs, some companies expense them as incurred, others capitalise some of them, some like Sovereign write unsuccessful costs off over the term of the licence.

2. The various treatments applied to the acquisition costs of licences. BP writes them off over the exploratory period, other companies do so over the estimated holding period of the licence.

The SORP on exploration and development activities requires that where a successful efforts policy is adopted:

1. Expenditure carried within each field be depreciated on a unit-of-production basis.
2. Licence acquisition costs should be written off over a maximum period of the licence.
3. Undepreciated costs should be reviewed annually for impairment.

There are subtle differences in the bases of the unit-of-production calculations employed. Some companies refer to 'proved / proven recoverable reserves', others to 'estimated recoverable reserves', or 'estimated recoverable reserves and estimated costs to develop those reserves', 'proved developed reserves', or 'proven and probable reserves'. This makes oil company accounts difficult, if not impossible, to compare.

Impairment: ceiling tests

The Companies Act 1985 (Sch 4 para 19) requires provision to be made where there is permanent diminution in the value of fixed assets. This is of particular importance in the case of oil and gas companies, and especially those using the full cost method.

It is difficult to estimate the value of future cash flows. Assumptions need to be made about prices and costs of production, exchange rates and taxation, many years hence. It is also necessary to decide whether to use a measure of the time value of money (ie discounting techniques), though the SORP recommends not to discount. The Oil Industry Accounting Committee has set up a standard method for ceiling test computations. Despite this, various methods are used. A number of companies use discounting techniques and a variety of reserve bases are employed making comparisons difficult.

Abandonment and site restoration

The large scale of oil production operations, and especially those in the North Sea, means the cost of their ultimate abandonment and associated site restoration have a significant impact on oil and gas companies. The matching concept requires that the cost of abandonment be considered a cost of production, and prudence suggests that an accounting provision should have been set aside by the end of the production stream.

A SORP on this addresses the problems involved in making current provision:

1. For costs which will not be incurred for many years.
2. When considerable doubts exist as to the ventual requirements of the authorities and the technology which will then be available.

Amongst other things, the SORP calls for separate disclosure of the abandonment charge (included, depending on format chosen, within 'cost of sales' or 'other operating charges'), and of the accumulated provision (under 'provisions for liabilities and charges'), and details of the policy adopted for accounting for abandonment costs and the principal assumptions made in respect of eventual work required, the total estimated liability at period-end prices, and the rate assumed for any tax relief.

Taxation of oil and gas companies

Oil and gas companies operating on the UK continental shelf are liable for both petroleum revenue tax (PRT) and corporation tax.

PRT is a tax based on profits of production from a field, less certain allowances. Due to the incidence and nature of these allowances (which are front-end loaded) the amount of PRT payable in a particular period may bear little relation to the underlying pre-tax profits derived from the same source disclosed in the accounts. Deferred taxation therefore raises its ugly head.

ED29 was issued in 1981 on accounting for PRT and in 1986 the Oil Industry Accounting Committee issued an ED of a proposed SORP. Neither was accepted by the industry. Various methods are found.

Companies operating in the Norwegian Continental Shelf are subject to Norwegian Special Tax, which operates quite differently from PRT. Again one finds deferred taxation provisions.

The 1993 budget reduced the rate of tax and also planned to change the rules, so that PRT would not apply to new discoveries.

Oil and gas reserves

The Disclosures SORP makes recommendations on the inclusion of reserve data, though this is not mandatory. Around half the companies in the industry, including most major oil companies, provide such data, but it is not usually comparable from one company to another.

Companies with a US listing or involvement tend to be the most forthcoming (as a result of SEC requirements).

A favourable find, particularly in the case of exploration and development companies, can cause the share price to move sharply upwards.

Financing arrangements

Oil and gas are highly capital-intensive, high risk, industries, and one finds a variety of risk-sharing joint venture and consortium arrangements.

A carried interest arises where one or more members of a consortium are financed by other members during the exploration and/or development phase of a project. Repayment may be required only out of future production, if any, from the carried party's licence interest, probably with some uplift to account for the financing cost, and ceases on a defined event (eg payback) when full benefit of the carried interest returns to the licensee.

Commitments under such a contract to bear future expenditure are dealt with as normal financial commitments. The carried party should not record expenditure that has been borne by the carrying party; so the liability to repay carried costs is not recognised in the accounts themselves (though the SORP calls the carry arrangements and the amount of the expenditure to date to be disclosed by both parties).

In a farm out agreement a company agrees to bear some or all of the costs of exploration and/or development of a licence holder in exchange for a share in the licence interest.

Net production interests occur when a smaller company participating in a discovery assigns part of its working interest in that licence in return for which the purchaser finances a disproportionate share of the development costs. In this way the vendor may retain an interest in profits while retaining rights to any upside potential of further exploitation of the licence.

What is termed project finance may be obtainable from banks, which offer limited or non-recourse loans, in exchange having first call on the cash flows from relevant production.

Builders of offshore platforms will sometimes provide the necessary finance (termed *contractor finance*).

Capitalisation of interest

Many oil and gas companies capitalise interest but they differ on whether this is interest on borrowings specifically raised to finance particular developments, or the general funding cost of expenditure on development policies. Capitalisation of interest often gives rise to deferred taxation consequences.

Integration

Oil companies differ greatly in the focus of their activity. They often use the terms upstream and downstream - particularly when talking of expansion or development – upstream meaning production-oriented, and downstream retail-oriented.

Many, like BP, are fully integrated, involved internationally in exploration, production, refining and marketing of petroleum and petrochemicals. Others concentrate largely on exploration and the early stages of development, often in partnership or as a joint venture with others to spread the risk, with a view to selling on once production begins or is ready to. Yet others, like CALOR concentrate on the manufacture, sale and distribution of oils (or gas). And there are a host of specialist companies providing things like specialist outfitting, insulation and fireproofing (CHIEFTAIN in Building Materials and Merchants), corrosion control (RAMCO), survey and positioning services (OCEONICS GROUP). Since the risk and financial implications (the need to provide funds to continue development) are entirely different, it is important, in studying a company to find out exactly what it does.

Effect of foreign exchange rates

Crude Oil, in particular North Sea Oil, is priced in US $, so even companies operating solely in the UK or on the UK Continental shelf are affected by the £/$ exchange rate.

Oil and gas companies operating internationally are affected both by local exchange rates and £/$ rates. So it is important to watch the effects of both of world prices and currency changes.

Oil and gas tends to be international, so analysts frequently make comparisons with US and other foreign oil groups.

Environmental costs

Oil, gas, mining, building materials, chemicals and pharmaceutical companies are all involved in one way or other with the environment, and are potentially damaging to it. More is beginning to be said in reports and accounts about groups' aims and standards in this regard; and a look out should be kept for any mention of a contingent liability (eg in respect of a tanker disaster like the Exxon Valdez or other oil spillage) – for it could be very damaging.

Effects of FRS 3

The Oil Industry Accounting Committee has issued a Guidance Note on FRS 3 and its application to oil and gas companies.

Analysts have traditionally tried to estimate a net asset value per share (though it is difficult to place an accurate value on reserves) and the improved information and consistency provided by FRS 3 and the Guidance Note may do something to assist in this.

Practice

Floated in 1984, Enterprise Oil is one of Britain's leading independent oil companies. Obtain a copy of its latest report and accounts.

1. In what countries does it have exploration acreage?
2. In 1990, oil prices, influenced by events in the Middle East, swung from over $40 a barrel to around $18. Consider the behaviour of oil prices in the year reported upon and more recently.
3. Any volatility of price is exacerbated by the need to express sales proceeds in sterling terms. How is Enterprise Oil affected by recent foreign exchange movements?
4. The accounts are typical of an operator with upstream interests. How are most exploration, development and production activities conducted?
5. The group adopts a 'successful efforts' policy of accounting. Explain how this differs from 'full cost'.

6. What are its accounting policies regarding:
   (i) ceiling tests;
   (ii) abandonment;
   (iii) capitalisation of interest.
7. Enterprise Oil normally has vast current asset investments. Explain why.

[Enterprise believes in long-term finance, in getting the finance in place before development begins. In this way it is not caught out changes in the capital market once the process has started – a copartner who at a late stage was unable to meet his commitments would be very unpopular with his coventurers. Great care is, incidentally, taken in negotiating the covenant structure to ensure that lenders do not so protect themselves that it becomes difficult to carry on the business of exploration.]

8. BP often makes substantial stockholding gains(losses). Why does not Enterprise Oil?
9. What can you find out about the reserves of oil? Are they growing or sinking? Why the change?

Chapter 26

BANKS AND MERCHANT BANKS

General overview

Banks form part of the Financials Group of the FT-SE Actuaries All Share Index. Just over 20 British banks have a full listing. The Big Four have in recent years become the Big Eight or Nine. Those currently in the FTSE-100 Index are:

HSBC HOLDINGS (subsidiaries of which include
  MIDLAND BANK AND HONG KONG & SHANGHAI
  BANKING CORPORATION)
LLOYDS BANK
NATIONAL WESTMINSTER
BARCLAYS
ABBEY NATIONAL

each with a market capitalisation at 7 February 1994 of £6–9 billion; and, less than half that size:

TSB
ROYAL BANK OF SCOTLAND
STANDARD CHARTERED
BANK OF SCOTLAND

We cover in this Chapter also merchant banks which, like banks, form part of the Financials Group of the FT-SE Actuaries All Share Index. Merchant banks tend to be much smaller in terms of market capitalisation. Only S.G.WARBURG and SCHRODERS had a market capitalisation at that date exceeding £1 billion, their main rivals in terms of size being:

KLEINWORT BENSON
HAMBROS.

Banks come in all sorts and sizes

A 'bank' is what is termed an 'authorised institution' under the Banking Act 1987. Banks differ greatly not only in size but in what they do. It is possible to classify them broadly as:

1. *Large clearing or high street banks*, such as Bank of Scotland, Barclays, Lloyds, Midland, NatWest and Royal Bank of Scotland, who between them operate over 10,000 branches in the UK, taking deposits, cashing and collecting cheques, making loans and providing overdrafts.

2. *Merchant banks* (or 'investment banks'), such as Barings, Hambros, Kleinworts, Lazards, Warburg and Schroders; who undertake wholesale banking business for large industrial and private clients and governments. They specialise in areas such as acceptance and similar credits for export business, corporate finance, and on matters such as mergers, acquisitions and new issues. They provide a fund management service, looking after the funds of pension funds, investment and unit trusts. They are also heavily involved in Eurocurrency and Eurobond business.

    It has been said that 'while a clearing bank lives off its deposits, a merchant bank lives by its wits'.

3. *British Overseas Banks*, such as Standard Chartered and Grindlay's, now a subsidiary of Australia & New Zealand Banking Group, with large numbers of branches overseas.

4. *Foreign Banks*, operating in London through subsidiaries, branches or representative offices.

5. *Nationwide retail banks*, such as Abbey National, TSB and National Girobank, whose origins differ somewhat from those of the clearers but which offer similar services.

The distinction between these categories, once fairly clear, has become blurred since 'Big Bang' which, by allowing banks and other financial institutions to own Stock Exchange firms, encouraged the purchase of a wide variety of related institutions with a view to offering, in a financial sense, one-stop shopping. Most clearers now have both merchant banking and overseas arms.

Central banks and bank supervision

Most countries have a central bank: for example the Federal Reserve System in the United States; the Deutsche Bundesbank in Germany; the Banque de France; the Bank of Japan. At the core of the City of London is the Bank of England, the UK's central bank. Central banks differ in their range of activities, powers and techniques, and in the nature of their relationship with government; but they all serve as bank to their countries' government and to its banking system.

Many central banks, including the Bank of England, are involved in supervising financial markets, banks and other institutions. Indeed, one of the Bank of England's most important tasks is the supervision of banks operating in the United Kingdom though this only became a statutory requirement in 1979. Before that the Bank exercised informal surveillance over institutions operating in the London market.

The main purpose of banking supervision is the protection of depositors and potential depositors rather than either bank shareholders or bank borrowers.

Under the Banking Act 1987, no one may take deposits from the public as part of a deposit taking business without express permission from the Bank of England ('the Bank').

In order to be and remain authorised, an institution has to satisfy the Bank that it has:

1. Adequate capital;
2. Adequate liquidity;
3. A realistic business plan;
4. Adequate systems and controls; and
5. Made adequate provision for bad and doubtful debts.

The Bank must also be satisfied that:

6. Its business is carried on with integrity and skill and in a prudent manner;
7. Its directors, managers and controllers are 'fit and proper' for the positions they hold.

Since *foreign banks* are already supervised by an overseas authority, the Bank of England sees its responsibility as secondary to that of the home supervisor, to whom the Bank looks for assurances on the overall soundness of the bank.

The Bank exercises *continuing supervision* through the collection of information from statistical returns, from reporting accountants' reports, and what are termed 'prudential visits'. It is not absolutely clear whether it is the Bank being prudent in keeping a eye on things, or the prudence of other banks, which is being referred to, or both.

Be that as it may, supervisors have to be satisfied that the downside risk is properly covered but they do not try to supplant a bank's management in judging the best strategy for the bank to follow.

Banks face developing competition

UK banks face increased competition from foreign banks. Many large loans are now syndicated, with foreign banks playing a leading role both in setting up the loan and the provision of funds. There are said to be more US banks represented in London than in New York; and competition between banks and between financial centres is intense.

British banks face. competition also from the building societies, which in addition to providing home loans, lend for other purposes and provide interest bearing current account facilities and cash points.

Large, and especially international, companies can frequently borrow more cheaply in the markets direct, than through a bank; their credit rating often being higher than that of their banks.

Reports and accounts of banks

Bank accounts are of interest to three main groups:

1. Investors;
2. Depositors;
3. Borrowers.

Groups 1 and 2 are for obvious reasons; group 3 because a banker under strain is an unpredictable lender, and may call in a loan or overdraft or refuse to renew facilities without the customer giving him good, or indeed any, cause. It is also not just an embarrassment to have an account with a bank which gets into trouble or, like BCCI, fails, it can be a disaster. If the account is in overdraft, it will be frozen; the liquidators will hold on to any security; and it will be very difficult to borrow elsewhere.

It is in the balance sheet that the major difference between bank accounts and those of trading businesses is found. Assets normally appear in order of realisability starting with the most easily realised (rather than in order of permanence).

The consolidated profit and loss account is little different from that of a non-banking company, but the notes tend to reveal far more about interest paid and received, and about provisions for bad and doubtful debts.

Banks have their own cash flow statement format (see the illustrations to FRS1).

Points to look for

Things we ask about are:

1. *What does the bank do and where?*

Banks differ in their approach to segmental information. Some, like National Westminster Bank take advantage of the exemptions in Companies Act 1985, Schedule 9, para 17 and SSAP 25. Most, like Abbey National treat UK Retail Operations as being managed on a unified basis and as a single segment, but provide separate information on Treasury Operations, Life Assurance and Estate Agency operations. Midland separates Commercial Banking from Merchant Banking and the Forward Trust. In many cases it is necessary to look specifically for the note on segmental information: it is not referred to in the profit and loss account.

It is important to study this segmental information to gain a sense of perspective. In 1992, for instance, Midland earned before tax £178m net (profits of £138m on total assets of £58,237m employed in commercial banking; losses of £33m on gross assets of £4,033m employed in merchant banking ...). In the same year, Abbey National made £564m before tax, £540m of it from UK Retail Banking. But it had lost (after exceptional items) £158m on Estate Agency Operations.

High Street banks have long sought additional sources of revenue (from trustee work, the handling of investments, factoring, leasing and insurance (though the latter was at one time regarded as a manager's perk – he often pocketed the commission personally). The move by many banks in the 1980s towards becoming a 'one stop money shop' has met with varying degrees of success. Nevertheless, some banks have made considerable progress (LLOYDS in 1992 reported that 16% of customers who bought insurance bought it through the bank, against 2% five years earlier).

An even more spectacular example is DIRECT LINE, which sells insurance, largely car insurance by telephone (and is famous for its TV advertisements featuring a little red telephone), a subsidiary of the ROYAL BANK OF SCOTLAND which made £50.2m for that group in 1993 – a year in which the group as a whole produced a profit, after provisions but before exceptional items, of £300.3m. A useful contribution indeed; and 1994 will show further growth.

2. *Liquidity*

Banks seldom hold enough ready money to meet all their obligations at once, but they must have enough ready money or 'liquidity' to meet their obligations as they fall due. This means: (i) holding enough cash and (ii) ensuring that the future profile of cash flows is appropriately matched. This again is an area upon which one has largely to rely on the Bank of England, though cash flow statements and ratios do provide some indication of strength or weakness.

3. *Credit risk and provisioning policy*

In satisfying itself the Bank of England looks at the bank's provisioning policy, at its methods and systems for monitoring credit risk and recoverability.

The Bank pays particular attention to *country debt*, ie loans made by a number of banks to less developed countries (LDCs), particularly in the 1970s and early 1980s, many of which have since been subject to a number of debt problems.

Some banks were, however, noticeably less willing to lend to Less Developed Countries than others (eg STANDARD & CHARTERED and BANK OF SCOTLAND had much smaller exposures than MIDLAND [now part of HSBC HOLDINGS] or LLOYDS).

A matrix, issued by the Bank in 1987 and since revised, offers a means of scoring exposures (and hence the level of provisions necessary) against a list of economic and financial factors.

Banks are, however, in a difficult position. If they write off or provide fully against country debt that will be seen as a sign to the nations involved that the banks have given up all hope of collection. On the other hand, prudence really demands this.

Most UK banks have raised their level of provisions against country debt to between 50% and 80% but it has taken them more than 10 years to reach this conclusion. Understandably, they are loath to abandon hope of recovery.

In looking at accounts, ask yourself in relation to provisions for sovereign debt: Do they look adequate? How much more may need to be written off in years to come?

The position as regards country debt is, however, tending to improve. A number of banks have achieved in 1991 and 1992 net releases in provision (LLOYDS: £122m in 1992; £40m in 1991).

4. *Large exposures and bad debt provisions*

Particular risks arise when a bank puts too many eggs in one basket and lends heavily to a single borrower or related group of borrowers. No single borrower or related group of borrowers should, the Bank of England believes, account for more than 10% of a bank's capital base – though the Bank permits more, but more than 25% only in the 'most exceptional circumstances'. Account can, for instance, be taken of good quality security, and there are special arrangements for banks underwriting capital market issues.

There is an old saw: 'Watch the banks. When they lend to a sector as though there is no tomorrow, sure as hell that sector is heading for trouble.' Time and again, banks both in the UK and the US have lent aggressively to a sector (like property in 1974 and again in 1988–89, or US oil and gas exploration in the 1970s) only to see it collapse, to their cost and that of their shareholders.

Accounting practice in the UK does not require banks to write off problem lendings as quickly as US banks do, and UK banks continue to accrue all interest in arrears until payment appears unlikely, whereas US banks do not.

Since banks do not normally mention large exposures until it is too late, it is usually necessary to rely on the Bank of England fulfilling its role. Past experience suggests that this may be unwise. Many banks do now show their exposure to particular sectors (LLOYDS and BARCLAYS show figures over a number of years, so one can see how the pattern has changed).

The recent recession succeeded in diverting attention from problems of sovereign debt to those nearer home. For example Barclays wrote off (net) £1,849m in 1992 (£1,208m in 1991) and at 31 December 1992 had made specific provisions of £2,247m and general provisions of £690m (exclusive of those country risks). A number of banks (formerly viewed as being 'as safe as houses' have been forced in the last couple of years into operating loss by the size of the provisions they needed to make. It is very difficult from the outside to tell just how badly a particular bank might be hit.

5. *Ratios*

In common with other bank supervisors, the Bank of England uses the free capital ratio developed by the Basle Committee on Banking Regulations and Supervisory Practices as a key supervisory tool and a number of banks refer to these ratios in the reports (see illustration alongside).

Other ratios provided by Barclays, and of value generally where they are available or can be calculated, are:

(i)   Prevailing average interest rates (Barclays base rate, LIBOR, 3 month sterling, 3 month Eurodollar and US Prime rate).

(ii)   Yields, spreads and margins (Gross yield: Group, Domestic, International); Interest spread: (Group, Domestic, International); Interest margin (split similarly).

Gross yield is the interest rate earned on average interest earning assets. Interest spread is the difference between the interest rate earned on average interest earning assets and the liabilities. Interest margin is net interest income

interest rate paid on average interest bearingas a percentage of average interest earning assets.

BARCLAYS *Extract from Financial Review 1992*

Capital ratios

	1992 £m	1991 £m
Tier 1		
Shareholders' funds (as defined for regulatory purposes)	5,164	5,656
Minority interests in tier 1	677	565
	5,841	6,221
Tier 2		
Fixed asset revaluation reserves	71	84
Qualifying undated capital notes and loan capital	3,668	3,097
	3,739	3,181
General provisions for bad and doubtful debts	690	468
	4,429	3,649
Less investments in associated undertakings and other supervisory deductions	703	731
Total net capital resources	9,567	9,139
Weighted risk assets		
On-balance sheet	84,918	86,263
Off-balance sheet	20,752	18,776
Total	105,670	105,039
Tier 1 ratio	5.5%	5.9%
Risk asset ratio	9.1%	8.7%

(iii) *Average* balance sheet figures for categories of assets (eg short-term funds, lendings to customers) and the average rate earned on each; and average balance sheet figures for categories of liabilities (eg current and demand accounts, savings accounts, loan capital and undated capital notes) and the average rate paid on each. In each case figures for offices in the UK are shown separately from those in offices outside the UK.

One tends to think of gearing and inflation as problems which afflict industry; but they affect the banks too. Lloyds, in its section of additional information, stresses the effect of these factors. While it shows figures for five years, 1988–92, we have room for only two.

LLOYDS *Extract from additional Financial Information 1992*

Relationship between key financial

ratios:	1991	1992
Leverage (times)	19.0	17.2
multiplied by		
Return on average assets after tax equals	0.79%	0.97%
Return on average total equity after tax	15.0%	16.7%
Return on average shareholders' equity after tax and minorities less	14.5%	16.9%
Dividend payout ratio equals	60.6%	52.9%
Internal generation of shareholders' equity	5.7%	8.0%
Average rate of inflation	5.9%	3.7%
Real return on average shareholders' equity after inflation	8.6%	13.2%

It will be seen that leverage (average assets divided by average total equity) improved to 17.2 times in 1992 (mind you it was 20.4 in 1990, which we don't show), and the return on average assets to 0.97% after tax (but it has still some way to go to return to the 1988 level of 1.27%).

The real return improved from 8.6% in 1991 to 13.2% in 1992. The part of the table we do not show made it clear that the trough was in 1989, when the real return on average shareholders' funds was negative, (28.2%).

This sort of table worth is worth studying, and producing, where possible, for other banks.

6. *Contingent liabilities*

Traditionally, banks write acceptances and provide guarantees, performance bonds and indemnities, interest rate and currency swaps, financial futures contracts, forward contracts for the purchase and sale of foreign currencies, option contracts and the like which, while giving rise to a contingent liability, are not reflected in the consolidated balance sheet.

The amounts involved are massive, as will be seen from the Barclays illustration alongside), running into tens of billions of pounds. Generally, however, no material irrecoverable liability arises and they are simply shown as contingent liabilities.

Banks vary in the information they provide, but the large clearing banks tend to provide quite a degree of detail. Barclays even shows the risk weighted amount used in calculating the ratios for the Bank of England.

BARCLAYS *Extract from Note 38 to the 1992 accounts. Comparatives not shown.*

	1992 Contract or underlying principal amount £m	1992 Risk weighted amount £m
Guarantees, accepances, endorsements and other items serving as direct credit substitutes	11,405	8,196
Other endorsements	255	–
Performance bonds and other transaction related contingencies	6,170	2,931
Documentary credits and other short-term trade related contingencies	869	154
Sale and repurchase agreements	245	113
Forward asset purchases and forward forward deposits placed	170	34
Note issuance and revolving underwriting facilities	653	181
Formal standby facilities, credit lines and other commitments to lend		
Less than one year maturity	31,789	–
One year and over maturity	9,958	4,810
Exchange rate related instruments		
14 days or less original maturity	16,273	–
Over 14 days original maturity	219,894	2,480
Interest rate related contracts	248,654	1,755
Exchange traded instruments and other off-balance sheet instruments	15,933	98
		20,752

The majority of these facilities are offset by corresponding obligations of third parties.

During the 1980s several clearing banks, in the normal course of business, entered into *swap transactions* with UK local authorities. The legality of such contracts was challenged in the High Court in February 1990, and it was held that transactions entered into by one authority (Hammersmith and Fulham) were unlawful. Pending the outcome of an appeal to the House of Lords, most banks have made full provision in respect of all outstanding swap transactions with local authorities, rather than treat them merely as a contingent liability.

7. *Is it a UK bank?*

If not:

(i)   Who is its main regulator?

(ii)   Where is its main business situated?

(iii) Do they coincide? In the case of BCCI they did not.

BANK OF SCOTLAND *Consolidated profit and loss account for the year ended 28 February 1993*

	Notes	1993 £m	1992 £m
Group operating profit			
before provisions		487.9	393.3
Provisions for bad and doubtful debts		371.7	252.8
Depositors' Protection Guarantee Fund			4.0
Group operating profit	1	116.2	136.5
Share of profits of associated undertakings		9.1	4.2
Profit before taxation		125.3	140.7
Taxation		47.3	50.1
Profit after taxation		78.0	90.6
Attributable to minority interests		1.3	1.2
Profit attributable to proprietors		76.7	89.4

...

This illustration continues alongside and on page 151.

(iv)   Is that regulator strong or weak?

(v)   Do widespread overseas branches, coupled with the fact that the group has many auditors, suggest a possible weakness?

Banks tend to be respected, but like any other organisation they can be incompetent. Over the years there have been a number of spectacular frauds. Would the auditors pick up fraud at the outset, or is the banking group's audit scattered among several firms in several countries, making discovery less easy?

8.   Cost cutting

Over the last 20 years, the large clearing or high street banks have made a major investment in computerisation. Electronic data interchange and funds transfer, cash points, and services like Switch have been developed. Staff numbers have fallen sharply (LLOYDS: by 1992 down 20% from a 1989 peak) and the number of branches has been reduced. Without this, a high street bank would not remain competitive.

9.   Additional information

UK clearing banks listed in the US file an annual report on Form 20-F with the Securities and Exchange Commission. Most make copies available to analysts. The US information is worth studying since it often sheds additional light. The British Bankers Association issues SORPs, which should be studied by anyone seeking to specialise in banks.

BANK OF SCOTLAND *Note 1: Group Operating Profit*

	Notes	1993 £m	1992 £m
Group operating profit comprises:			
Interest receivable		2,541.3	2,655.3
Income from investments			
– listed		18.6	18.3
– unlisted		17.1	12.9
		2,577.0	2,686.5
Interest payable			
– to depositors		(1,842.5)	(2,056.3)
– on loan capital repayable:			
within five years		(8.4)	(6.2)
after five years		(46.5)	(50.0)
		(1,897.4)	(2,112.5)
Net interest income		679.6	574.0
Provisions for:			
Bad and doubtful debts			
Specific	12	(361.9)	(235.3)
General	12	(9.8)	(17.5)
Depositors' Protection Guarantee Fund		–	(4.0)
		(371.7)	(256.8)
Net interest income after provisions		307.9	317.2
Profit on sale of investments		6.2	12.5
Other operating income		320.3	269.0
Total income		634.4	598.7
Operating expenses:			
Staff costs		(268.3)	(240.5)
Premises and equipment:			
Depreciation		(38.4)	(34.8)
Property rentals		(13.4)	(12.2)
Other expenditure		(46.7)	(39.9)
Miscellaneous expenses		(151.4)	(134.8)
Total operating expenses		(518.2)	(462.2)
Group operating profit		116.2	136.5

10.   Note issue

The only English bank allowed to issue notes is the Bank of England. Certain Scottish Banks (like BANK OF SCOTLAND, which we illustrate) still issue notes.

BANK OF SCOTLAND *Balance Sheet as at 28 February 1993*

	1993 £m	1992 £m
ASSETS EMPLOYED		
Cash and short term funds	5600.8	4722.7
Cheques in course of collection	203.5	180.9
Investments	509.1	396.5
Advances to customers and other accounts	22,006.3	18,995.7
Trade investments	18.9	39.3
Property and equipment	470.8	406.0
	28,809.4	24,741.1
FINANCED BY		
Liabilities		
Current deposit and other accounts	25,946.5	22,064.7
Notes in circulation	345.0	308.8
Corporate taxation	32.8	0.7
Proposed dividends	41.9	39.9
Deferred taxation	190.8	194.8
	26,557.0	22,608.9
Capital resources		
Issued capital:		
Preference stocks	200.0	200.0
Ordinary stock	289.3	287.1
Reserves	761.5	773.9
Proprietors' funds	1,250.8	1,261.0
Minority interests	4.3	3.7
Undated loan capital	386.8	312.6
Dated loan capital	610.5	554.9
	2,252.4	2,132.2
	28,809.4	24,741.1

BANK OF SCOTLAND *Note 12 Group Provisions for Bad and Doubtful Debts (extracts)*

	Specific £m	General £m	1992 Total £m
As at 28 February 1993	611.8	115.8	727.6
Revenue charge	367.8	9.8	377.6
Recoveries from amounts previously written off	(5.9)		(5.9)
Net charge to revenue	361.9	9.8	371.7

The general provision is augmented at around 1 per cent of the growth in risk advances.

The group's non-ECGD guaranteed lending to Lesser Developed Countries ('LDC'), together with the cumulative specific provisions attributable thereto, is as follows:

	1993 £m	1992 £m
Latin America	21.5	18.0
Eastern Europe	23.6	19.1
Other countries	2.0	1.6
	47.1	38.7
Cumulative specific provisions	38.0	29.9
Cumulative specific provisions as a percentage of the total sum outstanding	81%	77%

Practice

1. Obtain the report and accounts of a major clearing bank (say Lloyds). Ask the bank for a copy of Form 20-F which it filed with the Securities and Exchange Commission. Most companies listed in the US are able to provide copies of Form 20-F. Then:

   (i) Compute the key ratios.
   (ii) See what you can find out about:

       (a) customer spread;
       (b) where the profits are earned;
       (c) what other activities besides banking the company is engaged in;
       (d) how the bank handles sovereign debt;
       (e) whether it has (had) any large exposures.

2. Obtain the report and accounts of Hambros. Compare its size and range of activities with those of a clearing bank.

Chapter 27

INSURANCE AND LIFE ASSURANCE

General overview

Strictly, *assurance* provides payment on the happening of an event which is certain to happen, eg death of an individual, whereas *insurance* provides financial compensation in the event of a particular occurrence where there is only a risk that it might happen eg the possibility that your house may be burgled or destroyed by fire. In practice, both tend to be referred to as insurance, and the companies which provide them as *insurance companies*.

The City of London has long been a leading centre for international insurance; a market which can, for convenience be divided into two broad groups: *life* and *non-life*. These two markets can be further subdivided into the *primary market* which involves the sale of insurance to individuals and companies, and the *secondary* market, re-insurance. While the *reinsurance* market has strong international connections, the primary market is more restricted because cross-border selling is still comparatively difficult because of local internal regulation, particularly of life contracts. Nevertheless, UK insurance groups have traditionally been strong in the US and commonwealth countries. Some, like GENERAL ACCIDENT, have substantial overseas income.

The insurance industry in the UK is made up of:

1. Insurance companies;
2. Lloyd's of London;
3. Insurance brokers.

There are approximately 850 *insurance companies* authorised to sell in the UK, but half of them handle over 90% of the business. They provide a full range of insurance contracts including life, pensions, permanent health insurance, marine, aviation, fire, accident, motor, travel and household.

Lloyd's of London is a unique international market: a society of underwriters made up of some 25,000 members or 'names' who, as private individuals, accept insurance risks and are liable for claims to the full extent of their personal wealth. Unhappy experiences in recent years (involving fraud and incompetence as well as misfortune) have led to the questioning of this unlimited liability and to a fall in the number of names.

Members of Lloyd's are grouped into *syndicates* (of which there are currently about 350) and business is introduced to these syndicates by *insurance brokers*. Originally Lloyd's specialised in marine insurance. Today, it covers any risk, from oil refineries, aircraft, road vehicles and satellites to a wine-taster's palate.

Insurance brokers are intermediaries who look for the best cover for their clients and offer advice on insurance. Brokers place their business with the insurance companies and, if they are accredited, with Lloyd's.

Insurance and Life Assurance form part of the Financial Group of the FT-SE Actuaries All-Share Index.

In the Life sector, three companies stand out:

PRUDENTIAL
LLOYDS ABBEY
LEGAL & GENERAL

of which PRUDENTIAL with a market capitalisation of around £6.5bn is by far the biggest.

Among the Composites:

COMMERCIAL UNION
SUN ALLIANCE
GENERAL ACCIDENT
ROYAL INSURANCE
GUARDIAN ROYAL EXCHANGE

are the biggest with market capitalisations of £2 – £3.76 billion.

Brokers tend to be rather smaller, the biggest being:

WILLIS CORROON
SEDGWICK

with market capitalisations of above £900m.

How insurance and assurance work

The principle of insurance (eg fire, automobile or marine insurance) is simple. The insurer charges the insured a premium which, he believes, is commensurate with the risk he is underwriting, and he hopes that all the premiums he receives will exceed all the claims he has to pay out. If they do, the result is an underwriting profit. Frequently they don't and the result is an underwriting loss. This does not matter quite as much as one might think because the insurer does not rely solely on the underwriting result. The money received in premiums is invested so as to earn interest until it has to be paid out in claims. This investment income helps to offset any underwriting loss. Since insurance claims may take some years to finalise (and claims may arise a long time after the business was arranged) the income earned on provisions for future claims can be considerable. Insurance which (intentionally or unintentionally at the time it was written) results in claims over a long period is termed long-tail business.

Underwriting results, if you take a long enough period, are cyclical. Nevertheless, losses seem to have become almost habitual for most insurance companies, and in recent years have often exceeded investment income. But there are signs that some composites, as premiums are pushed up, may be coming out of the worst part of the cycle.

GUARDIAN ROYAL EXCHANGE *Extracts from 10 year review 1992*

	1992 £m	1991 £m	1990 £m	1989 £m	1988 £m
Investment income	296	279	279	291	225
Life underwriting	21	23	25	27	31
Non-life Underwriting	(314)	(512)	(461)	(170)	(17)
	-------	-------	-------	-------	-------
Profit (loss) before tax	3	(210)	(157)	148	239

Where an insurer is worried by the size of the risk he is underwriting, he can (like a bookmaker) lay off part of his risk, reinsuring it with another insurer. Since the risk laid off is 'top slice' of liability (eg an insurer accepts an overall risk of £100m, retains the first £40m, and reinsures the remaining

£60m), the rate of premium received by the reinsurer tends to be lower than that to the primary insurer – and if business passes through several hands there is a risk that it may get too thin.

Turning to *assurance*: companies provide a number of options:

1. *Term assurance* is in effect a straight bet with the assurance company. You pay premiums for an agreed period. If you die within that period, the company pays the sum for which your life was insured. If you don't die within that period you receive nothing.
2. *Whole life assurance* pays a lump sum when you die at any age. Premiums may continue until death or they may cease at, say, 65.
3. *Endowment assurance* is a method of saving for you and for providing as well protection for your dependents. You pay the premiums and at the end of the term of the insurance you receive an agreed lump sum. But if you die during that period, your dependents receive a lump sum.

Policies may be with or without profits. Where the policy is with-profits, the policyholder (or his dependents) is entitled to a share of the profits from the growth of the fund.

This share of profits accrues in two forms:

1. *Reversionary bonuses* which are added from time to time (say every three years) over the term of the policy – the amount of which at any time is known. It is known for reversionary bonuses to be paid out in cash at the time they are declared, but this is not usual.
2. *Terminal bonuses* which are added only at the end of the term.

Most assurance contracts are front-end loaded, ie the selling commission, which is high in the first year, and administration costs, are such that on surrender little or nothing is returned from the first two years' premiums. So it does not usually pay to surrender. Surrender values are, in any case, related to the premiums paid, age, life expectancy, the value of the policy at the end of its term, and any reversionary bonuses already accrued – but not any terminal bonus. Some companies pay out much more of their profits by way of reversionary bonus than others, but there seems to be a tendency away from this and towards higher terminal bonuses. This makes for substantial differences in surrender values. There has also been some reduction in bonuses.

LEGAL & GENERAL *Extract from the group chief executive's review of operations 1991*

Because of the lower investment returns which have been obtained over the past few years, and anticipated continued lower returns in monetary terms in the 1990s as a result of ERM membership, reversionary bonuses have been reduced. Terminal bonuses for policies with shorter terms have also been reduced whilst those for longer term policies have been increased. For example, for maturing 10 year endowment policies the payout will be reduced by 7.4%. For 25 year policies it will be increased by 1.1%.

In the words of the old proverb; 'Jam tomorrow, never jam today'.

Borrowers, and lenders, on endowment mortgages taken out in the mid to late 1980s, where the borrower borrowed up to the hilt, and bonuses were taken into account in the repayment calculation, have been embarrassed by short falls.

The Life Funds of a life company can be said to belong partly to the policyholders holding with profits policies and partly to the shareholders. Companies have in the past been surprisingly reticent in their accounts about the way in which profits are shared.

A major part of a company's life business tends to be pensions business.

Most life companies also write *annuities*, under which the purchaser pays a lump sum in return for which the company pays a specified sum to the annuitant periodically either for a fixed term or during that person's life (or possibly that of the last survivor of, say, husband and wife).

The premium income goes into the *life funds* of the assurance company where it is invested and earns income, and hopefully produces capital growth.

Life business is long term; and the way in which overall life funds grow is complex, being affected by a range of risks:

1. *Life expectancy*: The risk of a person dying at a specified age (or of surviving to a particular age) can be estimated but tends to change with time. People are tending to live long. This means that the risk of having to pay out on a life policy at a particular age is tending to fall. On the other hand, the risk of having to continue to pay an annuity for a longer period is tending to increase.

2. *Investment return*: This will reflect the performance of:

    (i) the stock market generally;
    (ii) the property market; and
    (iii) the investment management team of the assurance company.

    A delicate balance needs to be maintained. Assurance is a long term business, but investment performance tends to be looked at short term, both by the market and by those who seek to measure investment management performance.

    Investment return is affected also by:

    (i) *Taxation*: the reduction of ACT in 1993-94 meant that pension funds and other funds exempt from tax could reclaim rather less.

    (ii) *Exchange rates*: where investments are made overseas, the return is improved by any weakness in sterling.

    The heady days of the 1980s saw sharp rises both in Stock Exchange and property values, and life funds grew rapidly. A depression brought lower property prices, and the possibility that with lower rates of inflation there may also be less rapid growth in equity prices. Life companies will have difficulty in maintaining bonus levels – or even of meeting projections made employing the Financial Services Act return maxima.

3. *Premium growth*: This is influenced by the state of the economy, but not necessarily as one might expect. When times are hard people who are able to do save *more,* not less. But other factors are at work. Until comparatively recently, tax relief was given on life assurance (including endowment assurance) premiums, offering an incentive to save in this way, not least when purchasing a house subject to a mortgage. There is also a feeling that controls imposed by the Financial Services Act and by regulators may make the selling of life assurance more difficult, by making it seem less attractive.

4. *Competion*: This is coming currently not only from mutual offices (ie companies where the policyholders are the shareholders) but from overseas companies; and banks and building societies setting up life companies.

Things to look for in the accounts of insurance companies

The Association of British Insurers (ABI) has produced a SORP, 'Accounting for Insurance Business'. Another valuable source is Peat's Survey of 1991 Accounts of Major Composites.

Look in the report and accounts of insurance companies for evidence of:

1. *Exposure (undue exposure) to a particular category of risk:* for example, most insurance companies were involved to some extent with mortgage guarantee policies. Some limited their exposure to a defined percentage of the market. Others now wish that they had.

GUARDIAN ROYAL EXCHANGE *Extract from chief executive's review 1991*

High-profile losses on mortgage indemnity business have been a major feature of the market during the year. This type of insurance has a marked catastrophe component as a consequence of which we decided several years ago to contain our market share to approximately 2.5%. Even so, the cost to the group in 1991 in the UK exceeded that of the 1987 hurricane.

2. *Segments under stress* ie where recent experience has been unsatisfactory, and the action taken as a consequence.

GUARDIAN ROYAL EXCHANGE *Extract from chief executive's review 1991*

Reporting a second successive year of unsatisfactory performance ...

In my review last year I referred to the necessity to press for realistic pricing, for more stringent underwriting, and for further expense reductions...

United Kingdom private car premium rates for example were raised three times in 1991 and again early in 1992 – the cumulative increase over that period amounting to almost 40%. This was allied to action to improve underwriting and risk selection and had the effect of stabilising claims frequency and achieving a planned reduction in cars insured from 878,000 to 675,000.

GUARDIAN ROYAL EXCHANGE *Extract from chief executive's review 1991*

Subsidence claims remain a material contributor to losses in the household account. In recognition of this, the Group took a leading role in the introduction of differential geographic rating, linked to the incidence of subsidence and weather claims for buildings covers.

3. *Changes in marketing policy and structure.* Insurance companies have traditionally marketed their products through brokers and agents. Growing use is being made in an increasingly competitive and technically demanding environment of *tied* agents, possibly supported by insurance company staff, and direct writing by the company.

4. *The sharing of assurance profits between with profits policyholders and shareholders.* United Friendly only received a full listing in July 1991 but between February 1989, when they were first listed on the USM, the B shares rose from 144p to 653p (353%) and the market capitalisation rose from £88m to £535m. There were a number of reasons for.this. One important one was United Friendlies' avoidance of most of the pitfalls dug by other life companies at the time the Financial Services Act was introduced.

Perhaps more important was a bid by Pearl which led United Friendly to increase to the maximum readily possible the proportion of profits allocated to shareholders from with profits business, following the example of Prudential when its cash flow and ability to pay dividends were both being squeezed by estate agency losses.

5. *The allocation of, so called, 'orphan estate', wholly or partly to shareholders.* London and Manchester, a company faced with substantial losses from its mortgage finance and estate agency, began the practice: notionally allocating part of its orphan estate to shareholders and then transferring part of the investment return out of the life fund.

6. *The Life Fund and its 'embedded value' to shareholders.* Efforts are being made to show more realistic values of life funds. Some companies use what they term the 'embedded value' concept.

The Association of British Insurers has made proposals on trial basis for 'accruals accounting' disclosed in notes to the accounts, though no definitive standard has yet emerged Nevertheless companies are beginning to provide information along the lines suggested. It will be interesting to see what the attitude of the Inland Revenue is to this.

LEGAL & GENERAL *Extract from the group chief executive's review of operations 1992*

We have once again, published additional information relating to the Society Long Term Fund. From the combination of statutory and embedded value reporting, shareholders gain a considerable insight into the strength and performance of our UK Life and Pensions business and the value to them of this Fund.

At the end of 1992, our estimate of the value to shareholders (excluding goodwill) of their interest in the Long Term Fund was at least £1.84 billion, after tax. The value reported at the end of 1991 was £1.71 billion.

Under this reporting method, changes in assumptions will be required periodically, to reflect operating experience and the prospects for investment return and inflation. For 1992, the principal changes related to future rates of investment return, inflation and bonus. Taken together with a corresponding reduction in discount rate, the aggregate effect on the opening 1992 value was a small reduction of £20m.

The increase in the value to shareholders after tax during 1992, on the new assumptions, was £230m (1991, £200m), before the distribution of £75m, net of tax, to distributable profits. The change in value includes approximately £30m of value attributed to new business written during 1992 (1991, £40m). The balance is attributed to the management of business in force and the shareholders' retained capital.

We have taken extensive external advice to satisfy ourselves about the assumptions and values. Both Price Waterhouse, our auditors, and Tillinghast, independent actuaries, agree that they are reasonable

The methodology and key assumptions we have used are outlined below:

(i) The value of the shareholders' interest represents the discounted value of potential future transfers to shareholders from the Long Term Fund, both from profits related to the portfolio of in-force business and from shareholders' capital retained in the Long Term Fund.

(ii) This value is net of tax at current rates, including the present value of tax which would become
payable if the shareholders' capital retained in the Long Term Fund was eventually to be distributed.

(iii) The assumed future pre-tax investment returns are:

	1992	1991
Fixed interest	9.0% p.a.	10.0% p.a.
Equities and property	11.5% p.a.	12.5% p.a.

Investments matched to contractual liabilities are effectively valued on an amortised basis.

(iv) The risk discount rate used, which has regard to the investment returns, is 11.0% p.a. net of tax (1991, 12% p.a.).

(v) Expense inflation is assumed to be 6% p.a. (1991, 6.5% p.a.). RPI inflation of 5% p.a. (1991, 6.5% p.a.) has been assumed for indexation purposes.

...

The PRUDENTIAL devotes a separate booklet to the subject of the accruals method.

7. *The solvency ratios of composites.*

8. *The treatment of realised and unrealised investment gains.* Note, for instance, the approach of EAGLE STAR.

9. *Methods of providing for claims incurred but not yet reported.* DIRECT LINE, a subsidiary of ROYAL BANK OF SCOTLAND, claims that by seeking claims by telephone, and preparing the claim form on behalf of the insured, it largely overcomes this problem. Others may follow. Until they do, they have to estimate.

10. *The extent to which the insurer provides investment management, unit linked pensions and other services to pension funds.* Legal & General has long played an active role in this.

11. *The extent to which the insurer, emulating the banks, engages in provision of full financial services, eg mortgage services, estate agency and even banking.* And like them, had cause to regret it. PRUDENTIAL, as already mentioned, certainly did.

Analysts also keep a watchful eye on the returns made by insurance companies to the DTI.

A ratio to watch

Analysts often compare the free asset ratios of life companies:

$$\text{Free assets ratio} = \frac{\text{Solvency margin}}{\text{Total liabilities}}$$

where the statutory solvency margin is the minimum amount of assets in excess of the life fund's liabilities which the authorities require a life assurance company to hold in order to be allowed to trade.

Solvency margins Ratios 1991 and 1992

	1991	1992Est
	%	%
Britannic	56	62
Refuge	49	50
United Friendly	33	37
Legal & General	18	20

Source: Kleinwort Benson Research

The accounts

The consolidated profit and loss account of an insurance company is very similar to that of any other trading organisation but there is normally no turnover as such. Under the provisions of the Companies Act 1985 insurance companies are not required to show separately in their financial statements the amounts of their reserves and provisions or the amounts of the movements in them. However, when the EC Insurance Accounts Directive is adopted in the UK, harmonisation of the accounts of insurance companies in all member states will bring changes. Accounts will, for the first time, be required to present a true and fair view. We have already seen the application to insurance companies of FRS 1, FRS 3 (though a limited amendment exempts them from some requirements in FRED 5).

Insurance companies generally seek an actuary's report on their life fund each year, but most do not publish this. One that does is LEGAL & GENERAL. Where the Actuaries Report is published it should be studied..

LEGAL & GENERAL *Actuary's report1992 (extract)*

... it is our opinion that the aggregate amount of the liabilities in relation to the life and pensions insurance business of the Group at 31 December 1992 did not exceed the aggregate amount of the life and pensions insurance funds (including reserves and provisions), as shown in the Group's consolidated balance sheet, and that the bases of valuation of the liabilities have not been changed to an extent which is material to the Group.

In the UK a transfer of £197m was made from investment reserves to the revenue account primarily to enable bonuses to be declared to with-profit policyholders at rates which have regard to investment growth.

Insurance company balance sheets differ from those of other businesses because the major asset is investments; and the main 'source' of these assets is 'Insurance liabilities, provisions and reserves', as will be seen:

LEGAL & GENERAL *Extract from the consolidated balance sheet as at 31 December 1992*

	1992	1991
	£m	£m
Investments	21,281.1	18,010.1
Purchased interests in USA insurance funds	89.5	85.3
Mortgage lending	353.4	305.3
Other assets	931.7	985.1
TOTAL ASSETS	22,655.7	19,385.8
Securitised mortgages and related assets	259.9	331.5
Non-recourse funding	(259.9)	(331.5)
Borrowings		
For financing group operations	50.2	64.3
For financing mortgage lending	353.4	305.3
	403.6	369.6
Other liabilities and provisions	409.9	427.3
TOTAL LIABILITIES AND PROVISIONS	813.5	796.9
TOTAL NET ASSETS	21,842.2	18,588.9
Insurance liabilities, provisions and reserves		
Life and pensions	20,930.7	17,739.3
General insurance	649.3	609.1
TOTAL INSURANCE LIABILITIES, PROVISIONS AND RESERVES	21,580.0	18,348.4
SHAREHOLDERS' NET ASSETS	262.2	240.5

Domestic breakdown insurance

Domestic appliance breakdown insurance tends to be a specialist activity of companies such as DOMESTIC & GENERAL. Like general insurance companies, the funds employed by domestic appliance breakdown insurers tend to come largely from insurance funds rather than shareholders, but in their case the insurance funds mainly represent unearned premiums. Like the captive insurance companies and maintenance companies of groups like DIXONS, DEBENHAMS and many small computer companies, this sort of activity tends to be highly profitable.

DOMESTIC & GENERAL *Summary of consolidated balance sheet as 30 June 1993*

	1993	1992
	£m	£m
Fixed assets (including investments)	4,010	4,483
Net Current assets	55,354	43,026
Total assets less current liabilities	59,364	47,509
Creditors: Amounts falling due after more than one year	(442)	(610)
Provisions for liabilities and charges	(125)	(130)
Long-term business assets	1,248	1,091
Insurance funds:		
General insurance funds:		
Unearned premiums	(40,024)	(32,335)
Outstanding claims	(3,683)	(2,982)
Long-term business fund	(1,248)	(1,091)
Coinsurance management commission	(106)	(250)
Sub-total: Insurance funds	(45,061)	(36,658)
Net assets financed by Shareholders' Funds and Minority Interests	14,884	11,202
The profit and loss account showed the profit for the year before tax	7,684	6,191

Insurance brokers

The insurance broker acts as an intermediary between the insured and insurance or assurance company or Lloyd's syndicate(s). Traditionally, the broker received his reward from the company or syndicate in the form of commission, but there is a growing tendency for the commission to be handed on to the client and for the client to be charged a fee for the services of the broker eg in finding a company or syndicate prepared to write the risk most cheaply (or at all).

Keys to success are:

1. *The operating expenses / broking turnover ratio*
   – eg WILLIS CORROON: 85.78% in 1991; 93.05% in 1990 (the year they merged) – showing the benefits of merger.

   It is always difficult in a service industry, and broking is no exception, to reduce capacity (and fixed costs) if turnover falls.

2. *The broking operating profit / broking turnover ratio*

– eg WILLIS CORROON: 15.69% in 1991; 26.38% in 1990 (because interest and investment income fell from £60.4m in 1990 (when turnover was £310.8m) to £55.7 in 1991 (when it was £537.3m).

WILLIS CORROON are worth studying. They are involved in:

(i)   A major Lloyd's members agency;
(ii) Risk management consultancy eg in relation to oil rigs;
(iii) Insurance;
(iv) Reinsurance

– areas into which other brokers are likely to follow.

Many brokers have a large proportion of income in US$ so the £/US$ relationship is important.

3.   *A sound geographical spread of business.*
     Most brokers start as purely local organisations; but this means that they are subject to the economic fortunes of a particular region, and makes them a somewhat unattractive investment.

4.   Conringent liabilities and litigation. The notes to the accounts on these subjects should be read carefully in view of recent problems at Lloyd's.

Practice

1.   Obtain the latest report and accounts of Commercial Union. Assume that you are advising a small general unit trust. Make the case for acquiring a holding, representing 5% of the trust's funds, in Commercial Union. Your job is to make the case for BUY. Nevertheless, formulate in your own mind the opposing case: SELL and try to reject it.

2.   Obtain the accounts of either Sun Alliance or Pearl Group (a subsidiary of AMP which nevertheless publishes separate accounts). Compare Sun Alliance (or Pearl) with Commercial Union in terms of:

     (i)   What each does;
     (ii) The type of business it writes;
     (iii) Its premium income (whether annual premiums or single premiums);
     (iv) Its cost structure;
     (v)   Its investment policies (structure).

Chapter 28

PROPERTY

General overview of the sector

For FT-SE Actuaries Share Index purposes, Property forms part of the Financials Group. It is thus included in the All-Share Index but not in the Non-Financials Index.

At the time of writing, 40 of the securities out of the 105 in the Financials Group are Property companies, and they outweigh in number any other group in that sub-section. The sector is dominated by two companies with a market capitalisation (in February 1994) in excess of £2,000m:

> LAND SECURITIES and
> MEPC

In all there are about 100 property companies currently listed on the London Stock Exchange; though many are relatively small.

But not all investment in property is in the shares of property companies. Most industrial and commercial organisations, particularly stores and supermarkets, own large amounts of property which they occupy; and most insurance companies and many pension funds invest directly in property.

What makes property an attractive investment?

The main attraction of property as an investment is that, properly maintained, it is a long term hedge against inflation.

The value of rented property depends on two things: the rent payable and the expected yield. The rent will only change at periodic rent reviews, but values change also with changes in the expected yield.

The post-war years have been notable for spectacular growth in property prices generally, and in those of domestic housing in particular. But though the trend has been generally upward, there have

been sudden surges, such as the one that began in 1986. Shop rents more than doubled between the beginning of 1986 and mid-1989, and office and industrial building rents rose only a little less. This has brought major changes in yields (see example 28.1).

There have also been sharp falls in property values, notably in 1973–74 (the secondary banking crisis) and in 1990–91. In each case the cause was much the same: too much development financed by too much borrowing, largely short term or on overdraft – something many banks have lived to regret – which resulted in over-supply. The years 1990–92 saw around 10% of listed and over 20% of USM property companies go into receivership. Others were rescued by takeover.

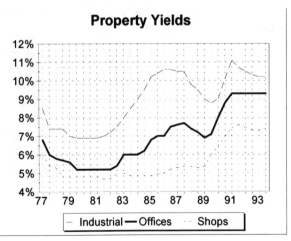

Example 28.1 Datastream IC Hillier Parker indices of property yields

A notable feature of the property market (which makes it attractive to some investors, eg insurance companies and pension funds) is that it provides a hedge against inflation which fixed interest investment does not, and it is usually safer than investment in companies, which can go bust. Shares in property companies do not, of course, have the latter advantage.

Investment property is seen as a growth investment in which the reward comes in the form of rents, rather than dividends. But the expectation in each case is that capital values will increase. Property takes more management than the ownership of equities, though in the UK commercial properties are normally let on a full repairing and insuring lease, effectively transferring the entire burden apart from rent collection and a very general oversight, onto the tenant.

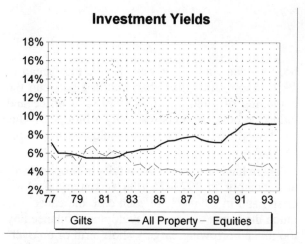

Investment Yields

Example 28.2 Investment yields: Property v Gilts and Equities (Data: Hillier Parker Research)

How property ownership is organised

In Britain the pattern of property ownership is complex, but fundamentally one can distinguish between:

> *Freeholds*, where (subject to any leasehold interest which has been granted) the property is owned outright by the landlord.

2. *Leaseholds*, where interests in the property are split: the owner of the original land or building having granted a lease to the leaseholder giving him the right, subject to a *ground rent*, to develop or redevelop the site or to occupy the building, for a stated period, say 99 years. At the end of the lease (subject to legal protections) the right to occupy the building reverts to the freeholder. At one time, leaseholds were granted for long periods, eg 999 years or 399 years, with the ground rent fixed in perpetuity. Such long periods are now uncommon and it is usual for the ground rent to be adjusted upwards at intervals.

The leaseholder may then let the building to a tenant at a *rack rent* (ie a market rent).

Commercial properties were at one time let on quite long leases but that has gradually changed. More recently a typical commercial lease was for a period of 20 or 25 years, with rent reviews, usually upward only, at 5 year intervals. This meant that at any time other than at the start of the lease and on completion of each rent review, the rent received by the landlord is likely to be less than that if the lease were renegotiated or the building were to be re-let. Currently, with the slump in rental and property values many tenants are paying above market rentals, and others are.seeking a reduction to market levels on renewal.

Property valuation

Properties are normally valued on a yield basis. The rent is usually expressed as £xx per square foot (of usable, ie exclusive of common areas such as stairs in a shared building, or of 'lettable area').

Thus, a 120,000 sq ft property in Central London, let at a rent of £30 per square foot, valued on a 5% yield, would be considered to be worth:

$$120,000 \times £30 \div 0.05 = £72 \text{ million}$$

The yield (5% in this case) reflects:

1. The position;
2. The relative desirability of the building;
3. Its condition ie its state of repair;
4. Any limitation on user;
5. Ease of access, and so on.

It will also reflect the nearness of the next rent review or of reversion to the landlord.

It is a matter on which both parties normally retain professional advisers (surveyors / estate agents / valuers).

Some idea of the pain suffered in the recent recession even by the stronger property companies, particularly those involved heavily in Central London offices, is given by the following extract and by Example 28.3, which shows the overall percentage yield (based on actual income) of LAND SECURITIES. Note the trough in 1989, reflecting peak values (and the lowest yield).

LAND SECURITIES *Chairman's statement 1992*

Never has the strength and security of rental income been more important. I am pleased to confirm that your group's rental income flow is strong and has increased by £44.3m to £380.7m during the year. There is a very high level of vacant space in Central London and no certainty that tenants will renew leases when they expire. It is therefore reassuring that over 70% of the rental income from that part of the portfolio is secured on leases expiring beyond the turn of the century without break clauses and with upward only rent reviews. The quality of lettings achieved in better times, the covenant strength of our tenants and the successful leasing of a high proportion of the Group's recent developments have all afforded protection from the worst effects of the depressed market.

...

Levels of future projected rentals are now substantially lower than those anticipated last year. Lease renewals are likely to be agreed at rents lower than those currently receivable.

We make a practice of following through this sort of comment.

LAND SECURITIES *Chairman's statement 1993*

Over 78% of our rental income is secured on leases, without break clauses and with upward only rent reviews expiring beyond the turn of the century: 81% in the City, 74% in West End and Victoria and almost 80% elsewhere in the United Kingdom meet these criteria.

However, £50m of current annual rental income from offices in Central London is subject to the effect of leases expiring before the turn of the century. Any income reduction as a result of this is expected to be offset largely by the receipt of additional revenue from rents already secured from lettings where there are currently unexpired rent free periods, from additional rents and reductions in irrecoverable outgoings generated by new lettings, and from the reversionary income still remaining in the portfolio, mainly in the retail sector.

The severe burden of void rates ... has not been alleviated despite strong representations ... The cost to your Group in the year under review was still over £3.1m despite the steps we have taken to reduce this liability.

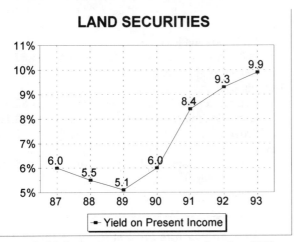

LAND SECURITIES

Example 28.3 LAND SECURITIES Annual review 1993

Commercial property falls into three categories:

1. Retail;
2. Offices; and
3. Industrial (factories and warehouses).

Unlike stocks and shares, insurance or commodities there is no marketplace for commercial prop-

erty. The market is centred upon major firms of estate agents, most especially Richard Ellis, Healey & Baker, Hillier & Parker and Jones Lang Wootton ('the Big Four').

Key players, besides the major property companies, are insurance companies and pension funds.

There are in fact two interconnected, overlapping, markets: the *letting market*, in which landlords let properties to tenants, and the *investment market*, in which completed, already let and income producing properties are acquired by financial institutions as long-term investments.

What property companies do

Property developers, property companies, financial institutions, or contractors, often acting together as consortia or joint ventures undertake property developments (which can involve acquiring an existing building, obtaining planning permission for a new user, demolishing it, designing, planning and constructing a new development (eg offices or a shopping complex), letting the completed buildings. They then have a choice: *investment* ie to retain the completed buildings themselves for the rent they will produce; or *trading* ie selling the development to another company or institution.

Some property companies are engaged in all these activities; but many specialise in one or two. Property is an opportunist industry. Property acquired for one purpose, for example letting as office space, is likely to be sold if the owner receives an offer he cannot refuse. Alternatively, if planning permission can be obtained, the site may be redeveloped, and turned, say, into a shopping complex, the operation often taking the form of a joint venture with a pension fund or insurance company; finance being provided partly by the partners and partly by bank borrowings (usually guaranteed by the joint venturers). In this way, the whole direction of a property group's activities often changes with time.

There are distinct markets: for commercial property, industrial property and residential property. Some property companies operate in all three; most specialise.

Many large property groups are involved not just in UK property but overseas, especially in Europe and the US.

What to look for in property company accounts

Study the report and accounts and then ask yourself these questions:

1. *What kind of property company is it?*

Property companies are usually either predominantly investment companies or predominantly development / trading companies.

In theory, the statement of main activities found in the directors' report should tell you what kind of property company it is but often the best place to look is the balance sheet:

(i)   If you find under 'Fixed Assets'

> TANGIBLE ASSETS:
> Investment properties   £xxx

then it is a property investment company.

(ii) If you find under 'Fixed Assets'

> TANGIBLE ASSETS:
> Investment properties
> – completed   £xxx
> – under development   £xxx

then it is a property investment company that handles its own development

(iii) If you find under 'Current assets':

> Stocks – trading properties   £xxx

then it is a property trading company.

(iv) If you find under 'Current assets':

> Stocks – trading properties   £xxx
>   – completed properties £xxx
>   – properties under
>   development £xxx

then it is a property trading company which develops properties for sale.

Some companies combine these roles. Balance sheet values then give an indication of the relative importance of the activities; so does the profit and loss account (but it is more affected by any slump in values).

It matters what kind of a company it is, for two reasons:

(a)   Property companies that are mainly developers / traders depend on being able to *sell* properties, so if the property market dries up, they are in trouble if interest payments exceed net rental income.

(b)   Property markets often do dry up just at the time interest rates rise (often as a result of that rise), which adds to the difficulties of property companies that are heavily borrowed at variable interest rates. As we shall see, accounting policies may allow such companies in their accounts to *roll up interest* on their developments in the short term, but their bankers, if they allow it at all, will not let them go on rolling up interest on their overdraft indefinitely.

2.   *Where are its assets?*

Groups differ in the extent to which they invest or develop overseas. Compare, for instance, Land Securities and Slough Estates.

As we see from the statement of principal activities alongside, Land Securities is a UK operation.

LAND SECURITIES *1992 Directors' Report*

1. **Business of the Group**

> During the year the Group has continued its business of property development and investment in offices, shops, out of town retail, food superstores and industrial and warehouse premises throughout the United Kingdom, together with the management of its properties.

Whereas, despite its name, Slough Estates has properties almost worldwide (in Belgium, France, Germany, Canada, United States, Austria, as well as other parts of the UK).

Even companies focused upon the UK have their own individual stamp and balance, which may make them very different from the average property company and give a very different risk profile. Consider, for example, GREAT PORTLAND ESTATES (below).

It is clearly a company specialising in freeholds and very long leaseholds of London (even Central London), office, commercial and shop property. But, partly as result of changes in the relative values of the various classes of property, and partly as a result of change of strategy, the perspective changed somewhat between 1990 and 1992.

GREAT PORTLAND ESTATES *Statistics given in the form of a series of charts in the 1990 and 1992 reports*

	1992	1990
Tenure:		
Freeholds and leases over 900 years	84.8%	87.6%
Leases 90–150 years	15.2%	12.4%
Geographical:		
Central London	66.6%	82.8%
Outer London & Suburbs	13.9%	12.1%
Provinces	19.5%	5.1%
User:		
Offices & Commercial	76.1%	85.5%
Retail & Showrooms	20.3%	13.0%
Light industrial	3.6%	1.5%

---

3.   *How do you rate the quality of its investment portfolio?*

A key factor in assessing any property company (and in particular estimating the risk of an investment) is the quality of its investment portfolio, if it is a property investment company, and of its land bank and planned developments, if it is a development or trading company.

Quality represents a combination of factors: location, suitability, age and status of construction and balance between shops, offices, residential property, leisure facilities such as golf clubs and marinas etc.

4. *How prudent are the company's borrowings?*

Most property companies borrow, and there is nothing wrong with borrowing if:

(i)   It is fixed rate or capped; and
(ii) Interest is covered by secure rental income.

The danger lies in borrowing for development or trading. Take, for example, DARES ESTATES. The year 1990 was a disastrous one for the group: There was a small loss on trading even before £27.248m was written off in exceptional items to recognise the diminution in value of property assets, and there were extraordinary items of £3.268m. Shareholders' funds fell as a result to £40.398m. By the end of the year, despite forced sales, borrowings had increased by more than 20% and had become mainly due within a year, while shareholders' funds had more than halved. The group was in negotiations with its bankers, and the auditors had qualified their report:

Study the extracts below, and ask yourself: what did the future hold for Dares?

DARES ESTATES *Extract from 1990 report and accounts*

Balance Sheet

	1990 £000	1989 £000
Current assets		
...		
Cash at bank and in hand	11,218	32,666
Current liabilities		
...		
Borrowings (secured)	(111,968)	(10,809)
Shareholders' funds	40,398	108,723

Note 30 Current financial position
As a result of the losses for the year and the diminution of asset values, the Group is in default of certain financial covenants and other provisions in its bank facilities and loan agreements.

Negotiations are in progress with the Group's principal bankers ...

The financial statements have been prepared on a going concern basis which assumes that:

1. Further property sales are achieved as planned.
2. The banking facilities of Associates will be restructured and its property will be leased as planned.
3. The Group's principal bankers will amend, extend and increase their facilities ...

Auditors' report
... As indicated in Note 30 the financial statements have been prepared on a going concern basis, which is dependent on the assumptions set out in that note.

Dares did in fact survive that crisis. At the time of writing it was still listed, but its shares stood at around 20p (after a low of 0.75p) – and it was still talking to its bankers.

5. *How prudent are the company's accounting policies?*

Property company accounts are not, on the whole, particularly informative. Even companies in the property sector with a similar type of business adopt widely different policies; which makes comparability difficult. Many property companies are inexplicably silent on matters which seem fundamental to understanding the performance of the business.

Things are not helped by the fact that the Companies Acts are designed with the average manufacturing business in mind and SSAPs and FRS (SSAP 19 and FRS 1 apart) do not really address the problems of the investment business, and in particular the fact that its success or otherwise is measured over many reporting periods in terms of capital growth and so does not lend itself to presentation in a conventional profit and loss account.

We focus on seven areas:

(i)   *Capitalisation of development costs, generally*

The analyst has to cope with a variety of ways of calculating cost of development properties, and frequently has to use his imagination in deciding what a stated accounting policy means.

For example, MERIVALE MOORE say:

'Properties held for development and resale as current assets are stated at the lower of cost and net realisable value...',

leaving the reader to decide what 'cost' is. Does it, for instance, include:

(a)   Legal, agency and other professional fees;
(b)   Administrative overheads;
(c)   Letting fees;
(d)   Ground rents;
(e)   Cost of obtaining finance;
(f)   Interest capitalised?

(ii) *Capitalisation of interest, in particular*

Most property companies involved in development capitalise interest. But some are noticeably more prudent in what they capitalise and more forthcoming in their explanations.

Example 28.4 overleaf depicts the main possibilities.

Example 28.4 Capitalisation of interest: prudent or imprudent?

TIME ——————————————————⇒		
Site purchased	Development begins	Development complete
⇓	⇓	⇓
| Bad to | capitalise	| Normal to | capitalise	| Bad if period | excessive

(iii) *Investment properties and depreciation*

SSAP 19 relates to investment properties generally, and applies to any company owning investment property, but it is of particular relevance to property companies.

Properties owned and occupied by a company for its own purposes, or let to other companies in the same group, are not investment properties.

An investment property is an interest in land and / or buildings, the construction and development work on which have been completed, and which is held for its investment potential (any rental income being negotiated at arm's length).

In the balance sheet, investment properties are to be included at their open market value. They should not be depreciated – an exception being leasehold property, which should be depreciated at least over the last 20 years of the lease period.

SSAP 19 does not require that the valuations be carried out by either qualified or independent valuers, but recommends that where investment properties represent a substantial proportion of the total assets of a major enterprise, the valuation be carried out annually by persons holding a recognised professional qualification with recent post-qualification experience in the location and category of properties concerned, and at least every five years by an external valuer.

Changes in the value of investment properties should be disclosed as a movement on an investment revaluation reserve; and if the investment revaluation reserve is insufficient to cover a deficit, any excess should be charged in the profit and loss account. In practice, companies often use the term 'revaluation reserve', or 'unrealised capital account' rather than 'investment revaluation reserve'.

The accounts should disclose prominently:

(a) The carrying value of investment properties; and

(b) The investment revaluation reserve.

Details of the valuation should be disclosed: its basis, the names or qualifications of the valuers, and if the valuation was made by an officer or employee of the group, that fact should be disclosed. Some companies publish part or all of the valuer's report.

(iv) *Reclassification of properties between trading or development and investment*

Trading or development properties are often transferred to the investment portfolio (or vice versa). Most groups do not spell out their accounting policy on this. In the past some groups placed a market valuation (possibly confirmed independently) on any transfer to the investment portfolio. Urgent Issues Task Force Abstract 5 prevents this. Assets transferred from current to fixed are to be made at the lower of cost and net realisable value at the date of transfer.

(v) *Related companies, joint ventures, consortia*

As we noted earlier, one feature of property company accounts is that developments are often undertaken by one-off development partnerships (or joint ventures) in which the company (or one of its subsidiaries) is an equity partner.

Under the provisions of the Companies Act 1989 and FRS 2, many such partnerships have become subsidiaries for group accounts purposes, thus negating one of the advantages of this form of organisation, ie that it was to some extent off-balance sheet.

But it does not affect the other advantage: that there is a degree of separation (if the so-called partnerships are limited companies) between the company and its development partnerships. So, if they get into financial difficulties, they can be allowed to go to the wall – subject always to the rules of fraudulent preference (ie that the venturers cannot prefer themselves knowing that the company is insolvent), to any bank guarantees given by the joint-venturers, and to any agreement to the contrary between them.

In the past, property companies in general have kept quiet about such agreements. OSSORY ESTATES was an exception.

OSSORY ESTATES Extracts from Note 22 to the 1991 accounts
Associated undertakings
Ossory Investments Shareholders Agreement states that in the event that a loss is realised by the Company the shareholders shall make good such losses in proportion to their equity shareholding by way of an interest free loan.

Developers may well try to get round the consolidation rules, so it continues to be important to read with care any notes on equity accounting and on associated or related companies (now termed 'participating interests' and 'associated undertakings') and on sales to them.

We would also be cautious where investment in, plus loans to related companies, is large in comparison to shareholders' funds. For example, ROSEHAUGH'S involvement in related companies (joint ventures) became increasingly, disproportionately and embarrassingly large, as it entered the 1990s.

ROSEHAUGH *Extracts from 1990 accounts*

Notes 11 and 12 Fixed asset investments

Fixed asset investments comprise the following:

Year to June	1987	1988	1989	1990
	£000	£000	£000	£000
...				
Related companies	77,534	159,201	259,507	263,962
Loans to related companies	37,332	74,358	47,054	125,541
...				
Five year record				
Shareholders' funds	264,676	366,958	476,085	470,874
Investment in related companies / Shareholders' funds	43.4%	49.0%	64.4%	82.7%

And in the accounts to 30 June 1991 the ratio had risen to 187.4%.

During this period Rosehaugh was run by a brilliant but somewhat dominant personality, Godfrey Bradman. In December 1991 the *Evening Standard* reported:

ROSEHAUGH *Extract from Evening Standard of 6 December 1991*

Godfrey Bradman is stepping down as chairman of property developer Rosehaugh, to become vice chairman, following news that the group plunged into pre-tax losses totalling £226 million in the year to June.

The losses are even greater than the £165.5 million run up in 1989–90. They result from exceptional write-offs against property schemes caused by the hard line surveyors are taking on property values these days.

Rosehaugh's accounts are being qualified by auditors Arthur Andersen because the company is in breach of its banking covenants following the losses, struck after exceptional provisions of £187 million.

Net borrowings currently total £310 million, against £340 million at the year end following disposals. Assets per share crashed from 373p to 130p.

Bradman is stepping down after the grand opening of Rosehaugh's Stanhope City Broadgate complex by the Queen ...

Remember what we said in Chapter 9 about being wary of companies whose prestigious new offices were opened by the prime minister? It seems equally true of major office or shopping complexes opened by the Queen.

(vi) *Methods of financing*

Because ordinary shares of property companies often stand at a discount to net asset value, property companies are one class of company which, when liquidity permits, often takes advantage of the rules which permit a company to acquire its own shares (and by doing so enhance net asset value per share).

The classic way of accelerating the growth of net asset value per share in a time of inflation is, however, to borrow long term, providing the debt can be serviced by good quality rental income from the property company's portfolio eg LAND SECURITIES.

In borrowing, the coupon or, if variable, the rate over base rate or LIBOR will depend not only on the quality of the company but on the security offered and the tightness of any covenants given (eg restrictions on other borrowing).

The loan capital of a property company can be very complicated and highly sophisticated. For example, MEPC raised £200 m in 1991 at a lower rate than obtainable in the UK by borrowing floating rate in the Eurodollar market and using swaps to convert the liability into sterling with a fixed rate of interest.

As an alternative to debt and to a rights issue of ordinary shares (which causes a sharp reduction in n.a.v. per share at conventional discounts), property companies frequently issue either:

(a) Convertible unsecured loan stock, which will have a lower coupon than straight debentures and requires no security; or

(b) Convertible preference shares, which have the advantages of a CULS, *and* which lenders have in the past been prepared to add to the equity rather than to borrowings, thus reducing rather than increasing the Debt / Equity ratio. Adoption of FRS 4, 'Capital Instruments', could change that.

Both can be issued with a conversion premium, which reduces or may even eliminate dilution of the n.a.v. on conversion.

Look with especial care at refinancing arrangements where a company is in breach of its banking / loan covenants and lenders (often the banks over-exposed to the property sector) have it over a barrel.

Indeed, the most interesting issues are often those in connection with refinancing arrangements. The rights attaching to shares issued in connection with any such arrangement should be studied with great care – and that is by no means easy.

Take, for example, the case of LONDON & METROPOLITAN. London & Metropolitan established its reputation in the field of commercial property development in the 1980s. Its developments included office, retail and business park schemes in the UK and in 1988 it extended its activities to developing the Pont Royal golf and leisure complex near Aix-en-Provence.

In September 1990 the group approached the banks with a view to reorganising the group's financial arrangements. Soon after this initial approach it was announced that County Hall Development Group, of which the company was a founder shareholder, had been unable to complete the purchase of County Hall and was to cease trading. This had a major impact on the company's shares, its prospects for raising new capital, and its negotiations with the banks. At the board's request, the company's listing was suspended in October 1990.

By the time refinancing arrangements were in place, the company was in breach of various covenants. Audited interim accounts to 30 June 1990 showed an operating loss of £4,546,000; but it was necessary to write off exceptional items totalling £83,957,000.

The refinancing arrangement involved the issue of redeemable preference shares (geared to LIBOR + 1.5%) and convertible preference shares (imposing various conditions upon the company – also geared to LIBOR + 1.5%). In the event of the company receiving an offer for its ordinary shares, holders of the convertible redeemable preference shares can convert into new ordinary shares of 1p (ranking pari passu with existing 5p ordinary shares as regards votes and dividends, but not in a winding up).

In addition the banks received warrants to subscribe at par in cash for 5p ordinary shares or new 1p ordinary shares at their option, enabling them to dilute the interest of ordinary shareholders by up to 15%. In the event of a change of control, the dilution could be as high as 49.9%.

(vii) *The distinction between 'capital' and 'revenue'*

A number of property groups, recognising the short-comings of normal accounts in presenting the results of a property company, long presented what were, in effect two profit and loss accounts: the first a traditional group profit and loss account; and the other, sometimes termed a group capital account, showed, usually under two heads, realised and unrealised, the capital surpluses and deficits. SLOUGH ESTATES did this. The overall balances of realised and unrealised capital surpluses (deficits) then each formed a single item in the note on reserves.

Investment property companies have vigourously resisted FRS 3 arguing that it makes a mockery of their reported figures. They believe that profits from investment companies should reflect the revenue earned from letting space, but should not include capital gains from churning the portfolio. They failed to persuade the ASC but both MEPC and BRITISH LAND continue to report headline profits, and to ignore capitasl items. The figures required by FRS 3 are there but given litle prominence. SLOUGH ESTATES uses the opportunity to present, in addition to normal earnings per share, the capital deficit for the year per ordinary share (basic and fully diluted); which we find helpful.

SLOUGH ESTATES *Extracts from Group profit and Loss Account and Group Capital Account for the year ended 31 December 1992*

	1992	1991
Earnings per ordinary share		
– basic	9.6p	8.0p
Capital deficit for the year per ordinary share – basic	(64.3p)	(36.9p)
Capital deficiit for the year per ordinary share		
– fully diluted	(53.7p)	(28.8p)

Net asset value

Acquisitions apart, accountants and accounting standards pay scant regard to asset value, arguing that the balance sheet is not a valuation statement, and that to divide shareholders' funds by the number of shares tells us nothing about value. FRS 3 and its reconciliation of movements in shareholders' funds could change that attitude.

MERIVALE MOORE *Extracts from ten year financial summary 1992*

	1983	1984	1985	1986	1987	1988	1989	1990	1991	1992
	£000	£000	£000	£000	£000	£000	£000	£000	£000	£000
Turnover	5,110	6,258	7,872	11,883	23,550	30,504	60,540	59,468	78,835	30,257
Gross rental income	601	851	1,000	1,723	2,620	2,753	3,815	5,052	5,044	4,078
(Loss)/Profit before tax	1,113	1,264	1,407	3,237	6,347	9,656	12,113	7,368	615	(12,975)
(Loss)/Profit after tax	826	1,004	853	2,363	4,525	6,511	7,863	5,153	1,741	(11,836)
(Loss)/Earnings per share	8.2p	10.0p	8.5p	17.0p	32.1p	46.2p	55.3p	35.8p	12.7p	(114.p)
Dividends per share (net)	1.0p	1.0p	1.5p	3.0p	4.5p	7.0p	10.5p	10.5p	10.5p	1.0p
Net assets	4,862	5,951	8,763	16,880	26,795	39,312	46,650	38,102	26,570	7,128
Net assets per share	48.2p	59.0p	86.0p	119.9p	190.4p	279.0p	331.2p	276.0p	194.9p	52.5p
Pro-forma net assets	–	–	–	27,731	44,530	71,212	90,773	71,003	34,700	10,565
Pro-forma net assets per share	–	–	–	197.0p	316.4p	505.4p	644.6p	514.3p	254.5p	77.3p

But that lack of interest was not found in certain sectors, such as investment trusts and property companies, where most of the assets are of a single type, a market exists which provides an indication of their value and which is adopted for accounting purposes. It is common in the UK therefore (other countries reject revaluation for balance sheet purposes) to compute the net asset value of a property company and use it as an indication of capital growth (the purpose for which many investors choose property companies in the first place). Although whether asset value (based on expert opinion at a single point in time, and taking account of the letting value of voids and that of future reversions and rent reviews) is a more useful indicator than share price (which is based on market knowledge from day to day), is a matter for debate.

Two problems exist when using net asset values:

1. Just as earnings per share of a company with convertibles are computed and disclosed on *both* a net and a fully diluted basis, so we believe should net asset values.
2. While revaluation of fixed assets is permitted for balance sheet purposes in the UK, revaluation of current assets at net realisable value where that is greater than cost certainly is not. This means that in the case of a mixed property company (ie one with both trading and investment property) some property appears in the accounts at cost and some at valuation. Some companies (like MERIVALE MOORE and ASDA PROPERTIES) get round this in n.a.v. calculations by publishing (outside the accounts, and hence outwith the audit) a proforma balance sheet in which trading properties are stated at professional valuation.

   In itself this is not unreasonable. But to publish the n.a.v. in the directors' report or 5 year summary on this basis only, as some companies do, is undesirable, and to do so without qualification, unfair.

It is instructive to study the ten year financial summary of MERIVALE MOORE (above), a company which, through its subsidiaries, invests in, develops and sells both residential and industrial property.

It is easy to see from this why property companies were so attractive to many fund managers in the 1980s: turnover, rental income, profits, earnings per share, dividends, net assets (especially proforma net assets), and net assets per share all grew spectacularly – but the crunch was equally painful when it came.

Property companies are among those which have their own illustrative format for FRS 1 purposes; and it is instructive to study the cash flow statement of MERIVALE MOORE for the year to 30 June 1992 (on the next page) and the notes which accompanied it. One can feel the strains, the pain, the disappointment.

MERIVALE MOORE *Note 32, 1992 accounts*

(a) Reconciliation of Operating (Loss) / Profit to net cash inflow from Operating Activities

	1992 £000	1991 £000
Operating (loss) / profit before exceptional items	(3,345)	1,841
Write back of acquisition cost of subsidiary undertaking	–	34
Depreciation charges	128	192
Interest payable classified as an extraordinary item	(475)	(636)
(Loss) / profit on sale of commercial investment properties	(709)	488
Cost of investment property sold	5,408	1,640
Write down of investments	72	–
Profit on sale of listed investments	–	(13)
Interest charges	9,138	11,060
Interest receivable	(1,332)	(676)
Decrease in stocks	23,053	35,420
Decrease in debtors	3,650	1,870
Decrease in creditors	(22,846)	(18,948)
	12,778	32,304

MERIVALE MOORE *Cash flow statement for the year ended 30 June 1992*

	1992 £000	1991 £000
Net cash inflow from operating activities	12,778	32,304
Returns on investment and servicing finance		
Interest received	1,332	676
Interest paid	(9,138)	(11,060)
Dividends paid	(1,146)	(1,438)
Net cash outflow from returns on investments and service of finance	(8,952)	(11,822)
Tax received (paid)	108	(3,450)
Investing activities:		
Payments to acquire investment property	(556)	(970)
Payments to acquire subsidiary undertakings	–	(352)
Payments to acquire investments	–	(28)
Payments to acquire sundry fixed assets	(55)	(53)
Receipts from sales of sundry fixed assets	57	91
Receipts from sales of investments	–	1,107
Net cash outflow from investing activities	(554)	(295)
Financing:		
Purchase of own share capital	–	(376)
Decrease in net borrowings	3,380	16,451

In studying the extracts, observe the way the brackets are used (eg cash and bank balances: brackets equals 'in hand' not 'overdrawn'). Note how very different the net cash inflow from Operating Activities is from the Operating (Loss) / Profit before Exceptional Items.

Useful ratios

In analysing property company accounts the standard general purpose ratios of:

(i)   Gearing; and
(ii) Interest cover

can be seriously distorted by the revaluation of properties and by the capitalisation of interest.

NOTE 32 (continued)

(b)   *Analysis of changes in net borrowings during the year:*

	1992 £000	1991 £000
Balance at 1 July 1991	52,709	69,160
Net cash inflow	(3,380)	(16,451)
Balance at 30 June 1992	49,329	52,709

(c)   *Analysis of net borrowings as shown in the balance sheet*

	1992 £000	1991 £000	Change in year £000
9.5% Unsecured Loan notes 1996	469	761	(292)
Bank loans and overdraft due within one year	34,491	36,896	(2,405)
Bank loans due after more than one year	16,483	11,538	4,945
First Mortgage Debenture Stock	12,900	12,900	–
Bank Balances and Cash	(15,014)	(9,386)	(5,628)
	49,329	52,709	(3,380)

The problem of capitalised interest can be solved by adding back the interest capitalised in the calculation of interest cover:

$$\text{Interest cover} = \frac{\text{Profit including investment income before interest and tax}}{\text{Interest}}$$

A more draconian measure is *overhead cover*:

$$\text{Overhead Cover} = \frac{\text{Rental Income} + \text{Interest Receivable}}{\substack{\text{Interest Payable} + \text{Capitalised Interest} \\ + \text{Administration costs} + \text{Dividends} \\ \text{(preference and ordinary)}}}$$

Clearly, any property company which depends on trading income and/or on capitalising interest to cover interest charges, overheads and dividends is more vulnerable than one which does not. It seems that overhead cover provides early warning for those willing to take it, though the market was somewhat slow to react in the early 1990s.

Things to look out for

1.   *Profit and Loss Account.* Assess the Overhead Cover.
2.   *Group balance sheet: Consider:*

    (a)   The proportion of borrowings that are short term;

(b) The significance of any sharp jump in borrowings.

3. *Note on Fixed Asset Investments.* Especially investment in, and loans to related companies, as a percentage of shareholders' funds

4. *Note on capital commitments.* Are they substantial?

5. *Note on contingent liabilities.*   Study:

(i) Guarantees in respect of borrowings of associated undertakings, related companies or joint ventures;

(ii) Other guarantees, particularly those given in respect of secured loans made to third-parties on developments in which the company had an interest, or has a continuing interest.

6. *Any suggestion* (such as a reserve for property insurance) *that the company is its own insurer* (as MOUNTVIEW ESTATES). If no individual property represents a significant part of the portfolio, and the properties are scattered in location, this could save money. But the bigger the investment in each, and the nearer properties are one to another, the greater the risk of a calamity of catastrophic proportions, eg the destruction of an entire shopping mall.

7. *Any mention of pre-letting arrangements (or pre-selling of developments).* If such arrangements exist this is a plus point: they reduce risk.

Practice

Obtain the latest accounts of:

1. Land Securities;
2. Slough Estates; and
3. Dares Estates.

Compare the companies, specifically:

(i) their area of activity, the quality and spread of investment, financing and methods of operation;

(ii) their accounting policies; and

(iii) recent performance.

INDEX

AAH HOLDINGS, 134
ABBEY CREST case study, 54
ABBEY NATIONAL, 145
Acquisition accounting, fair values in, 67
Acquisitions, 57
 and disposals, keepoing track of, 74
 and mergers, 63, 69
 deferred consideration, 66
 keys to success in understanding, 65
 over-ambitious and ill-timed, 46
 post-acquisition audit, 66
 visionary and opportunistic, 64
 why companies make, 63
Actuaries' report, 156
Administration costs, reducing, 52
Admission of Securities to Listing, 104, 116
AIRTOURS, 26, 125
AITKEN HUME INTERNATIONAL, 67, 94
ALLIED-LYONS, 82
Altman, Edward, 48
AMPS, 40
AMSTRAD, 48
ANGLIAN WATER SERVICES, 103
Annual general meetings, attendance of, 19
ARGYLL, 126
ASB Discussion Paper, 'The Role of
 Valuation in Financial Reporting', 101
ASDA GROUP, 126
Assets, 14
ASSOCIATED NURSING SERVICES, 134
Association of British Insurers,
 proposals, 155
AT&T, 133
AUSTIN REEED, 127
B&Q, 127
BAA, 94
BANK OF SCOTLAND, 150
Bank supervision, 146
Banker's view of a company, 37
Banks, 145
 capital ratios, 148
 contingent liabilities, 149
 credit risk, 147
 note issue, 153
 relations with, 37
 reports and accounts, 146
 what to look for in the accounts, 147
BARCLAYS, 145, 149
BARRATT DEVELOPMENT, 115
BAT, 91 103

BCCI, 84
Bevan Judi, 48
BHS, 127
BLUE CIRCLE, 115
BM GROUP, 95
Board of directors, resignations from, 47
BOC, 80, 83
Body language, 18
BODY SHOP, 48, 127
Boesky, 19
BOOKER, 90
BOOTS, 126, 127
Borrowings, excessive, 47
Borrowings, short-term, 47
BP, 102, 140
BPB INDUSTRIES, 116
Brackets, use of, 20
BRITISH GAS, 140
BRITISH LAND, 93
Brokers' circulars, 1
BRYANT, 115
BT, 132
Building materials and merchants, 116
 extraction, 117
 manufacture, 116
 merchants, 117
BURMAH CASTROL, 140
BURNETT & HALLAMSHIRE, 2
BURNFIELD, 96
BURTON, 127
CABLE & WIRELESS, 132
Cadbury Report, interim reports, 108
CADBURY SCHWEPPES, 80
Capital and revenue, distinction between,
 156
Capital instruments, unusual, 39
Capital requirements, projection of future,
 32
Capital, cost of, 39
CARADON, 115
Case studies
 Abbey Crest, 54
 ASDA, 43
 Courts, 112
 Inchcape, 68, 70
 Lucas, 32
 Medeva, 136
 Wilding Office Equipment, 6
Cash, shortage of, 55
Cash flow statements, 29

Cash flow, per share, 63
 effects of profit improvement, 57
 under FRS1, 62
Catering, 122
Central banks, 146
CHLORIDE, 72
Closure, why companies resort to, 71
COLOROLL, 48
COMET, 127
Commercial risk, 14
COMMERCIAL UNION, 153
COMMUNITY HOSPITALS GROUP, 134
Companies
 cannot neatly be categorised, 110
 some have it, others don't, 51
 UK trading abroad, 81
 which grow too fast, 46
 why they buy and sell overseas, 81
COMPASS GROUP, 124
Competition, asking about, 18
Consideration, deferred, 66
Construction companies, what to look for in
 the accounts, 119
Consultants, use of, 51
Continuing activities, 57
Contracting and construction, 115, 118
Controlling shareholding, 15
Convertible capital bonds, 40
Convertible debt, 40
Corporate objectives, statements of, 51
COURTAULDS, 68
COURTS case study, 112
Currency risk, 14, 81
Current cost accounting, 103, 132
Current Purchasing Power Accounting, 103
Danger signals, 49
DARES ESTATES, 163
Debt issued with warrants for ordinary
 shares, 40
Deep discount bonds, 40
Demergers, 75
Depreciation, investment properties, 164
Derecognition, 42
Development costs, capitalisation of by
 property companies, 163
DIRECT LINE, 156
Directors' share purchases and sales, 15
Directors, non-executive, 78
Discontinued operations, 57
Discontinued operations, reporting, 71, 72

Disposal, why groups dispose of subsidiaries and activities, 71
DOMESTIC & GENERAL, 157
Dominant characters, 48
Down but not out, 50
EAGLE STAR, 156
Earnings per share, 58, 61, 74
  normalised, 62
  under FRS 3, 62
  underlying, 62
ED 51, 'Accounting for Fixed Assets and Revaluations', 101
Electricity, 131
  power generators, 131
  regional electricy companies (RECs), 131
Electronic funds transfer and point of sale (EFTPOS) equipment, 53
Electronic point of sale (EPOS) equipment, 53
ELLIS & EVERARD, 109
ENTERPRISE OIL, 140
Environmental costs, 143
Equities, why invest in? 12
EUROPEAN LEISURE, 95
Exchange rates, effects on oil and gas companies, 143
Expansion, too fast, 47
Exploration and development expenditure, 140
Extraordinary items, 58
Eyes and ears, use of, 3, 18
Factoring, 42
Factory visits, 18
Failure, factor of age and size, 46
Failures, company, 106
Fair value adjustments, 67
Finance Director
  needs to find money at the drop of a hat, 36
  points to consider in raising money, 37
  role of, 77
  foreign exchange, 83
Financial risk, 14
FIRST TECHNOLOGY, 15
Food retailers, 126
  points to look for in the accounts, 128
Foreign
  operations, 81
  companies, investment in, 84
  currency transactions, in the accounts of the individual company, 85
Foreign currency transactions, in the group accounts, 87
Foreign exchange, doubts on convertibility, 86
Foreign exchange, forward market, 82
Foreign exchange, playing the currency markets, 82
Foreign exchange, temporal method, 90
Foreign exchange, translation differences, 87
Foreign operations, methods of organising, 85
Form 20-F (SEC), 150
Format, adoption of standard for reports, 26
FORTE, 73, 122
FRED 4, 42
FRS 1, 'Cash Flow Statements', 68, 104, 167, 168
FRS 1, cash flow under, 62
FRS 2, 90
FRS 3, 'Reporting Financial Performance', 57, 72
  and interim reports, 105
FRS 3, effects on ouil and gas companies, 143
  normalised earnings per share under, 62

FRS 3, transitional problems, 60
FRS 4, 40
FT–SE Actuaries
  Non-Financials Share Index, 110
  All Share Index, 13
GAMING, 124
Gearing, effects of, 38
GEC, 80
GENERAL ACCIDENT, 153
GENERAL ELECTRIC, 111
GEORGE WIMPEY, 115
Getting a first impression, 5
GKN, 88
GLAXO, 134
Goodwill, treatment of on disposal of a business, 75
GRANADA, 122
GRAND METROPOLITAN, 43, 108, 123, 124
Graphical presentation
  bar charts, 23
  semi-logarithmic charts, 24
  standards of, 22
  unfair, 23
GREAT PORTLAND ESTATES, 162
GREAT UNIVERSAL STORES, 126
GREENACRE GROUP, 134
Gross profit, increasing, 52
Groups
  closure, reasons for, 71
  changes in shape, 72
  disposals, 71
  methods of control of large, 76, 79
  non-executive directors, 78
  philosophy, 76
  rationale for existence of, 78
  succession, 78
Growth, graphical demonstration of, 24
GUARDIAN ROYAL EXCHANGE, 153, 155
GUINNESS, 19, 102
HABITAT, 127
Habits, forming the right, 12
HAMBROS, 145
HANSON, 51, 80
Health care, 134
HI-TEC SPORTS, 3
High Street, Take a walk down the, 3
Hire purchase contracts, 43
Historical cost basis of accounting, 98
Historical summaries, 102
Holidays, overseas, factors affecting, 125
Hooper, David, 1
Hotels, sector, 122
Hyperinflation, 88
ICELAND FROZEN FOODS, 126
ICI, 80
Improvement of the existing business, 52
INCHCAPE case study, 66, 69
INCHCAPE, 62, 68
Income bonds, 40
Independence, 76
Index linked loans, 40
Inflation
  accounting for, 103
  and rents, 101
  depreciation insufficient in times of, 99
  difficulty of measuring, 98
  effect of on components of working capital, 102
  effect of rate of, 13
  effects of, 97
  gains on borrowed money, 101
  high, 88
  historical summaries, adjustment of, 102
  is revaluation the solution, 100
  stock profits, 102
  why the present position is unsatisfactory, 98

Information
  need for, 28
  ways of conveying, 22
Insider dealing, 19
Inspectors' reports, learning from, 48
Insurance
  brokers, 157
  companies, accounts format, 156
  companies, solvency margins, 156
  sector, 152
  ratio to watch, 156
  domestic breakdown, 157
  embedded value, 155
  how it works, 153
  orphan estate, 155
  types of, 153
Interest
  caps, 82
  capitalisation of by property companies, 163
  capitalisation of by oil and gas companies, 143
  reducing cost of, 52, 55
Interim reports
  lack of a balance sheet, 104
  shortcomings, 104
  true and fair view, 105
  use of, 104, 106
Interim statements, audit of 105
Investment yields, 160
Investment, operational, 84
Investment, portfolio, 84
Investors, seek a diversified portfolio, 110
J SMART (CONTRACTORS), 118
JAMES WILKES, 105
Jay, John, 48
JEYES, 134
Just in time supply (JIT), 53
Key ratios, developing useful, 15
KINGFISHER, 57, 126
KLEINWORT BENSON, 145
KWIK SAVE, 126
LADBROKE, 122
LAND SECURITIES, 159–162
LASMO, 140
Leases and hire purchase contracts, 43
LEGAL & GENERAL, 154, 157
Leisure, sector, 122
Leisure and hotels, accounting features of, 123
Lenders, requirements of, 38
Limited recourse debt, 40
LINCOLN HOUSE, 66
LLOYDS' OF LONDON, 152
LLOYDS ABBEY, 152
LLOYDS BANK, 145, 149
LONDON INTERNATIONAL GROUP, 134
Longer Look, 12
LONRHO, 93
LOWNDES QUEENSWAY, 49
LUCAS case study, 32
M&W, 128
Management buyouts, 74
Management, 15
Management, meeting, 17
MARKS AND SPENCER, 126
MAXWELL COMMUNICATION CORPORATION, 91
Maxwell, Robert, 1, 91
MC CARTHY & STONE, 23, 119, 121
MEDEVA case study, 136
MEDEVA, 77, 134
MEPC, 159
Merchant banks, 145
MERIVALE MOORE, 167
MIDLAND BANK, 145
MILLER, STANLEY, 48

MIRROR GROUP NEWSPAPERS, 1, 91
MOLINS, 94
Money
  laundering, 84
  FD's need to find at the drop of a hat, 36
  finding the, 36
  internal sources v external, 36
MOTHERCARE, 127
Nadir, Asil, 2
NATIONAL WESTMINSTER, 145
Net asset value, and property
  companies, 166
NEXT, 49
Non-pharmaceutical health care companies,
  what to look for in the accounts, 135
Occupational Pensions Board, 92
Off-balance sheet finance, 41
Oil and gas distribution sectors, 140
  effect of exchange rates, 143
  environmental costs, 143
  full cost accounting, 140, 141
  impairment ceiling tests, 142
  integration, 143
  points to look for in accounts, 141
  reserves, 142
  successful efforts accounting, 140, 141
  taxation, 142
Oil Industry Accounting Committee SORPs,
  140, 142
Operating costs, reducing, 52
Operational risk, 14
Operational statistics, 133
Opportunities, seizing, 17
Overseas investment, risks of, 85
OWNERS' ABROAD, 125
Package tours and holidays, 124
PARKFIELD, 106
PEARSON, 62
Pension costs and the concept of prudence,
  97
Pension funds, 57
  actuarial methods, 94
  inflation a key problem, 93
  self-investment, 96
  surplus, who owns? 93
  things to look out for, 95
  trustees, relying on, 92
  who calls the tune, 92
Pension Scheme Surpluses (Administration)
  Regulations 1987, 94
Pension schemes,
  defined contribution, 91, 92
  sex equality, 96
  types of, 91
  unfunded, 91
Pensions, problems with, 91
Perpetual debt, 40
Personal skills, scepticism, 1
Pharmaceutical companies, what to look for
  in the accounts, 135
PILKINGTON, 115, 116
Political risk, 14
POLLY PECK, 2, 48, 89
Post-acquisition audit, 66
Prediction of failure, scientific
  methods of, 48
Preparation, need for thorough, 17
Presentation
  separate, 43
  accounts and tables, 20
  linked, 43
  methods of, 20
Price earnings ratios, sector differences in,
  110
Privatisation, 130
Privatised organisations, features of, 130
Product strength, 14

Products, own label, 53
Profit improvement plans, adverse short
  term effects on profitability, 56
Profitability
  improving, 51
  questionable improvements in, 55
Properties, reclassification of, 164
Property companies
  capital and revenue, distinction between,
    166
  methods of financing, 165
  points to look for in accounts, 161, 169
  useful ratios, 168
  what they do, 161
Property values, 160
Property ownership, how organised, 160
Property
  sector, 159
    what makes it an attractive investment,
    159
  yields, 159
Prospects, assessing a company's, 14
PROTEUS INTERNATIONAL, 134
PRUDENTIAL, 152, 156
QUALITY CARE HOMES, 134
Quarterly statements, would they be better?
  108
Quick Look, 5
RANK ORGANISATION, 122
Ratios to watch, profit and loss account, 54
Ratios, banks, 148
RATNERS, 48
RECKITT & COLMAN, 90, 134
Reconciliation of movements on
  shareholders' funds, 60
REDLAND, 115
Reference material, essential, 25
Related companies, joint ventures and
  consortia, used by property groups, 164
Reporting Financial Performance (FRS 3),
  57
Reports, in-depth, 25
Research and development, 135
Retailers, food and general, 126
REUTERS HOLDINGS, 90
RICHARDS, 127
RMC, 115
ROSEHAUGH, 165
ROYAL BANK OF SCOTLAND, 96, 145
SAINSBURY, 53, 126, 128
Sales based ordering, 53
Scepticism, 1
SCHOLL, 134
SCOTTISH WIDOWS' FUND, 92
SCHRODERS, 145
SEARS, 126
Seasonal businesses, 106
Sectors
  how to choose, 13
  getting to grips with one, 109
  how they differ, 109
  where to start, 110
Securities and Investments Board (SIB), 48
Securitised assets, 42
SEDGWICK, 152
Segmental analysis, 109, 111
Segmental information, use of, 111
SFAS 52, 89
Shape, changes in, 14, 72
Share price performance, 15
Shares or loan capital, the choice, 37
SHELL TRANSPORT AND TRADING, 93, 140
SKETCHLEY, 127
SLOUGH ESTATES, 166
SMITH & NEPHEW, 134
SMITH (WH), 126, 127
SMITHKLINE BEECHAM, 68, 134

Societe General Strauss Turnbull, 2
SOCK SHOP, 48
SOUTHERN ELECTRIC, 103
SSAP 20, 89
SSAP 24, 'Accounting for Pension Costs',
  91
SSAP 25, 'Segmental Reporting', 85, 111,
  119
SSAP 6, 'Extraordinary Items and Prior Year
  Adjustments', 57
Statement of total recognised gains and
  losses, 57, 59
Stepped interest bonds, 40
Stock Exchange 'Yellow Book', 41
Stock, consignment, 42
STOREHOUSE, 127
Stores companies, points to look for in the
  accounts, 127
Stores, sector, 126
Style, analyst's concern with, 80
Style, pitfalls, 80
Styles of strategic management, 79
Subordinated debts, 40
Subsidiaries
  assessing progress of foreign, 87
  foreign registered, 83
SUN ALLIANCE, 153
SUPERDRUG, 127
Supermarkets, points to look for in the
  accounts, 128
SUTHERLAND, 67
Swaps, 82
TARMAC, 80, 115
TATE & LYLE, 83, 89
Taxation
  oil and gas companies, 142
  special factors affecting charge, 58
TAYLOR WOODROW, 115
Telephone Networks, 132
Terrington, Derek, 1
Terrorism, effects of, 125
TESCO, 53, 126, 128, 129
THOMSON, 125
THORN EMI, 122
Third World, lending to, 64
TI GROUP, 60, 62
Total return, 13
Track record, 14
TRAFALGAR HOUSE, 61
TSB, 145
UNICHEM, 134
Urgent Issues Task Force (UITF)
  Abstract 3, 75
  Abstract 5, 164
  Abstract 6, 96
Utilities, sector, 130
Valuation, role of in financial reporting, 101
Van Wezel, Franz, 3
VODAPHONE, 132
Warning signs, 48
Water, 132
WELLCOME, 83, 134
WESTMINSTER HEALTH CARE HOLDINGS,
  136.
WESTMINSTER SCAFFOLDING, 119
What goes up ..., 490
What you know or whom you know?, 3
WHITBREAD, 108
WILDING OFFICE EQUIPMENT case study, 6
WILLIAM MORRISON, 126
WILLIS CORROON, 153
WILSON BOWDEN, 115
WILSON CONNOLLY, 115, 120
WORLD OF LEATHER, 127, 128
WPP, 48
Z score, 48
Zero coupon bonds, 40